Public Insurance and Private Markets

Public Insurance and Private Markets

Jeffrey R. Brown, Editor

The AEI Press

Publisher for the American Enterprise Institute

WASHINGTON, D.C.

Distributed by arrangement with the Rowman & Littlefield Publishing Group, 4501 Forbes Boulevard, Suite 200, Lanham, Maryland 20706. To order call toll free 1-800-462-6420 or 1-717-794-3800. For all other inquiries please contact AEI Press, 1150 Seventeenth Street, N.W. Washington, D.C. 20036 or call 1-800-862-5801.

NRI National Research Initiative

This publication is a project of the National Research Initiative, a program of the American Enterprise Institute that is designed to support, publish, and disseminate research by university-based scholars and other independent researchers who are engaged in the exploration of important public policy issues.

Library of Congress Cataloging-in-Publication Data

Public insurance and private markets / Jeffrey R. Brown, editor.

p. cm.

Includes bibliographical references and index.

ISBN-13: 978-0-8447-4325-7

ISBN-10: 0-8447-4325-9

1. Disaster insurance—United States. 2. Insurance—Government policy—United States. I. Brown, Jeffrey R.

HG9979.3.P83 2010

368.400973—dc22

2010001639

14 13 12 11 10 1 2 3 4 5

Printed in the United States of America

Contents

List of Illustrations

Figures

Tables

Introduction: What Role Should the Government Play in Insuring Private Market Risks?

Jeffrey R. Brown

The economic and financial-market events of 2008–2009 should remove any lingering doubt about whether the U.S. government's role as an insurer of private market activity has consequences for taxpayers and economic efficiency. The government has made explicit its previously implicit guarantee of the government-sponsored enterprises Fannie Mae and Freddie Mac. The Federal Deposit Insurance Corporation (FDIC) has (at least temporarily) increased the insured limits on bank deposits. The U.S. Treasury has agreed to insure money market mutual funds. Government actions that would have been politically inconceivable as late as spring 2008 (such as the federal government taking equity positions in private firms on a massive scale, or using taxpayer funds to bail out troubled mortgage buyers and sellers) are now a reality.

Whether or not these interventions achieve their short-term goal of halting the general decline of the U.S. economy, the consequences of decisions about public versus private risk bearing are now very clear and tangible. The events of 2008–2009 should inform our analysis and policy debates about the appropriate role of government in insuring private market risk for decades to come.While recent interventions have been unprecedented in size, the role of the government (and thus the taxpayer) in insuring financial risks generated in the private market is not a new one. Indeed, even prior to these events, the U.S. government could fairly be called the largest insurance company in the history of the world. After all, the federal government operates the world's largest pension and disability insurance system (Social Security) and the world's largest health care insurance programs (Medicare and Medicaid), and it provides explicit or implicit insurance against a broad range of risks, such as pension funding shortfalls, crop losses, and property damage from natural disasters, to name a few. This is on top of the general risk exposure that taxpayers already share through the income tax system.

The government's role as a risk bearer is typically justified using the theory of market failures. Indeed, the study of market failures is as old as the study of markets themselves. Even Adam Smith, typically viewed as the father of modern economic thought, recognized that markets can occasionally fail to achieve optimal social outcomes. Over the years, the class of market failures, and our understanding of them, has grown. In the twenty-first century, virtually any first-year PhD student in economics worth his or her salt knows how to write a simple model showing that in the presence of market failures, whether they arise from imperfect competition, externalities, asymmetric information, or other sources, an omniscient and benevolent government may improve social welfare by mandating, regulating, or incentivizing optimal behavior.

Of course, governments—even democratically elected ones—are not consistently omniscient or benevolent. Government policies, as well as private markets, can and sometimes do fail to achieve socially desirable outcomes. Well-intentioned policies often have unintended consequences that mitigate their efficacy or solve one set of problems at the expense of creating new ones. In the words of Milton Friedman, "The government solution to a problem is usually as bad as the problem."

All too often, our policy debates reduce to ideological grandstanding. Many free-market advocates tend to ignore the possibility of real market failures. Many critics of markets believe that market failures are ubiquitous and that only the government has the power to set the world right again. A talented economic theorist can construct formal models justifying either position. To truly understand whether government intervention in markets—in this case, insurance markets—is harmful or beneficial on net, it is necessary to go beyond general ideological statements and assess the facts on the ground. For better or for worse, there are numerous U.S. government interventions in insurance markets available for study. This book looks at six of these interventions in an attempt to assess whether they are truly needed and how they might be improved.

An Overview of the Volume

The goal of this book is to bring economic theory and evidence to bear on existing U.S. government policy in six areas of public and private risk bearing, and to suggest policy options to improve the efficiency of public policy in these areas. These studies generally recognize that private markets are capable of failing to function efficiently. However, they are also forceful and expansive in their criticism of the poorly designed government programs in place.

In chapter 1, George Pennacchi examines the structure of the Federal Deposit Insurance Corporation. He points to the positive aspects of deposit insurance—namely, the protection of small, unsophisticated investors and the enhancement of overall financial-market stability through the prevention of bank runs. However, he also discusses the important economic distortions caused by politically induced limits on the FDIC's ability to price deposit insurance accurately—based on the underlying risks. He finds that the FDIC's attempt to set deposit insurance premiums to target deposit insurance fund reserves leads to excessive systematic risk taking by banks. He also discusses the limited progress toward combating the "Too Big to Fail" (TBTF) incentive for bailing out large banks.

Pennacchi considers several reform options that would combat the distortions created by the current FDIC system and help improve efficiency in the banking system. The first would centralize the clearing process for derivative contracts as a way of reducing counterparty risk. This reform would make it harder to assert the TBTF rationale for bailing out distressed banks, because a common justification for TBTF assistance (used in the case of Bear Stearns, AIG, Wachovia, and CitiGroup) is that counterparty risk in derivatives contracts serves to interconnect institutions, and the failure of one would trigger losses and potential failures at others. An advantage of a clearinghouse is that it allows parties to "net" their positions with their many counterparties, thus providing more expertise and cost efficiencies in setting margin requirements. The second reform would emphasize charging appropriate risk-adjusting premiums to banks by using more market information and possibly collateralization of deposits. The third reform would either abolish the Deposit Insurance Fund (DIF) or use market mechanisms such as swaps to transfer the risk of targeting DIF reserves to investors outside of the banking industry.

In chapter 2, Andrew Biggs and I analyze the Pension Benefit Guaranty Corporation (PBGC), an agency of the federal government that insures private-sector defined-benefit pension plans against the bankruptcy of the sponsoring employer. We find that the PBGC does not adequately risk-adjust premiums and so encourages risk taking by plan sponsors, that it fails to ensure adequate funding, that it does not provide timely and appropriate information to pension plan participants or financial markets, and that it is likely to impose substantial costs on future taxpayers. We also highlight how the PBGC's 2008 decision to increase equity exposure is precisely the wrong medicine for curing the funding shortfalls facing the agency.

Looking to the future, we discuss both incremental and wholesale reforms aimed at increasing market discipline in the program. At the top of the list: Congress should authorize the PBGC to risk-adjust the premiums that it charges to plan sponsors. There is no good economic justification for charging the same premium per participant to a very healthy plan sponsor with an overfunded pension plan invested in a portfolio that immunizes the plan against changes to its funding status, and to a financially distressed firm invested in a risky portfolio of assets that could worsen its funding status just when the firm is likely to dump its pension liabilities on the PBGC. Other incremental reforms include allowing the PBGC to use private reinsurance or securitization to reduce some of its exposure and increase pricing transparency; requiring that pension promises be given seniority over other liabilities in bankruptcy proceedings; or further limiting PBGC coverage. We also discuss the more far-reaching reform possibility of eliminating the PBGC and replacing it with a government-mandated, but privately run, pension insurance system, though we acknowledge that doing so would not eliminate the large implicit debt overhang that already exists in the system.

In chapter 3, Dwight Jaffee and Thomas Russell discuss the market for insurance against losses arising from terrorist attacks. Explicit federal involvement in this market emerged in the aftermath of the September 11,

2001, attacks, when insurers realized that their insurance pricing models were seriously inadequate and when foreign reinsurers withdrew from this segment of the property and casualty insurance market. Thus, a purportedly "temporary" government insurance program was created in 2002 to provide the industry with a backstop against large losses. Perhaps unsurprisingly, this "temporary" program has already been extended twice. Because it is virtually impossible for a fully functional private reinsurance market to emerge when the government is giving away "free" reinsurance, it will always be possible for proponents of government intervention to justify further extensions by pointing to the lack of a private market alternative. The authors discuss the important resource allocation costs that occur when subsidies prevent individuals and firms from bearing the true economic costs of their decisions. Supporters of the federal program often argue that the resource allocation costs are limited in this context, because a policyholder is far removed from a terrorist's decision about whether to attack the U.S. Such a view, however, ignores the myriad of decisions that can influence the likelihood that an attack succeeds (e.g., how much to spend on security) or the damages that result (e.g., whether to upgrade sprinkler systems). Like it or not, such decisions will be affected in aggregate by the marginal cost of investing in these activities relative to the cost of insuring against the loss.

Jaffee and Russell note that the current federal terrorism insurance program covers losses from conventional attacks, but excludes chemical, nuclear, biological, and radiological (CNBR) attacks. The authors argue that the magnitude of losses from a conventional attack could be absorbed by private markets, but that the CNBR losses are of a magnitude large enough to warrant an explicit government role. The authors recommend that, when the current legislation ends in 2014, responsibility for conventional acts of terrorism be returned to the private market, with no government subsidy, and that the government shift its focus to covering CNBR risk, although not simply by using the existing terrorism insurance model; the authors discuss a range of ways that the government can partner with private investors to help recapitalize private insurers in the aftermath of a large CNBR event. In the event that the government does not see fit to exit the market for conventional terrorism losses, the insurance should at least be provided at an appropriate, risk-adjusted cost to the insured businesses.

Kunreuther and Michel-Kerjan analyze the tremendous growth in financial losses arising from natural catastrophes in recent decades, which they attribute to a combination of increasing urbanization, increased concentration of economic value in risk-prone areas, and possible changes in weather patterns. Looking forward, they suggest that the growth in future losses is likely to continue to increase, posing important market and public policy changes.

Although the federal government has programs in place to deal with other types of risks discussed in this book, it has no comprehensive program to insure against catastrophe *ex ante*. (One exception—flood insurance—is discussed in detail in chapter 5.) As such, rather than analyzing an existing program, the authors lay out a number of principles for how any future intervention into catastrophe insurance markets should be structured; they call specifically for premiums that reflect risk, the use of grants (rather than price subsidies) to deal with equity and affordability issues, taking steps to ensure sufficient insurance demand, and appropriate solvency regulation.

The authors acknowledge that individuals often fail to invest in effective mitigation activities. Rather than using this fact to justify the direct provision of insurance by the federal government, however, Kunreuther and Michel-Kerjan propose the creation of a new financial product. Specifically, they suggest moving from the standard one-year insurance contract for homeowners to long-term insurance contracts, which would provide financial incentives for individuals to undertake efficient mitigation efforts. They propose flood insurance as a natural candidate for implementing this idea. If a long-term (e.g., twenty-year) flood insurance policy were tied to a particular property, then the homeowner could take out a twenty-year home improvement loan, invest in risk mitigation, and achieve a net increase in cash flow for cost-effective mitigation efforts through the resulting reduction in the flood insurance premium.

In chapter 5, Mark Browne and Martin Halek discuss the National Flood Insurance Program (NFIP) in detail and explore a range of reform options. They trace the origins of the modern-day NFIP from the government's approaches to flood control in the 1800s through the policies of today. They point out the flaws of the existing program, notably the mispricing of insurance, and show that many flood insurance policies are underpriced relative to the risk they insure, with some policies receiving a 60–65 percent subsidization rate. (Indeed, the extent of mispricing is even worse than these figures suggest, due to "grandfathering" of rates and other design flaws.) Given its inadequate pricing model, it is not surprising that the NFIP is underfunded on an annual basis.

The authors explore various routes by which the efficient transfer of flood risk could be accomplished through private-market alternatives, including the use of private reinsurance, alternative risk-transfer mechanisms (such as catastrophe options, industry loss warranties, or contingent capital agreements), and, most directly, private insurance provision.

In chapter 6, Vincent Smith and Barry Goodwin examine the federal government's role in providing insurance against agricultural losses. The authors discuss how federal crop insurance programs have been driven by political considerations from the beginning, when President Roosevelt proposed the creation of multiple-peril programs in 1936. Over the past three decades, the programs have been expanded to offer subsidized coverage for more crops (and, recently, even some livestock); the result is a wider range of available insurance products, and an increase in subsidies—the taxpayer now provides approximately 60 percent of the actuarially fair premium. The authors explain that Congress's primary rationale for expansion was to increase participation enough so that ad hoc disaster programs would be unnecessary. However, even though participation in federal crop insurance has increased to include over 80 percent of eligible crop acreage, Congress nonetheless included a disaster relief program in the 2008 farm bill while maintaining subsidy levels.

The authors find little evidence of a market failure that would justify government intervention in this market. Recognizing the political reality that federal intervention in this market is unlikely to go away, however, they offer a number of principles to guide how a government program should be designed and implemented, such as limiting moral hazard through controls on coverage levels and using a rational pricing mechanism that limits the distortions to production patterns. They also discuss some of the changes that would be required to bring the program into compliance with world trade agreements.

Lessons Learned

Taken as a whole, these six studies provide a number of both constructive and cautionary lessons for policymakers considering new government insurance programs or reforms to existing ones. While the details of each particular market matter, a number of general themes emerge from the analyses.

Government Intervention Must Be Justified. One of the themes that emerges involves the economic justification for government intervention in insurance markets. The mere existence of a market failure does not necessarily mean that the government is in a position to overcome this failure, even on theoretical grounds. For example, one common source of market failure in insurance markets is moral hazard, the well-known phenomenon in which individuals engage in riskier behavior when they know that they are insured against the downside loss. Having the government rather than the private sector provide insurance does nothing to overcome this source of inefficiency. Indeed, given the government's apparent inability to properly price insurance, government provision may exacerbate this problem. Of course, even if the government is able to overcome the source of the market failure in theory, a discerning analyst must also question whether a government insurance program will be able to improve the situation in practice, given the political nature of the policy and regulatory process.

There are three potential justifications for government intervention that arise across the multiple insurance markets analyzed in this book. The first is adverse selection, a type of asymmetric information in which the potential insurance purchaser knows more about his risk than the insurance seller, and in which it is possible that only the more risky individuals will purchase the insurance. In theory, adverse selection can cause a voluntary market to completely unravel (Akerlof 1970; Rothschild and Stiglitz 1976). To combat adverse selection, the government has one tool in its arsenal that no private insurer has—the power of compulsion. Specifically, the government can mandate that all individuals or firms participate in a particular market, thus removing self-selection from the equation. For example, the government can require all sponsors of defined-benefit pension plans to purchase insurance, or all homeowners to insure their residences against floods. As has been frequently noted in the economics literature, however, just because the government may have an important role in mandating insurance coverage, that does not mean that the government must be the one to provide the insurance. A government-mandated but privately run insurance program may be the most efficient answer.

A second rationale that frequently appears in discussions of government insurance programs is known as the "Samaritan's Dilemma" (Buchanan 1975). The Samaritan's Dilemma is quite simple: it arises when individuals can increase future benefits from an altruistic government (or altruistic individuals) by behaving in a manner that is socially inefficient. After a loss, be it one arising from a terrorist attack, a hurricane, or a widespread failure of pension plans, it is politically difficult for a democratically elected government to do nothing. There will be political pressure for the government to step in as the "Good Samaritan" to offer some form of aid (whether in the form of disaster relief, victim compensation funds, financial bailouts, or any number of other policies). If there is a widespread *ex ante* belief that such relief will be forthcoming after a bad event, then individuals will behave as if they are insured. This is essentially a form of moral hazard, but one due to a political failure (i.e., the inability to credibly commit to not intervene) rather than a market failure. In light of this, it is often suggested that having an explicit, well-defined, *ex ante* government role makes it easier for politicians to resist *ex post* relief. If the *ex ante* insurance program that provides appropriate incentives for risk mitigation is more efficient than *ex post* relief, then an explicit government program may actually reduce the taxpayers' ultimate exposure.

Of course, using the Samaritan's Dilemma to justify intervention presupposes that intervention will truly lead to a more efficient allocation of resources even after accounting for all behavioral responses of the affected population and the policymakers. Given that the *ex ante* government programs are often designed inefficiently themselves, and that politicians may still step in with *ex post* assistance even in the presence of a preexisting insurance program, the jury is still out on whether the evidence supports this justification for a government role. Even if it is determined that an *ex ante* program is desirable, one still must choose whether the government should directly provide the insurance, or whether a minimalist approach of ensuring that the private market operates effectively (such as by mandating participation and/or regulating the insurers) would be sufficient.

A third rationale that economists often use to justify a role for government is that the government has the unique ability to diversify risk across generations through fiscal policy. Some risks are large and systematic, meaning that they cannot be diversified away simply by insuring more individuals or firms. Furthermore, in some cases, effectively insuring a risk can influence the extent to which it becomes systematic: for example, one rationale for deposit insurance is to prevent financial distress at one bank from causing negative externalities on other participants in the financial system.

While the government has no advantage over the private sector in diversifying risk within a given generation, it is uniquely situated to contract across generations. As noted by Bohn (2006, 11), "Welfare improvements are possible because a government's power of taxation gives it a unique ability to make commitments on behalf of future generations." However, there are at least three reasons to observe caution when using the intergenerational risk-sharing argument to justify a government insurance program. First, while intergenerational risk sharing has the theoretical potential to spread risk more efficiently, it does not eliminate the risk. As the Congressional Budget Office (2004, 5) has noted: "Risk is not reduced by the government's power to print money, because financing credit losses by creating money substitutes an inflation tax for a pecuniary tax. In the end, someone must bear the consequences of unpredictable financial returns, and markets determine a price for assuming that risk." Second, as Bohn (2006, 11) points out, "The government's power to oblige future generations also creates potential for abuse. Risks might be shifted haphazardly onto future generations by governments catering to current voters." Third, as noted by Brown and Orszag (2006), the possible advantage of spreading risk more efficiently *across* generations must be weighed against the fact that fiscal policy may not spread risk efficiently *within* each generation. Markets use price signals to spread risk efficiently so that it is borne by those most willing to bear it. Fiscal policy spreads risk based on a host of political factors that may not bear any relation to the preferences of those chosen to bear the risk.

Other arguments in favor of government intervention in insurance markets are less convincing. For example, it is often argued that parameter uncertainty, particularly when there is the possibility of rare events, makes it difficult for the private market to function. In the immediate aftermath of the 9/11 attacks, insurers expressed concern about their inability to accurately model the risk distribution of terrorism losses. Especially at the time, no one knew whether 9/11 was a rare event unlikely to repeat itself in our lifetimes, or whether the world had entered a new era when large-scale attacks would be more common.

While it is true that parameter uncertainty makes insurance pricing more difficult, the government rarely has a comparative advantage in overcoming this uncertainty. Even in the unique case of terrorism, in which the government as a whole has access to security-relevant intelligence that is not available to private insurers, the Treasury Department (which runs the terrorism insurance program) cannot price insurance more effectively than private markets unless the intelligence community shares with it detailed information about the probability distribution of possible terrorist attacks that it is unwilling to share with private markets. That Treasury receives such information is unlikely. First, it has been well documented that the U.S. intelligence community has had difficulties sharing appropriate intelligence efficiently even across agencies within the intelligence community.[1] Second, if the intelligence community does not want to share relevant information about the probability distribution with private markets, then it would also be hesitant to use this information to price a government-run insurance program, since market participants might infer the information from the prices charged by the government. Third, as Jaffee and Russell's chapter in this volume documents, whatever information advantage the government may possess has certainly not translated into appropriate insurance pricing, as the premium charged under the current program is zero.

A more subtle information-based argument, and one used to make the case for government involvement, is that some information required to effectively price insurance has a "public goods" aspect to it. For example, having good meteorological data helps all insurers to price catastrophe insurance more effectively, and if each individual firm is left to collect this data independently, such information might be underprovided. If on the other hand the government collects the information centrally, or allows insurers to work cooperatively to collect the information themselves, it might help ensure the optimal investment in the public good. But once that information has been provided, the provision of insurance need not be done by the government.

Government insurance provision is also sometimes justified on the basis of consumer protection. For example, proponents of government intervention may claim that small, unsophisticated investors need the protection of the FDIC, or that unsophisticated pensioners need the protection of the PBGC. Once again, however, the desired objective can be achieved through less intrusive steps than direct government provision. Concerns about myopic consumers failing to purchase insurance can be overcome through mandates or automatic enrollment. Concerns about insurer solvency and transparency can be overcome through government regulation of private insurers.

Risk-Adjusted Premiums Are Essential. A second conclusion drawn by all six studies in this volume is that, in those cases where policymakers decide that the government should be involved in the direct provision of insurance, insurance should be priced on an economically appropriate, risk-adjusted basis. The appropriate pricing of risk is critical to ensuring the efficient allocation of resources in the economy. Utility-maximizing individuals and profit-maximizing firms will, when making decisions about risk, trade off the cost of insuring against the cost of mitigating a risk. If insurance prices are too low, they will overinsure and invest too little in risk mitigation—thereby increasing society's exposure to the risk.

There are two important aspects of the pricing issue. First, it is important that the average level of premiums be appropriately adjusted for systematic risk. Several government insurance programs are designed to be "self-financing," which too often is interpreted to mean that their goal is to break even over time—in which case the premium is typically set so that the expected losses are equal to the expected premium revenue over some period. This is precisely the wrong goal, however, when the risk being insured is systematic risk. Failures of banks and pension-plan sponsors, for example, are more likely to occur during times of economic distress, which is just when society places a relatively higher value on additional resources (or, in economic parlance, when the marginal utility of income is high). Finance theory is clear that a positive risk premium should be incorporated into the price to reflect this systematic risk. The government has a tremendous disadvantage in pricing systematic risk, because in most years the insurance program will appear to be earning a profit, which in turn will lead the insured industry (e.g., plan sponsors in the case of the PBGC) to demand that premiums be reduced.

The second issue that must be considered when doing appropriate risk-based pricing is the heterogeneity of risk in the insured population. Even if we were to hold constant the average level of the premiums being charged, which may or may not contain a risk premium depending on the level of systematic risk, different individuals or different firms should face different prices depending on the risk characteristics that they present. For example, a better-capitalized bank with a more conservative lending strategy should pay less for insurance than a worse-capitalized bank with an aggressive lending strategy. Similarly, a mom-and-pop diner in rural Kansas ought to pay substantially less for terrorism insurance than a diner across the street from a national landmark in New York City or Washington, D.C.

If there is a single theme that comes through loud and clear in all six chapters in this book, it is that the government has a terrible track record at appropriately pricing risk. In the FDIC insurance program, Pennacchi shows, premiums have often been set too low, which leads an increasing proportion of the financial system to seek access to artificially cheap credit, and in turn worsens the stability of the financial system. Brown and Biggs show that the lack of risk-adjustment in the PBGC program encourages firms to overinvest in risky assets and discourages them from fully funding their pensions. Russell and Jaffee note that the government does not even pretend to try to price terrorism insurance effectively—on an *ex ante* basis, it simply gives away the insurance free of charge. Kunreuther and Michel-Kerjan note the importance of pricing risk accurately in order to avoid, among other things, overdevelopment in risk-prone areas. Browne and Halek suggest that the flood insurance program has likely led to overdevelopment in flood zones. Goodwin and Smith discuss the land-use misallocation that arises from mispricing in the crop insurance programs.

The insight that the government has difficulty setting risk-based premiums is not new. As Pennacchi reminds us, Stiglitz (1993, 114) noted that "government . . . faces a tremendous disadvantage in assessing risks and charging premiums based on risk differences." The reason is that risk assessments are subjective:

> Is it plausible to believe that the government could charge banks in Texas a higher premium for insurance than banks in Idaho . . . ? Any such differentiation might be quickly labeled unfair. The market, by contrast, makes such differentiations all the time, converting the subjective judgments of many participants into an objective standard. . . . If some bank in Houston complains about the risk premium it is being charged by the market . . . there is a simple reply: Provide evidence that the risk has been overestimated, and the market will render a verdict. If the information is credible, the risk premium will be reduced. (Stiglitz 1993, 114–15)

The True Taxpayer Burden Must Be Recognized. Government insurance programs impose what economists call "contingent liabilities" on taxpayers. By virtue of the fact that these programs are insuring uncertain outcomes, the actual loss imposed on taxpayers is contingent upon the realization of the loss. Such a contingent loss exposure represents an accounting challenge for policymakers, because federal budget accounting is essentially a complex version of cash flow accounting. The result of using expected values of cash flows in connection with programs designed to be self-financing is that many of these programs *appear* to have little aggregate budgetary impact. But economists know that the full, risk-adjusted costs of these programs can be substantial, and these costs do not appear on the government's books. A failure to formally recognize these liabilities, however, does not make them go away. A full analysis of the budget treatment of these programs, and recommendations for how to reform those budget procedures, is well beyond the scope of this book. Nonetheless, an important conclusion of these analyses is that the true economic cost of these programs must be fully accounted for.

Markets Can Transfer Risk Efficiently. Many of the programs analyzed in this book are decades old. The FDIC program was created in the depths of the Great Depression. The NFIP was created over forty years ago, in 1968. The PBGC was created by the Employee Retirement Income Security Act of 1974. The basic infrastructure of these programs was built in an era that predates much of the modern literature: the famous Black-Scholes option pricing paper was not published until 1973 (Black and Scholes 1973) and the seminal paper on imperfect information in insurance markets was not published until 1976 (Rothschild and Stiglitz 1976). In the time since the programs under discussion were created, the world has witnessed tectonic shifts in the way that private markets can package and transfer risks.

This increased ability of markets to price and transfer risk opens up possibilities for reform that simply did not exist in years past, and the analyses presented in this book draw on these possibilities. In the context of FDIC insurance, Pennacchi suggests that the swaps market can be used to transfer the risk of targeting deposit reserves to investors outside the banking industry. Biggs and Brown suggest that the PBGC ought to make use of financial markets to off-load some of its risk exposure and gain information about the price of pension default risk. Jaffee and Russell recommend the issuance of new securities to help recapitalize insurers at times of highly stressed financial conditions. Kunreuther and Michel-Kerjan recommend the private issuance of new long-term insurance contracts.

Undoubtedly, there will be market skeptics ready to suggest that the use of financial instruments to repackage risk is the proximate cause of the recent turmoil in financial markets; they will therefore view direct government provision of insurance as a better solution. A full debate on the causes of the financial crisis could fill several separate volumes, but at least a few general points are worth noting here in response. First, economic theory is clear that more "complete" markets generally lead to welfare improvements, and instruments for transferring risk are an important tool for helping make markets more complete. Nothing about the recent financial-market turmoil changes the fact that having more efficient and effective ways of transferring risk to parties most willing to bear it has the potential to improve economic efficiency. While financial-market regulation may be required to overcome negative externalities affecting the broader financial system, it is important that we not throw out the baby with the bathwater in response to the financial crisis.

Second, it is worth reminding the reader that the government itself bears a nontrivial share of responsibility for the ongoing trouble in financial markets. To cite one example out of many, Fannie Mae and Freddie Mac were able to profitably engage in excessive risk taking in the mortgage market in large part because they were implicitly backed by a federal government guarantee and thus partially shielded from the discipline of market forces. The fate of these entities underscores the importance of structuring government insurance programs in a manner that provides appropriate incentives for efficient risk taking.

Of course, recent events also underscore the dangers of having an inefficient and inconsistent regulatory system watching over complex and dynamic financial markets. In the context of the programs discussed in this volume, an increased reliance on private insurance markets and private capital markets would need to be accompanied by a more coherent and unified regulatory system. For example, given the increasingly national and global nature of many of the risks being insured, an insurance regulation system that relies on fifty different state regulatory agencies is unlikely to be the most efficient approach to achieving effective risk-management solutions.[2]

Conclusion

Risk is inherent in any economic system, and a key choice that any society faces is how to allocate risk. In a well-functioning market-based system, risks will be spread efficiently so that they are borne by those most willing to bear them in return for an appropriate risk premium. Unfortunately, it is well known that markets can, and often do, fail to spread this risk efficiently due to a variety of information problems and other market failures. In a subset of these cases, economic theory suggests that appropriately structured government intervention has the potential to improve outcomes.

Unfortunately, governments can also fail to spread risk efficiently. In some cases, such as in the presence of moral hazard, the government has no comparative advantage over markets in addressing the source of the problem. Even in those cases where the government does have a clear theoretical advantage through its power of compulsion or its ability to spread risks intertemporally, there is no guarantee that it will succeed in practice. Indeed, because the government operates according to political rather than market imperatives, it is in many cases uniquely *unable* to bring about effective risk transfer in the economy. Historical experience with government-run insurance programs in the United States makes clear that policymakers are unwilling or unable to implement risk-based pricing across a wide range of programs, a failure that leads to resource misallocation, excessive risk taking, and potentially enormous burdens on current and future taxpayers.

Given this history, it is by no means clear that public insurance systems outperform private ones, even in cases where there is evidence of market failures. This lack of clarity should, at a minimum, give policymakers, academic researchers, and analysts pause when they consider whether the government ought to enter a new area of insurance, such as insurance against natural catastrophe losses. The findings in these chapters point to the importance of utilizing market-based principles in designing new or reforming existing insurance programs. The imposition of market discipline, such as through risk-based pricing, is critical to improving the allocation of risk in the economy.

Taken as a whole, the analyses in this volume suggest three basic principles that should guide the government's role in insurance markets. First, the government should intervene in insurance markets only when there exists a clear market failure that prevents the private insurance market from efficiently transferring risk on its own. Second, after accounting for likely government failures in the design of the intervention, the government should have a very clear comparative advantage over the private market in overcoming the market failure and facilitating efficient risk allocation. Third, the government program should be designed to reproduce the outcomes that would have been delivered by a competitive market in the absence of any market failure. If the government's "value added" arises from its ability to transfer risk across generations, then to the extent possible the risk allocation within each generation should still be done according to market principles. Restricting the government's role to the limited set of situations where these principles can be met would improve the efficiency of risk allocation in the economy, and thus improve the overall economic well-being of present and future generations.

Notes

1. For example, the *9/11 Commission Report* outlines a number of specific recommendations designed to address problems related to information sharing across federal agencies. See National Commission on Terrorist Attacks upon the United States (2004), 416–19.

2. Grace and Scott (2008) provide a useful discussion of the reasons that the United States may wish to consider the optional federal chartering of insurance companies.

References

Akerlof, George A. 1970. The market for lemons: Quality uncertainty and the market mechanism. *Quarterly Journal of Economics* 84 (3): 488–500.

Black, Fischer, and Myron Scholes. 1973. The pricing of options and corporate liabilities. *Journal of Political Economy* 81: 637–54.

Bohn, Henning. 2006. Who bears what risk? An intergenerational perspective. In *Restructuring retirement risks*, ed. David Blitzstein, Olivia S. Mitchell, and Stephen P. Utkus, 10–36. Oxford: Oxford University Press.

Brown, Jeffrey R., and Peter Orszag. 2006. The political economy of government-issued survivor bonds. *Journal of Risk and Insurance* 73 (4): 611–31.

Buchanan, James M. 1975. The Samaritan's dilemma. In *Altruism, morality and economic theory*, ed. Edmund S. Phelps, 71–85. New York: Russell Sage Foundation.

Congressional Budget Office. 2004. Estimating the value of subsidies for federal loans and loan guarantees. August. www.cbo.gov/ftpdocs/57xx/doc5751/08-19-Credit-Subsidies.pdf.

Grace, Martin, and Hal S. Scott. 2008. Optional federal chartering of insurance: Rationale and design of a regulatory structure. Paper presented at "The Future of Insurance Regulation," AEI conference, July 10, Washington, D.C.

National Commission on Terrorist Attacks upon the United States. 2004. *9/11 Commission Report: Final Report of the National Commission on Terrorist Attacks.* Washington, D.C.: Government Printing Office. http://govinfo.library.unt.edu/911/report/ 911Report.pdf.

Rothschild, Michael, and Joseph Stiglitz. 1976. Equilibrium in competitive insurance markets: An essay on the economics of imperfect information. *Quarterly Journal of Economics* 90 (4): 629–49.

Stiglitz, Joseph. 1993. Perspectives on the role of government risk-bearing within the financial sector. In *Government risk-bearing*, ed. Mark S. Sniderman, 109–30. Boston: Kluwer Academic Publishers.

1

Deposit Insurance Reform

George G. Pennacchi

The U.S. government funds its operations by auctioning U.S. Treasury securities, which are considered to be free from default risk. It also gives banks the right to issue default-free debt in the form of deposits insured by the Federal Deposit Insurance Corporation (FDIC). FDIC insurance is valuable to banks because they pay investors lower interest rates on default-free debt than on comparable default-risky debt. FDIC backing is particularly valuable during economic downturns (recessions), when a "flight to quality" increases the demand for default-free investments. During 2008, many nonbank financial institutions applied for conversion to bank or thrift holding companies, in large part to obtain access to insured funding.[1] Because a greater share of the financial system is now protected by the safety net of deposit insurance, the FDIC's impact on the financial system has grown.

The goal of this chapter is to examine the nature of deposit insurance and suggest reforms that can improve the efficiency and stability of the financial system. Much of its focus is on the appropriate premiums that banks should pay for deposit insurance. Often this issue is neglected when deposit insurance, and bank regulation more generally, is discussed.[2] It is an important one, however, because it impacts the stability of the financial system as a whole. When premiums are set too low, as they often are, deposit insurance becomes available at a subsidized rate. This subsidization gives intermediaries the incentive to switch from uninsured debt to insured

The author thanks Mark Flannery for valuable comments.

deposits, a switch that became easier during the current decade due to legislation that liberalized the formation of bank holding companies.[3] With an increasing proportion of the financial system gaining access to artificially cheap insured deposits, there is likely to be a decline in financial system stability and a greater likelihood of taxpayer bailouts.

The plan of the chapter is as follows. The next section reviews justifications for government deposit insurance, which include its ability to provide a safe savings vehicle for small, unsophisticated investors and to prevent bank runs, and also considers its costs, which derive from the insurer's difficulties in assessing banks' risks. The third section gives a brief history of federal deposit insurance in the United States. As a prelude to highlighting the shortcomings of FDIC insurance, the fourth section discusses the risk characteristics of deposit insurance and how premiums should be set to avoid subsidies and their resulting distortions.

The fifth section considers how FDIC insurance falls short of an ideal deposit insurance system and why it tends to be subsidized. While FDIC insurance is promoted as being financed entirely by the banking industry, in practice it has received taxpayer infusions. Part of the taxpayer subsidy occurs when large banks—considered "Too Big to Fail" (TBTF)—are assisted. The sixth section discusses reforms that would minimize counterparty risk between financial institutions and investors and that would mitigate, if not eliminate, TBTF assistance. It also suggests alternative reforms for how deposit insurance premiums should be set in order to reduce subsidies, reduce the risk of banks paying higher premiums during economic downturns, and reduce the likelihood of taxpayer bailouts.

Rationale for Government Deposit Insurance

Government provision of deposit insurance has been justified by two main arguments. One is that deposit insurance creates a safe savings vehicle for financially unsophisticated individuals. If such individuals lack access to low-risk investments other than bank deposits, then deposit insurance transforms their default-risky bank debt into an investment that is default free. In the absence of deposit insurance, some individuals may be able to seek and monitor creditworthy banks in which to place their savings, but many people lack the ability to do this at low cost. It may be more efficient for a government to provide deposit insurance and for it, rather than many small savers, to supervise banks (Merton 1977). A related reason for deposit insurance involves banks' role in providing a liquid transactions account (checking deposit) for small, uninformed customers (Gorton and Pennacchi 1990). A bank's ability to create liquid transactions deposits can break down if its capital declines and default risk rises. In this circumstance, deposit insurance restores deposit liquidity by making deposits default free.[4]

The second main rationale for deposit insurance is that it may increase financial and monetary stability. The reasoning is as follows. Besides serving small savers, another role for banks is to efficiently lend to "opaque" firms and individuals: those borrowers whose creditworthiness needs to be evaluated and monitored in order to avoid excessive defaults. As Diamond (1984) shows, banks provide a low-cost means of screening the credit of loan applicants and monitoring borrowers on the behalf of many small savers (depositors). However, the private information about borrower credit risk that banks gain when making such loans can make loans illiquid. If a bank needs to sell such loans prior to maturity, value can be lost by liquidating them. This occurs due to an adverse selection problem where loan buyers suspect that a bank is selling its worst-quality loans. Alternatively, after selling a loan, a bank will lack the incentive to efficiently monitor the borrower, increasing the likelihood that the loan will default. In either case, loan buyers will discount the value of the loan so that loan sales will occur at fire-sale prices.

Banks' role in making illiquid loans then can conflict with their role in providing liquid deposit accounts. Bank runs occur if individuals decide to withdraw their deposits en masse in an attempt to avoid individually suffering losses should the bank need to liquidate its loans. Runs not only cause disruptions to bank-dependent borrowers. If individuals shift out of bank deposits and hoard currency, runs also have a monetary impact that is deflationary (Friedman and Schwartz 1963). Deposit insurance eliminates the incentive to start a bank run and thereby avoids the excessive liquidation of bank loans (Diamond and Dybvig 1983).

Protecting small savers and eliminating bank runs are the main benefits of government deposit insurance. But government deposit insurance also entails costs. It exposes the federal government to losses from bank failures and therefore requires the government to supervise and regulate banks (Flannery 1982). If government supervision and regulation of banks is lax, bank failures may be more likely than in the absence of deposit insurance. Banks are like any other limited-liability firm that issues debt: they may have moral hazard incentives to make excessively risky investments that, when successful, return high profits to shareholders but, when unsuccessful, return losses to debt holders or the government insurer. When a bank's debt is uninsured, debt holders have an incentive to limit this risk taking by restricting the bank's investments via covenants or by charging higher credit spreads on risky banks' debt. However, insured depositors lack the incentive to impose this market discipline. Hence, there is a need for the government insurer to regulate an insured bank's capital structure and investment policy, and to mimic the market discipline of risk-related credit spreads by charging risk-related deposit insurance premiums.

Unfortunately, political concerns impinge on a government's ability to adequately monitor financial institutions and assess their risks. Compared to market investors, government regulators face constraints that limit their ability to discriminate between banks having different risks of failure. Because of these limitations, deposit insurance premiums and bank regulation are unlikely to reflect the true cost of the government's guarantee. Stiglitz (1993, 114–15) argues this point:

> Government . . . faces a tremendous disadvantage in assessing risks and charging premiums based on risk differences. The reason . . . is that risk assessments are basically subjective. . . . No matter how rational the risk assessor may be, there is always a subjective element in choosing the relevant base for making such judgments. . . . Is it plausible to believe that the government could charge banks in Texas a higher premium for insurance than banks in Idaho . . . ? Any such differentiation might be quickly labeled unfair.
>
> The market makes such differentiations all the time, converting the subjective judgments of many participants into an objective standard. . . . Government inevitably has to employ relatively simple rules in assessing risk—rules that almost certainly do not capture all of the relevant information, since

> political considerations will not allow government to differentiate on bases that the market would almost surely employ.
>
> The difficulties government has in assessing risk, and that citizens face in evaluating the government's performance on this score, provide an opportunity for granting huge hidden subsidies.

In principle, deposit insurance might be provided by private insurers, who face fewer political constraints when assessing a bank's risk. However, unsophisticated depositors may lack the ability to evaluate the creditworthiness of private insurers and may have greater confidence that the federal government, with its power to tax and print money, can fulfill its deposit guarantee.[5] This confidence is especially important for insuring against bank defaults because, as will be argued below, bank failures tend to be correlated with one another and with large-scale economic downturns, making deposit insurance losses undiversifiable. A private insurance company may need a large amount of capital to ensure that it can make good on its promise and prevent incentives for bank runs.

One possibility for turning deposit insurance over to the private sector would be for private insurers to insure multiple banks' deposits and then have the federal government guarantee the private insurers' policies against default. While government supervision and regulation of the private insurers would be required, such an arrangement would likely be less complex for a government and subject to fewer distortions compared to directly regulating and monitoring each bank. If competitive private insurers were capitalized sufficiently, they would have an incentive to properly assess banks' risks and set fair premiums.

Another public-private arrangement would allow private insurers to insure a "first loss" piece of bank losses while the government covered catastrophic losses. Under this plan, private insurers could be required to put up collateral equal to the total amount of losses to which they are exposed, thus eliminating the possibility of their default. The arrangement would then be very similar to a credit-linked note or a subordinated debt requirement. Several proposals have been advanced to require that banks regularly issue subordinated debt.[6] A similar proposal would require that a bank issue subordinated debt that automatically converts to new shareholders' equity when the value of its original shareholders' equity declines (Flannery 2005).[7]

For all of these proposals, the larger the required private subordinated insurance/debt piece, the smaller any distortions resulting from government mispricing of the catastrophic loss piece.

Recent technological change and financial innovation make it possible to ask whether other financial structures can provide the same benefits as insuring bank deposits but with lower complexities and costs. For example, new financial arrangements have weakened the argument that traditionally insured bank deposits are necessary to provide small savers with a safe liquid transactions account. As discussed in Gorton and Pennacchi (1992, 1993), money market mutual fund shares can substitute for bank deposits. Because U.S. Securities and Exchange Commission (SEC) rules require money market funds to be invested in high-credit-quality, short-term instruments, rather than longer-maturity, credit-risky loans and investments, they have much lower default risk.[8] Any remaining default risk that money market funds do possess is relatively transparent and easy to assess, even by a government regulator. Government insurance of money market mutual funds could provide extra confidence to investors at much lower cost than deposit insurance.[9]

As outlined in Pennacchi (2006), banks could offer insured money market shares to their customers wanting a liquid, safe account by following SEC rules and fully collateralizing these accounts with money market instruments. These banks' remaining loans and investments would need to be funded with uninsured debt, such as wholesale certificates of deposit (CDs) and commercial paper.[10] Such a plan could be most easily implemented for the largest of U.S. banks, since most of their liabilities are already in the form of uninsured debt. As is the case today, during times of financial crisis the Federal Reserve can act as a lender of last resort to support wholesale CD and commercial paper markets in order to avoid runs by institutional investors.

In summary, the rationale for government deposit insurance is weaker now than when the FDIC was created in 1933. Structural changes in the financial system have created greater scope for private alternatives. The federal government may still have a role as a backstop, but it should leave the lion's share of risk assessment to private investors and/or insurers who can better perform this function. Alternatively, a government deposit insurer could emphasize the use of market information to assess banks' risks; that is, it could mimic private investors' risk assessments of particular banks. This topic is explored below, in the section on proposals for reform.

Brief History of U.S. Federal Deposit Insurance

Federal deposit insurance began under the (Glass-Steagall) Banking Act of 1933, which created the FDIC to insure deposits in commercial banks. The National Housing Act of 1934 created a parallel insurer for thrift institutions, the Federal Savings and Loan Insurance Corporation (FSLIC). In the wake of the savings and loan crisis in the 1980s, the FSLIC was abolished by the Financial Institutions Reform, Recovery and Enforcement Act of 1989 (FIRREA), and its insurance duties were transferred to the FDIC. Because the FSLIC's administration of deposit insurance was similar to that of the FDIC, our description of U.S. deposit insurance will focus on the FDIC.[11]

Through most of the FDIC's history, deposit insurance premiums did not depend on the creditworthiness of individual banks, largely because of the government's difficulty in assessing risk. From 1935 to 1990, each FDIC-insured bank was assessed one-twelfth of 1 percent of its total deposits (approximately 8.3 cents per $100 in deposits; that is, 8.3 basis points). However, the effective FDIC insurance premium per deposit paid by all banks was typically lower because, starting in 1950, a portion of it usually was rebated. This rebate was adjusted in order to target the amount of reserves in the FDIC's Deposit Insurance Fund (DIF).[12] FDIC reserves are invested in U.S. Treasury securities, and these reserves increase due to interest payments from these securities and due to banks' net premium payments. Reserves decline due to insurance claims arising from bank failures. The FDIC's reserves began in 1934 with a $289 million capital injection from the U.S. Treasury and the Federal Reserve.[13]

From the start, the banking industry generally wanted deposit insurance assessments to be set at a relatively low level (Federal Deposit Insurance Corp. 1984, 56). The FDIC, on the other hand, desired premiums to be high enough to maintain sufficient reserves for covering future claims from bank failures and to reduce the likelihood that additional funds from the U.S. Treasury would be required.[14] Thus since the creation of the FDIC there has been a focus on its reserves (the DIF) as a separate account within the overall federal government's balance sheet, and premiums have been adjusted to manage the DIF's level. In 1980, the DIF was given a range of between 1.1 and 1.4 percent of the banking industry's total insured deposits. Following depletion of the DIF due to the large number of bank failures during the 1980s (see figure 1-1), the 1989 FIRREA legislation mandated that premiums be set to eventually achieve a designated reserve ratio (DRR)—the ratio of reserves to total insured deposits—of 1.25 percent.

The costly bank failures of the 1980s and early 1990s, which required over $100 billion in taxpayer funds to resolve, ultimately led to reforms that included more stringent supervision of problem banks. The 1991 Federal Deposit Insurance Corporation Improvement Act (FDICIA) instituted several nondiscretionary supervisory interventions, known as "prompt corrective action" provisions, which required problem banks to quickly increase their capital ratios or be closed.[15] The act also required the FDIC to deal with problem banks and failed banks in a manner that would impose the least cost to the DIF. FDICIA made one exception: these "least cost" provisions could be lifted only when imposing them "would have serious adverse effects on economic conditions or financial stability."[16] This systemic risk exception requires approval by at least two-thirds of the FDIC Board, two-thirds of the Federal Reserve Board, and the U.S. Treasury Secretary after consultation with the U.S. president.

FDICIA also required that the FDIC establish risk-related premiums. The outcome of this requirement was a schedule where premiums differed depending on the level of a bank's capitalization (well capitalized, adequately capitalized, or undercapitalized) and its supervisory rating group (rating 1 or 2; rating 3; or rating 4 or 5). As a result, banks could in principle pay any of nine different levels of insurance premium depending on their capitalization and supervisory rating. Unfortunately, this assessment plan failed to effectively discriminate between different banks' riskiness; from 1996 to 2006, well over 90 percent of all banks were categorized in the lowest-risk category (well capitalized, rating 1 or 2).

FDICIA and the Deposit Insurance Funds Act of 1996 further specified that if DIF reserves exceeded the DRR of 1.25 percent, the FDIC was prohibited from charging any insurance premiums to banks in the lowest-risk category. In addition, if DIF reserves fell below 1.25 percent, all banks

FIGURE 1-1
NUMBER OF FAILURES AND FDIC ASSISTANCE TRANSACTIONS: COMMERCIAL BANKS AND THRIFTS, 1934–2009

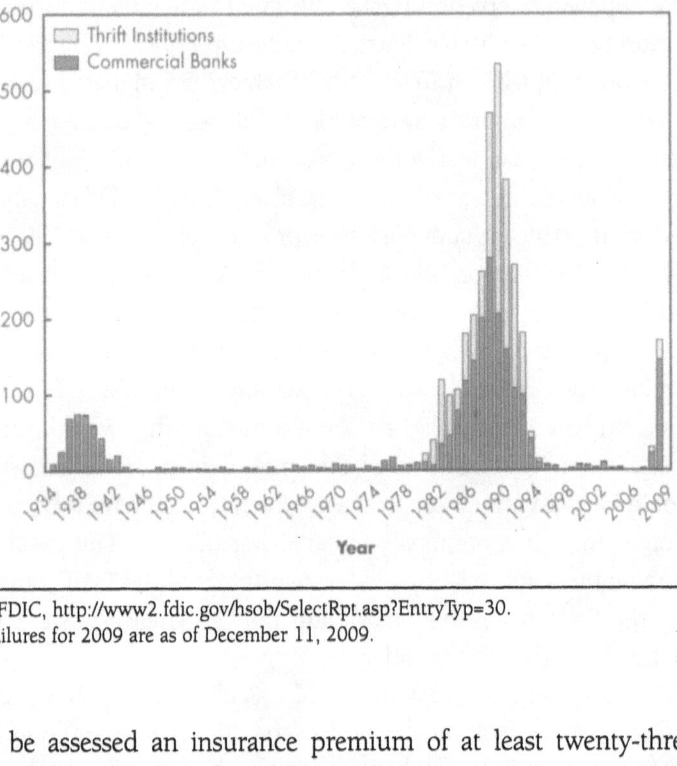

SOURCE: FDIC, http://www2.fdic.gov/hsob/SelectRpt.asp?EntryTyp=30.
NOTE: Failures for 2009 are as of December 11, 2009.

would be assessed an insurance premium of at least twenty-three basis points per $100 of deposits until the 1.25 percent target was restored. During the entire 1996 to 2006 period, DIF reserves were above 1.25 percent of insured deposits, and the vast majority of banks were classified in the lowest-risk category. Hence, during this decade, all but a small minority of banks paid nothing for deposit insurance.

The Federal Deposit Insurance Reform Act of 2005 (FDIRA) instituted two major changes regarding the setting of insurance premiums. First, this legislation allowed the FDIC to revise the risk-based classification system so that premiums could be charged for banks categorized as least risk even when DIF reserves were above target. The revised risk categories continue to be based on capital levels and supervisory ratings, but additional information (on financial ratios and, for large banks, the credit rating of long-term debt) is also used. At the time of adoption, approximately 45 percent of banks were charged the minimum rate. The initial proposal permitted base risk-related rates to range from two to forty basis points.[17]

Second, instead of a hard target of 1.25 percent, the DRR was now given a looser range of 1.15 percent to 1.50 percent. Reserves are managed to satisfy this DRR range as follows: when DIF reserves exceed 1.50 percent (1.35 percent), a rebate of 100 percent (50 percent) of the surplus is paid to banks. If DIF reserves fall below 1.15 percent, the FDIC must establish a restoration plan that raises premiums to a level sufficient to return reserves to the DRR range within five years. The reserves of DIF did fall to 1.01 percent of insured deposits on June 30, 2008, and the FDIC presented a restoration plan that assessed rates from twelve to forty-five basis points, depending on risk category.[18]

During the last quarter of 2008, the FDIC established temporary insurance programs. The Emergency Economic Stabilization Act, which created the Troubled Assets Relief Program (TARP) and was signed into law on October 3, 2008, also raised the basic per-account deposit insurance coverage from $100,000 to $250,000 until December 31, 2009 (the deadline was later extended until December 31, 2013). In addition, the FDIC gained approval for a systemic risk exception under FDICIA to create its Temporary Liquidity Guarantee Program (TLGP). TLGP is a voluntary program that has two main provisions. First, for a deposit insurance premium surcharge of ten basis points on balances exceeding $250,000, a bank can obtain unlimited insurance coverage for non-interest-bearing transactions accounts until December 31, 2009. Second, until June 30, 2009, banks and bank holding companies can issue senior unsecured debt that is guaranteed against default, with coverage limited until June 30, 2012.[19] The insurance premiums for debt having an initial maturity of between 30 and 180 days, 181 and 364 days, and 365 days or greater are fifty basis points, seventy-five basis points, and one hundred basis points, respectively.[20]

The amount of insured bank and bank holding company liabilities under these temporary programs will not be included in insured deposits when calculating the DIF reserve-to-insured-deposit ratio. However, because the TLGP was established under FDICIA's systemic risk exception, any net losses from the program must be covered by a special assessment charged to all banks. Any net surplus generated by TLGP would be added to the DIF. Note that a systemic risk exception was also invoked on November 23, 2008, when the FDIC made up to $10 billion in loan guarantees to assist Citigroup, so that any net losses from these guarantees would also require a special assessment paid by all banks.

At the end of 2008, the DIF had fallen to 0.40 percent of insured deposits, and the FDIC forecast that the fund would be wiped out in 2009 unless premiums were raised further. On February 27, 2009, the FDIC board approved a one-time, twenty-basis-point surcharge that would raise total premiums from thirty-two to seventy basis points, depending on risk category. An immediate outcry by the banking industry that such a large increase was unfair forced the FDIC to suspend this increase. However, by the first quarter of 2009, the DIF had further declined to 0.27 percent of insured deposits, and in May 2009 the FDIC approved a one-time premium equal to five basis points of a bank's total liabilities excluding Tier 1 capital.[21]

Nature of Deposit Insurance Risks

Several types of financial contracts provide insurance against default and are closely related to deposit insurance or guarantees of nondeposit bank debt. One type that has a long history in international trade is a financial guarantee called a standby letter of credit. Standby letters of credit are guarantees typically made by a financial institution to insure one party in a contract against the default of a second party's obligation in the contract. Often, this obligation is for the second party to make a future payment in return for a good delivered or service rendered by the first party. Hence, a letter of credit insures against the second party's default risk. Another type is municipal bond insurance: a guarantee by a financial institution against the default of a bond issued by a state or local government. The insurer guarantees to investors (the first party) the full promised payment on a municipal bond should the municipality (the second party) default.

Another very similar contract is a credit default swap (CDS). Under this contract, the insurer is called a "protection seller" and receives periodic premiums over the life of the insurance contract from a "protection buyer"—the first party. Should a second party default on a debt obligation, the protection seller pays the protection buyer the difference between the promised payment (or par value) of the second party's debt and the debt's current market or recovery value. Thus, if a CDS is written on a bank's senior unsecured debt, the contract's protection seller is providing the same insurance as that provided by the FDIC under its TLGP guarantee of the bank's senior unsecured debt. Similarly, a CDS contract written on a bank's uninsured, wholesale CD provides the same guarantee against default as does FDIC insurance of a CD.

Let us consider by way of the following example how the fair market premiums paid on CDS contracts and deposit insurance relate to yields on default-free and default-risky debt. Suppose that a newly issued, default-free Treasury note maturing in five years sells at par and makes periodic coupon payments at an annual rate of 4 percent. Also, a five-year note newly issued by a default-risky bank sells at par, but it must promise to make periodic coupon payments at an annual rate of 6 percent. The extra 2 percent in promised yield, defined as the bank note's "credit spread," provides fair market compensation to an investor for the bank note's default risk.

Indeed, one can see that this 2 percent credit spread would equal the fair CDS premium to insure the bank note. This is because an investor desiring a default-free note would be indifferent between purchasing the Treasury note at 4 percent or purchasing the default-risky bank note at 6 percent along with buying five years' of credit protection and paying a CDS premium of 2 percent. Similarly, an investor desiring a default-risky note would be indifferent between purchasing the bank note at 6 percent or purchasing the Treasury note at 4 percent and selling five years' of credit protection and receiving a CDS premium of 2 percent. Thus, we see that the spread between the default-risky bond's yield and the default-free bond's yield equals the fair premium for default insurance; that is, it equals the fair CDS premium. Similarly, we can think of the spread between the interest rate on a bank's uninsured deposit and the interest rate on the same bank's insured deposit as equal to the fair premium for deposit insurance.

This example helps to make clear that deposit insurance is exactly a CDS contract written on a deposit, but one where the bank pays the CDS premium to the protection seller (deposit insurer) on behalf of the depositor. Since the insured deposit is now a default-free investment, the depositor is willing to accept the default-free interest rate (e.g., 4 percent on a five-year CD) while that bank pays the credit spread (e.g., 2 percent), so that the bank's all-in cost would be approximately the same as if it issued an uninsured deposit (e.g., 6 percent). Interestingly, even the periodicity of premium payments for FDIC insurance and the typical CDS contract are the same: they are both assessed on a quarterly basis.

Deposit insurance and CDS guarantees on bank debt have risk characteristics that differ in important ways relative to most other forms of insurance such as life insurance and property or casualty insurance. The risks from underwriting many term life insurance policies or automobile collision policies can be diversified away by pooling the risks of several policies together. This is not the case for deposit insurance. The risks of deposit insurance losses due to bank failures cannot be diversified away by pooling the risks of many banks together, because deposit insurance loss claims are not independent or uncorrelated events. Bank failures are linked to macroeconomic conditions which tend to create financial distress at many banks at the same time. This is not surprising, since bank assets consist largely of real estate, commercial, and consumer loans, which experience higher default rates during economic downturns. Thus bank failures and deposit insurance losses rise during recessions and decline during expansions, so that they bear systematic risk.

Figure 1-1 (see page 28) shows the number of insured commercial bank and thrift institution failures during each year since the start of U.S. federal deposit insurance. Clearly, failures are clustered and are not independently distributed across years.[22] There were many years when the FDIC suffered few or no losses, but a significant number of years when its losses were substantial. This pattern of skewed risk differs substantially from the pattern shown by automobile or term life insurance policies, where loss rates from underwriting a large pool of insured individuals are relatively similar from one year to the next. These other forms of insurance have loss events that are much closer to being independently distributed, so that the law of large numbers applies and the average loss rates for the insured pool during any particular year are highly predictable.

When insurance is written on a pool of independent risks, a competitive insurer can set premiums equal to the annual expected losses and, due to the high predictability of these losses, experience minimal variation in net profits each year. This is not the case for deposit insurance because of the skewed nature of bank failures. If premiums are set to expected losses at the beginning of a year, the insurer will tend to experience small net profits in most years that will be wiped out by significant net losses in a smaller number of years.

Moreover, because bank failures tend to occur during economic downturns, the net profits and losses of underwriting deposit insurance will have risk that varies systematically with the economy and the value of other assets.

In terms of the capital asset pricing model (CAPM), underwriting deposit insurance is a positive beta investment: during economic expansions (recessions) when stock market returns are high (low), a deposit insurer will make profits (experience losses) because premiums will be greater (less) than loss claims from bank failures. Thus to compensate an insurer for the risk that losses will be highest during severe recessions, *fair premiums must exceed expected losses.* In other words, fair market deposit insurance premiums will contain a systematic risk premium in addition to expected losses so that a deposit insurer charging fair premiums will earn positive average profits. Importantly, empirical evidence finds that firms' actual credit spreads on uninsured debt contain, in addition to an expected loss component, a significant systematic risk premium (Elton et al. 2001). These uninsured debt holders, then, who can be viewed as investing in default-free debt along with underwriting debt insurance, earn average returns greater than a holder of only default-free debt.

As a result, if a deposit insurer does not include a charge for systematic risk when setting premiums, insured deposits will be subsidized relative to other forms of uninsured funding. This leads to two financial system distortions that excessively expand deposit insurance: banks will prefer financing using insured deposits rather than uninsured deposits or debt, thereby reducing market discipline; and nonbank financial intermediaries will lose market share relative to subsidized banks, in part as nonbank institutions convert to banks.[23]

The relationship between fair premiums and expected losses is illustrated in figure 1-2. The graphs are examples based on the simple Merton (1977) model, but their qualitative features hold for more realistic models.[24] The horizontal axis shows a bank's capital-to-debt ratio over the range of 15 percent to –5 percent, while the vertical axis gives annualized premiums and losses as a proportion of the bank's total debt. In each case, the graphs assume the annualized standard deviation of a bank's capital-to-total-liabilities ratio is 5 percent. The baseline assumption is that the bank's assets have systematic risk such that the expected rate of return on bank assets exceeds the default-free interest rate by 1 percent per annum.[25]

FIGURE 1-2
ANNUALIZED FAIR INSURANCE PREMIUMS (OR CREDIT SPREADS) AND EXPECTED LOSSES

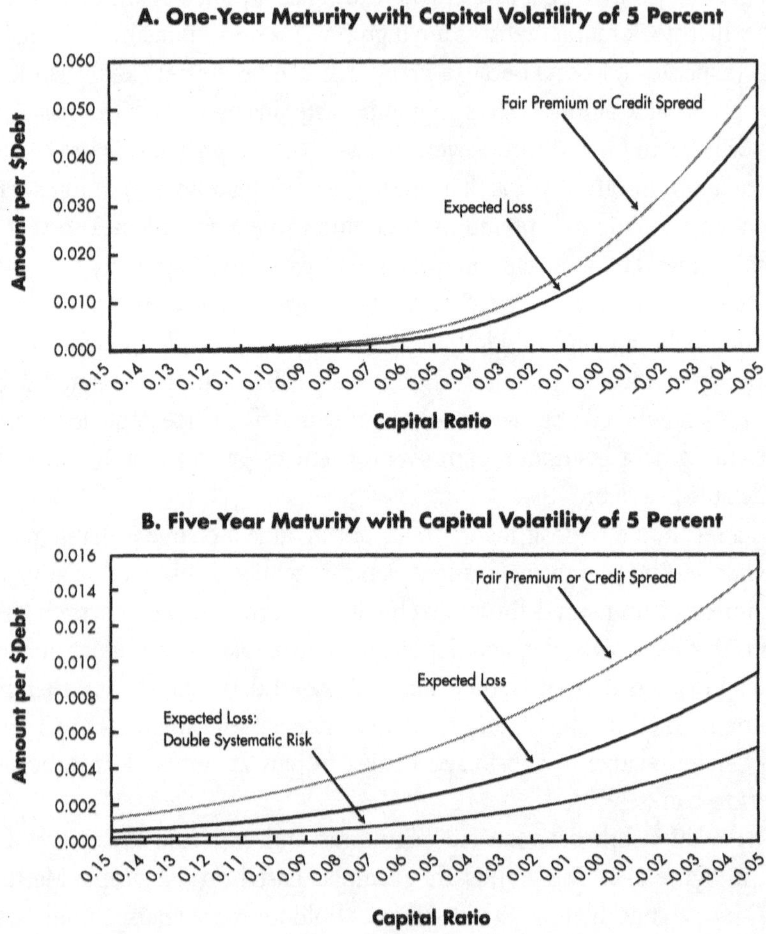

SOURCE: Author's calculations.

NOTE: The graphs are based on Merton (1977) and assume that a bank's capital-to-liability ratio has an annual standard deviation of 5 percent and that the expected return on bank assets is 1 percent greater than the default-free interest rate, except in the case of double systematic risk (shown in panel B), where the expected return on bank assets is 2 percent greater than the default-free interest rate.

Panel A considers the case of a one-year insurance contract horizon and shows how fair premiums and expected losses increase as a bank's capital ratio declines. However, due to systematic risk, fair premiums rise faster than expected losses. The difference between these two curves is the systematic risk premium required to compensate for the likelihood that the insurer's losses are incurred during economic downturns, while its profits are received during economic upturns. Panel B is a similar graph but for a five-year insurance contract horizon. Here, we see that both annualized premiums and annualized expected losses are greater than in panel A, and the difference between fair premiums and expected losses for any particular capital level is greater. Fixing a premium over five years rather than one year is unattractive to an insurer because it does not allow for adjustments upward if economic conditions worsen after the first year.

Panel B also represents the case where a bank's assets are assumed to have double the systematic risk such that their expected rate of return exceeds the default-free interest rate by 2 percent. Importantly, we maintain the assumption that the bank's capital ratio volatility remains at 5 percent, so that the fair premium is the same as the alternative case where systematic risk is less. However, assets with higher systematic risk, and therefore a higher expected rate of return, produce average insurer losses that are less, so if expected losses are used as a measure for setting insurance premiums, it would appear that the bank with more systematic risk is safer and should be charged a lower premium. But this approach is incorrect: while on average the bank imposes fewer losses on the insurer, when it does impose losses they are likely to occur during severe economic downturns.

This last example points to a third distortion that arises if insurance premiums are set to a bank's expected losses and fail to include a systematic risk premium: banks making loans and investments with higher systematic risk enjoy a greater financing subsidy relative to banks making loans and investments with lower systematic risk. As detailed in Pennacchi (2006), this systematic risk subsidy distorts the financial system's allocation of resources in favor of investments with excessive systematic risk, thereby magnifying the amplitude of economic cycles. If banks herd into investments with high systematic risk, there is a greater tendency for them to fail at the same time, creating more severe banking crises; that is, more "systemic" risk.

Shortcomings of the Current FDIC System

The 2005 FDIRA gave the FDIC slightly more flexibility in setting premiums. As mentioned earlier, it abolished the hard target for DIF that required premiums to rise (fall) sharply when the DIF fell below (rose above) a DRR of 1.25 percent. FDIRA also led to greater variation in premiums for banks having different risk attributes. But the current framework for setting premiums continues to produce needless distortions to banks' costs of financing and, more generally, to the financial system's allocation of credit. Finance theory provides no rationale for linking fair premiums to the level of an insurer's reserves. DIF reserves reflect past premiums and past insurance losses. Fair insurance premiums should be forward-looking, reflecting the likelihood and risk of future insurance losses.

Setting deposit insurance premiums to target DIF reserves (even if the target is a soft range of DRRs) implies that premiums tend to rise during economic downturns when bank failures rise and the DIF is depleted (Feldman 1998; Pennacchi 2000). This is what happened in 2008–2009. In contrast, premiums tend to fall during economic expansions when bank failures decline, as was the case prior to 2008. Thus, tying premiums to the DIF reserves can amplify economic cycles, as insured deposit funding becomes cheaper (more expensive) during expansions (recessions).

One argument for setting premiums to maintain a target level of DIF reserves is that such a practice insulates taxpayers from having to fund deposit insurance losses: premiums paid by banks will be raised to replenish the DIF so that taxpayers will not be at risk. However, the political economy of banking crises is incompatible with such a commitment by the banking industry. As we saw when FSLIC loss claims soared, surviving depository institutions argue that they should not be responsible for the imprudent behavior of their failed members.[26] In the 1989 FIRREA, legislators accepted this argument and agreed that taxpayers should help cover the thrift industry's losses. Curry and Shibut (2000) calculate that as of year-end 1999, resolving the savings and loan crisis cost the thrift industry $29 billion, but cost the taxpayers $124 billion.

During the current economic crisis, there is a similar lack of commitment to having the banking industry cover all deposit insurance losses. Potential deposit insurance losses from banks are again being transferred to taxpayers. Take the case of Wachovia. In late September 2008, Wells Fargo and Citigroup were negotiating with the FDIC for assistance in return for taking over the distressed bank Wachovia. However, Wells Fargo pulled out of the negotiations, leaving Citigroup as the only bidder. On September 29, Citigroup made a $2.2 billion bid to acquire Wachovia with FDIC assistance given under FDICIA's systemic risk exception.[27] The next day, September 30, the U.S. Treasury issued Internal Revenue Service (IRS) Notice 2008-83, which abolished limitations on tax shelters derived from an acquiring bank's use of an acquired bank's prior losses.[28] Shortly afterward, on October 3, Wells Fargo reentered the bidding for Wachovia with a $15.4 billion offer that required no FDIC assistance. The FDIC and Wachovia, siding with Wells Fargo, nullified the Citigroup deal.

What motivated Wells Fargo to reenter with such an attractive bid? Under the prior tax rule, Wells Fargo would have been limited to deducting Wachovia losses of $930 million a year for twenty years. However, under the new rule Wells Fargo can deduct all $74 billion of Wachovia losses. At a 35 percent corporate tax rate, the extra $55.4 billion in deductible losses represents roughly a $19.4 billion taxpayer infusion to Wells Fargo and Wachovia. This is likely to be more than the value of the assistance that the FDIC would have provided to Citigroup; yet the assistance to Wells Fargo does not affect the DIF and will not be borne by the banking industry in the form of higher future insurance premiums.

This targeted Treasury tax ruling subsequently benefited two other banks acquiring distressed banks. Tax experts estimate that the takeover of distressed National City by PNC, announced on October 24, 2008, will cost taxpayers $5.1 billion in lost revenue from PNC's expanded deductions.[29] Similarly, Banco Santander, which announced on October 13, 2008, that it would fully acquire Sovereign, will receive several billion dollars of tax benefits as a result of the Treasury's ruling. The 2009 American Recovery and Reinvestment Act (stimulus legislation), signed into law on February 17, 2009, repealed IRS Notice 2008-83 for future acquisitions, but it grandfathered the tax benefits received for these prior acquisitions.

Taxpayers are also now expected to assist Citigroup. On November 23, 2008, the U.S. government agreed to cover 90 percent of losses above $29 billion on Citigroup's $306 billion portfolio of mortgage-related assets. However, the first $5 billion of any U.S. government losses are absorbed by the U.S. Treasury via assistance through the TARP, while the next $10 billion are absorbed by the FDIC. Hence, rather than Citigroup's assistance being provided solely by the FDIC and affecting the DIF, taxpayers are first in line to bear losses.[30] In January 2009, the Congressional Budget Office estimated that the present value of taxpayer losses for all TARP assistance to Citigroup is $5 billion (CBO 2009). More generally, taxpayer assistance provided to other banks through the TARP Capital Purchase Program (CPP) very likely will take the place of FDIC losses that would have been incurred from resolving failed banks. CBO's estimate of taxpayer losses from other CPP assistance is $32 billion.

Thus, political pressure to aid the banking industry makes it doubtful that a DIF targeting scheme will, in fact, commit the banking industry to cover all its losses. When losses become large, government officials find either direct or indirect ways to let the banking industry off the hook and transfer the cost of bank failures to taxpayers. Perhaps this is why the banking industry has been in favor of a DIF targeting scheme: during economic expansions banks receive premium rebates of the DIF surplus, but during economic recessions banks are released from bearing the full brunt of paying higher premiums to replenish the DIF. By itself, then, a DIF targeting policy leads to a subsidy of the banking industry. In contrast, a policy in which premiums are set fairly and independent of the DIF would, by definition, involve a zero subsidy, and taxpayers would, on average, make profits from providing deposit insurance.[31]

This is not a contradiction. As discussed earlier, the expected profits earned by taxpayers provide compensation for their exposure to systematic risk. Pennacchi (2000) shows that if insurance premiums were set fairly, the value of the DIF should under most scenarios be expected to grow indefinitely. In other words, a stable DIF ratio is incompatible with fair pricing for deposit insurance. This is another argument for ignoring the DIF and allowing the U.S. Treasury to retain any premiums in excess of deposit insurance losses and to cover any deficits. Under fair premiums the Treasury should profit, on average.

Another reason for ignoring FDIC reserves is that highlighting them is likely to undermine the very confidence in bank safety the FDIC was designed to create. If reporting reserves furthers the myth that they are essential for insuring bank deposits, runs by insured depositors can result from falling DIF reserves during financial crises.[32] In the words of many banks and the FDIC Web site, "FDIC deposit insurance is backed by the full faith and credit of the United States government," and it should be this fact alone that supports FDIC insurance viability and pricing.[33]

While a reserve targeting policy contributes to subsidizing deposit insurance, the current FDIC framework for determining how premiums should vary with respect to a given bank's risk may also subsidize systematic risk. For the most part, the models underlying the FDIC's premium schedules are based on either the probability of a bank's experiencing a supervisory rating downgrade, or the bank's credit rating on its long-term debt. Unfortunately, the probability of a rating downgrade does not account for the sensitivity of a bank's downgrade risk to overall economic conditions—that is, its systematic rather than its idiosyncratic risk. Similarly, the credit rating of a bank's debt reflects the rating agency's view of the probability of default or the expected default loss. It does not measure the systematic risk of default—that is, the sensitivity of default to economic conditions.[34]

As illustrated in figure 1-2 (see page 34) and discussed in Duffie et al. (2003), the required systematic risk component of fair deposit insurance premiums can be large. Also as noted earlier, failure to incorporate this systematic risk component creates incentives to excessively issue insured deposits and motivates banks to make investments in loans and securities with high systematic risk. Moreover, failure to account for systematic risk is likely to provide a relatively greater deposit insurance subsidy to large banks: Demsetz and Strahan (1997) find that larger banks typically possess greater systematic risk than do smaller ones. Their finding is consistent with what is occurring during the current financial crisis, which has centered on systematic losses at primarily large banks.

In addition to deficiencies in setting insurance premiums, insufficient progress has been made in reducing the Too Big to Fail problem. A TBTF policy directly affects deposit insurance, because the systematic risk exception to FDICIA allows the FDIC to circumvent the resolution method that would minimize deposit insurance losses. Often, the course taken to assist a TBTF bank ends up protecting investors in the troubled bank's uninsured debt. If such investors expect that the bank is TBTF, so that they are de facto insured, the default risk premium (credit spread) that the bank pays on its debt will be smaller than in the absence of this expectation. Hence, the implicit insurance deriving from a TBTF policy represents another subsidy to large banks.[35]

The FDIC has made progress in improving how large banks report the amounts of their insured and uninsured deposits, so when banks fail it can quickly determine which accounts qualify for immediate availability of funds. However, as Stern and Feldman (2004) make clear, there are many other measures that could have been implemented to prevent the losses at one large financial institution from spilling over to others. It is the fear that these spillovers will create systematic risk that provides the main justification for TBTF bailouts.

Reform Proposals

Because the reach of federal deposit insurance has expanded during the recent financial crisis, reducing its distortions should be a major focus of regulatory reform. Failure to address the deficiencies of the current system could prove costly and hasten the next crisis. This section makes several recommendations for reform. Some proposals are alternative ways of reaching the same goal, which is to manage and price insurance fairly, thereby creating a level playing field between various types of financial intermediaries and markets.

End TBTF Assistance. Distortions arise when the U.S. Treasury or the FDIC assists large, interconnected financial institutions. The potential for TBTF assistance results in moral hazard by creating incentives for financial institutions to grow large and complex, perhaps through inefficient acquisitions. It also creates incentives for excessive risk taking, since uninsured debt holders of these institutions are de facto insured and thus do not penalize the institution by requiring that it pay a credit spread commensurate with its risk.

The resort to TBTF bailouts is not inevitable. In recent TBTF assistance to Bear Stearns, AIG, Wachovia, and Citigroup, the justification was that the failure of these institutions would lead to losses at other financial institutions because of complex interconnectedness, primarily arising from counterparty risk in over-the-counter (OTC) derivative contracts. Therefore, removing the negative externality of OTC contracts would be the most important reform designed to end TBTF assistance.

In principle, parties in derivative contracts might research the creditworthiness of their trading partners and set appropriate margin (collateral) requirements. However, as noted by Merton (1995), many customers of large financial institutions lack the desire or expertise to evaluate the institution's default risk.[36] Hence, there may be significant cost efficiencies from having a central clearinghouse with expertise in setting appropriate margin requirements for OTC derivative transactions. Clearinghouses have an excellent record of preventing contract defaults, even during times of extreme market volatility. A central clearinghouse also has an information advantage that enables it to net the various positions that a particular party has with many different counterparties. Netting can reduce the amount of margin required by a party if some of its derivative positions are offsetting.

In addition to central clearing of derivatives, a further step to eliminate TBTF assistance would be to encourage or require exchange trading, rather than over-the-counter trading, of derivatives. While the ability to customize the terms of OTC contracts offers some benefits, there is an obvious downside to OTC trading: where a particular financial institution has a significant share of the market making in a specific type of OTC contract, TBTF might be invoked even in the absence of counterparty risk because that institution's failure could significantly reduce the market-making capacity for that contract. If, instead, the contract was traded on an exchange, the market structure for the contract would remain intact following any financial institution's failure. Another well-known benefit of exchange trading is that standardization of contracts increases contract liquidity and makes for more competitive and transparent pricing.

Establish Fair Market Pricing. As noted earlier, governments face political constraints when assessing risk (Stiglitz 1993). One step toward insulating the FDIC from charges of unfairness in rate setting is to rely on market prices when determining insurance premiums. Recently, the UK treasury made an important advance in this regard. On October 8, 2008, it announced its Credit Guarantee Scheme (CGS), similar in form to the FDIC's TLGP for insuring banks' senior unsecured debt. However, instead of following the FDIC's policy of setting the same premiums for all qualifying banks, the CGS charges an annual premium for a bank's senior unsecured debt equal to fifty basis points plus the bank's median five-year-maturity CDS spread during the twelve months prior to October 8, 2008.[37] Because CDS spreads differ across banks, this premium-setting method discriminates between high- and low-risk banks. Furthermore, because CDS spreads are likely to incorporate a systematic risk premium, this method also avoids subsidizing systematic risk.

A potential criticism of using market information such as CDS spreads to set insurance premiums is that such a practice would create excessive volatility in the premiums paid by banks.[38] However, this view fails to account for differences in the types of insurance contracts that can be offered. Pennacchi (2005) shows that insurance contracts, and therefore fair premiums, can vary based on a contract's maturity. An insurance contract's maturity can be compared to the maturity of a firm's uninsured debt. A firm could choose to issue all of its debt with a one-year maturity and each year roll over all of its debt into new debt having a one-year maturity. In such a case, the credit spread that the firm pays on its debt could change dramatically each year because its creditworthiness and the market price of default risk change annually. But another firm could issue debt having a five-year maturity; each year only one-fifth of its total debt matures and is rolled over into new five-year debt. A firm with five-year overlapping debt contracts would pay an average credit spread that is much smoother over time.

Figure 1-3 illustrates the fair insurance premiums that five different banks would have paid on their senior unsecured debt during the 2004 to 2009 period. The premiums equal the individual banks' market CDS spreads having maturities of one or five years. In panel A of the figure, banks are assumed to have one-year insurance contracts, while in panel B, the banks are assumed to have five-year overlapping contracts. It is apparent that the five-year overlapping contracts produce a smoother time series of insurance premiums. However, the cost to the bank for this greater stability is a greater average premium for the longer-maturity contract. The reason is that an insurer providing long-maturity contracts bears greater systematic risk: its premiums do not rise much during bad economic times, when a bank's default risk is likely to rise. Therefore, to compensate the insurer for greater net losses during bad years, the average long-maturity premium must exceed the average short-maturity premium.

While CDS markets typically exist for major banks' senior unsecured debt, market information on these spreads is not directly applicable to setting insurance premiums on deposits, because deposits are an even more senior claim on a bank's assets. This seniority of deposits was established

FIGURE 1-3
FAIR INSURANCE PREMIUMS

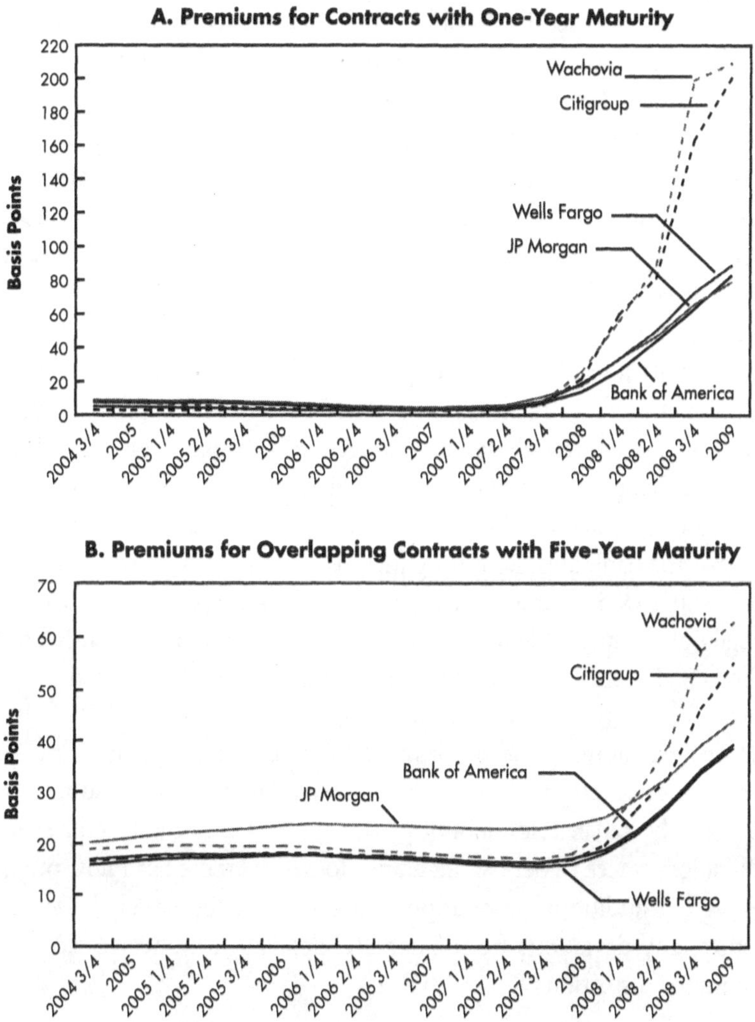

SOURCE: Author's calculations using credit default swap data obtained from Bloomberg.

under the Omnibus Budget Reconciliation Act of 1993 and is known as "depositor preference."[39] However, models exist for converting the CDS spreads on less senior debt to fair insurance premiums on more senior deposits. Furthermore, if the bank has publicly traded equity (stock), information on stock prices can be used to determine fair deposit insurance rates. Falkenheim and Pennacchi (2003) and Duffie et al. (2003) provide techniques for estimating fair deposit insurance rates for privately held banks.

As discussed in the second section, a structural change that would greatly simplify the setting of premiums for insured deposits is to take the concept of depositor preference further and give FDIC-insured deposits a secured (collateralized) claim on high-credit-quality bank assets. There is precedent for this practice. When the Federal Reserve lends to banks through the discount window, it requires banks to pledge high-quality securities to secure its loans. Similarly, when Federal Home Loan Banks (FHLBs) make advances to banks, they require that these loans be secured with mortgage-related assets. Because of this pledged collateral, the Federal Reserve and the FHLBs have higher priority than the FDIC's unsecured claim on a bank's assets in the event that the bank fails. Requiring that insured deposits be collateralized by high-quality money market instruments allows fair deposit insurance rates to be negligible, comparable to the one-basis-point premium currently charged by the U.S. Treasury to insure the shares of money market mutual funds.[40]

Another alternative that would simplify the setting of FDIC deposit insurance premiums is the subordinated debt or private insurance requirement mentioned earlier. If banks had substantial amounts of subordinated (and possibly convertible) debt or private insurance that covered a substantial "first loss" piece of deposit insurance losses, then the fair FDIC premium for covering additional catastrophic losses would be small.[41] Given this structure, any deviations from fair FDIC deposit insurance pricing would cause minor distortions.

Divorce Premiums from Deposit Insurance Fund Reserves. As stated earlier, the setting of fair market deposit insurance premiums, which prevents subsidies and distortions to banks' costs of financing, is possible only if premiums are divorced from DIF reserves. The most straightforward way to prevent DIF reserves from impinging on the fair pricing of insurance is to abolish the DIF. Without a DIF, the FDIC's net income from providing deposit insurance would be transferred each year to the U.S. Treasury, just as the seigniorage revenue from money creation is transferred to the Treasury from the Federal Reserve. In years when this net revenue is negative, the FDIC would receive an opposite transfer from the Treasury. However, since fair insurance premiums exceed expected insurance losses due to their systematic risk component, when the FDIC sets fair premiums its expected transfer to the Treasury will be positive.

If it is politically infeasible to allow for FDIC funding from the Treasury during the minority of years when its net revenues are negative, it could still set fair premiums (as if the fund did not exist) but operate a separate reserve targeting scheme. Specifically, the fair premiums charged to banks by the FDIC would continue to augment DIF reserves, and the FDIC's deposit insurance loss claims would continue to deplete DIF reserves. However, the FDIC would charge a separate assessment to replenish the DIF when it is below the DRR range and pay a separate dividend from the DIF when it is above the DRR range. Importantly, the participants in this reserve targeting scheme *need not be banks*. The FDIC could sell shares in the DIF that require the shareholder to contribute funds when the DIF is below the DRR range and to receive dividends when the DIF is above the DRR range. If the FDIC charges fair premiums, the market value of these shares will be approximately zero when the DIF is at the midpoint of the DRR range.

Banks could participate in this reserve targeting scheme, but from a risk-management point of view, it would be better if they sold their current shares to investors outside the banking industry who are better able to bear the risk. Because reserve targeting assessments tend to rise when bank failures are high, banks should diversify away from this risk, which requires them to draw down their capital when they are likely to want to increase it. Transferring the risk of reserve targeting outside the banking industry would undoubtedly improve banking stability.

A similar reserve targeting mechanism that would transfer risk is an FDIC industry assessment swap market.[42] Note that banks pay quarterly assessments to the FDIC, and due to reserve targeting, the average assessment per deposit across all banks is stochastic, rising (falling) when the DIF falls below (rises above) target. An industry assessment swap market allows a bank to swap a future FDIC industry-average assessment for a payment that is known today. In terms of a standard (interest rate) swap, banks would want to be fixed-rate payers and floating-rate receivers, where they receive the future industry-average assessments required by the FDIC during future quarters. Like other derivative markets, a centralized clearinghouse would determine appropriate margin requirements to mitigate the swaps' counterparty risk.

Conclusions

Federal deposit insurance provides benefits by protecting small, unsophisticated savers and by mitigating bank runs. However, because governments are politically constrained in their assessment of banks' risks, government deposit insurance is usually priced unfairly and administered inefficiently. As a result, government deposit insurance can create financial system distortions. If deposit insurance is to be fairly priced, premiums need to be divorced from the DIF reserves and must include a systematic risk component that compensates the insurer (taxpayers) for bearing loss claims during economic downturns.

Unfortunately, current FDIC practice continues to link premiums to DIF reserves and fails to incorporate a systematic risk premium, thereby subsidizing systematic risk. In addition, a TBTF policy results in preferential assistance to large, interconnected financial institutions, thereby subsidizing size and complexity. These subsidies led to distortions that helped create the current financial crisis.

Deposit insurance subsidies and their resulting inefficiencies can be reduced. An essential reform is to minimize TBTF assistance, mainly through central clearing and exchange trading of derivatives. A second set of reforms would reduce the mispricing and distortions of deposit insurance through mandatory subordinated and convertible debt, private insurance with a federal backstop, reliance on market information to set deposit insurance premiums, and mandatory collateralization of insured deposits.

The recent expansion of the deposit insurance safety net makes clear that changes are needed now more than ever; the current crisis shows how tempting it is for government to resort to taxpayer bailouts—and how unwise. Hopefully, the current crisis will motivate structural improvements to deposit insurance that will increase the financial system's efficiency and stability.

Notes

1. Financial institutions that have applied for bank or thrift holding company status include investment banks (Goldman Sachs, Morgan Stanley, Raymond James), finance companies (American Express, CIT, GMAC), and insurance companies (Aegon, Genworth Financial, Hartford Financial, and Lincoln National). Besides gaining access to insured deposits, institutions with this status become eligible for insurance on their senior unsecured debt, as will be discussed later.

2. In the past, bank regulation has emphasized setting appropriate capital standards (such as the Basel I and II international capital standards) far more than setting proper deposit insurance premiums. But theory such as Flannery (1991) implies that setting both capital standards and deposit insurance premiums is required for optimal bank regulation.

3. Specifically, the (Gramm-Leach-Bliley) Financial Services Modernization Act of 1999 eased consolidation between banks, securities firms, and insurance companies.

4. This need for deposit insurance is supported by Laeven's (2004) empirical findings that insurance coverage is significantly higher in countries where banks tend to be poorly capitalized and where depositors tend to be poorly educated.

5. During the 1980s, as bank failures mounted, there was some anxiety about whether the U.S. government stood behind federal deposit insurance corporations. In an attempt to quell this fear, Title IX of the Competitive Equality Banking Act of 1987 formally stated that "deposits up to the statutorily prescribed amount in federally insured depository institutions are backed by the full faith and credit of the United States." *Competitive Equality Banking Act of 1987*, Public Law 100-86, *U.S. Statutes at Large* 101 (1987): 552.

6. See Evanoff and Wall (2000) for a review of proposals that require banks to regularly issue subordinated debt. DeYoung et al. (2001) show that subordinated debt yields, as well as supervisory ratings, provide valuable information about a bank's risk.

7. An attractive aspect of this proposal is that a bank is not forced into default and receivership when its original shareholders' equity declines: its convertible debt serves as "contingent capital." This is not unlike the February 2009 conversion of the U.S. Treasury's preferred shares of Citigroup into new Citigroup common shareholders' equity. Kashyap, Rajan, and Stein (2008) present a related contingent capital proposal.

8. This statement holds true despite the recent "breaking of the buck" by the Primary Reserve Fund. This money market fund's loss of 1.5 percent of its asset value resulted from its large position in defaulted Lehman Brothers commercial paper, which had been rated A2/P2. Current SEC regulations require at least 95 percent of a fund's holdings to be rated A1/P1 and at most 5 percent to be rated A2/P2. The fund's loss could have been prevented by tighter SEC rules, such as disallowing obligations rated A2/P2 or requiring more diversification across companies if they are rated A2/P2.

9. In September 2008, the U.S. Treasury established a temporary program to guarantee money market mutual fund shares for an annual premium of one basis point (one cent per $100 of insured shares). See Bullard (2009) for arguments favoring money market mutual fund insurance over deposit insurance.

10. There is theoretical research that seeks to explain banks' practice of funding illiquid loans by uninsured, short-maturity deposits as an optimal contract. This work includes Diamond (1984), Calomiris and Kahn (1991), and Diamond and Rajan (2001). However, this research models bank deposits simply as short-term bank debt, so that these justifications for a bank's structure hold for wholesale CDs and commercial paper as well as uninsured bank deposits.

11. A third federal insurer, the National Credit Union Share Insurance Fund (NCUSIF), was created in 1970 to insure the shares (deposits) of credit unions. Its administration of share insurance closely follows the FDIC's administration of deposit insurance.

12. Prior to 2005, there were two insurance funds: the Bank Insurance Fund (BIF) covering commercial banks and the Savings Association Insurance Fund (SAIF) covering thrifts. The Federal Savings and Loan Insurance Corporation (FSLIC) operated an insurance fund that became known as the SAIF when it was taken over by the FDIC in 1989. The funds were merged as the DIF in 2005.

13. By 1951, the FDIC had repaid with interest this initial capital injection.

14. The Banking Act of 1935 provided the FDIC with a $975 million line of credit from the U.S. Treasury. Currently, this line of credit is formally set at $30 billion.

15. Prompt corrective action provisions were a response to the view that thrift and commercial bank regulators had delayed the closure of undercapitalized banks. This "regulatory forbearance" had added to the ultimate cost of resolving failed banks and led to the taxpayer bailout.

16. *Federal Deposit Insurance Corporation Improvement Act of 1991*, Public Law 102-242, *U.S. Statutes at Large* 105 (1991): 2236. The quotation is from Section 141(a)(I)(G)).

17. *Federal Register* 71, no. 141, July 24, 2006.

18. *Federal Register* 73, no. 201, October 16, 2008.

19. In most cases the FDIC will approve issuance of debt that is no greater than 125 percent of a bank's debt as of September 30, 2008. This debt can include promissory notes, commercial paper, and interbank funding having a maturity of at least thirty days.

20. The TLGP was extended until October 31, 2009, with debt issued during this extension period subject to a surcharge of up to fifty basis points.

21. *Federal Register* 74, no. 102, May 29, 2009.

22. Using a sample of sixty-eight publicly traded U.S. banks over the 1987 to 1996 period, Pennacchi (2000) finds that the average monthly correlation between banks' market values of capital (net worth) is 37.5 percent.

23. A prime example occurred after passage of the Financial Services Modernization (Gramm-Leach-Bliley) Act of 1999, which allowed securities firms to acquire banks.

Recall that during the period 1996 to 2006, deposit insurance premiums clearly were subsidized, because they were set at zero for the vast majority of banks. As a result, retail securities firms chose to transfer hundreds of billions of dollars of their customers' sweep accounts out of money market mutual funds and into FDIC-insured money market deposit accounts (MMDAs). From the end of 1999 to the end of 2004, balances in MMDAs grew at a 16.4 percent annual rate, while assets of retail money funds *declined* at a 3.0 percent annual rate, a phenomenon that Crane and Krasner (2004) refer to as "re-intermediation."

24. Pennacchi (2005) gives estimates of fair premiums and expected losses for forty-two large U.S. banks based on a multiperiod extension of the Merton (1977) model.

25. Historically, returns on banks' assets have averaged approximately 1 percent more than banks' interest payments on their debt and deposits. See Pennacchi (2000) for a discussion.

26. As FDIC loss claims have risen during the current financial crisis, the same arguments are being made by banks that face the possibility of higher FDIC premiums needed to replenish the DIF. For example, see Joe Adler, "FDIC's New Assessment Lambasted as Unfair," *American Banker,* March 2, 2009.

27. The FDIC would absorb all losses above $42 billion on a $312 billion portfolio of Wachovia loans in exchange for a $12 billion stake in Citigroup. Any net cost of this FDIC assistance would require a special assessment charged to the banking industry.

28. In order to prevent mergers that were motivated only by tax benefits, Congress had intended to restrict the amount of an acquired firm's losses that an acquiring firm could deduct. The Treasury's ruling exempted from this restriction only loan losses of acquired banks. Some have questioned whether the U.S. Treasury had the authority to amend this tax law. See "Obscure Tax Breaks Increase Cost of Financial Rescue," *Wall Street Journal,* October 18, 2008.

29. See "PNC Stands to Gain from Tax Ruling," *Wall Street Journal,* October 30, 2008.

30. For this guarantee, the U.S. Treasury obtains $4 billion in Citigroup preferred stock and the FDIC obtains $3 billion in Citigroup preferred stock. Of course this preferred stock may end up being worthless if the U.S. government has to make good on its guarantee. There are other provisions to the assistance involving a $20 billion preferred stock injection by the Treasury.

31. If federal government budgets are appropriately based on accrual accounting rather than cash flow accounting, the cost of federal deposit insurance should be recorded when the government's liability for providing that insurance is incurred. In turn, the present value of premium revenue received from providing the insurance will equal that same cost if premiums are set equal to their fair market values.

32. Cook and Spellman (1994) provide evidence that FSLIC-insured depositors demanded a risk premium to cover the possibility that the FSLIC would be unable to fulfill its guarantee.

33. For the FDIC Web site, see www.fdic.gov/consumers/banking/confidence/symbol.html.

34. Coval, Jurek, and Stafford (2009) emphasize this point and discuss how a focus on credit ratings resulted in the creation of structured financial instruments with excessive systematic risk.

35. A TBTF subsidy is often cited by small bank owners, often to lobby for an increase in the insured deposit limit. Recently, small bank owners have complained of the FDIC's systematic risk exceptions, since both small and large banks could be burdened with a special assessment if such assistance proves costly to the FDIC. See "Prospect of Citi Premium Fuels Anger," *American Banker,* November 25, 2008.

36. For example, a customer who wishes to take a position in an interest rate swap or a CDS on a third-party corporation may not have the desire or expertise to evaluate the credit of the OTC dealer who is taking the other side of the derivative contract.

37. The guarantee can be used to cover CDs, commercial paper, and senior unsecured bonds and notes. The Treasury can apply its own estimate of an appropriate CDS spread if public data for the bank's CDS spreads are unavailable.

38. A similar criticism is often made for market value accounting.

39. See Marino and Bennett (1999) and Osterberg and Thomson (2003) for the consequences of this legislation.

40. Pennacchi (2006) discusses the feasibility of requiring such collateralization.

41. Note that issuance of mandatory subordinated debt could be designed to resemble the overlapping longer-maturity insurance contracts discussed above.

42. A similar derivative security exists for the property insurance industry and is called an industry loss warrant.

References

Bullard, Mercer. 2009. Federally-insured money market funds and narrow banks: The path of least insurance. Working paper. University of Mississippi School of Law. Available at http://ssrn.com/abstract=1351987.

Calomiris, Charles, and Charles Kahn. 1991. The role of demandable debt in structuring optimal banking arrangements. *American Economic Review* 81: 497–513.

Congressional Budget Office. 2009. *The Troubled Asset Relief Program: Report on transactions through December 31, 2008.* Washington, D.C.: Congressional Budget Office. January. http://www.cbo.gov/doc.cfm?index=9961.

Cook, Douglas, and Lewis Spellman. 1994. Repudiation risk and restitution costs: Toward understanding premiums on insured deposits. *Journal of Money, Credit and Banking* 26: 439–59.

Coval, Joshua, Jakub Jurek, and Erik Stafford. 2009. Economic catastrophe bonds. *American Economic Review* 99 (3): 628–66.

Crane, Peter, and Michael Krasner. 2004. *Brokerage cash sweep options: The shift from money funds to FDIC-insured bank deposit accounts.* iMoneyNet, Inc., special report. November.

Curry, Timothy, and Lynn Shibut. 2000. The cost of the savings and loan crisis: Truth and consequences. *FDIC Banking Review* 13 (2): 26–35. December.

Demsetz, Rebecca, and Philip Strahan. 1997. Diversification, size, and risk at U.S. bank holding companies. *Journal of Money, Credit and Banking* 29: 300–313.

DeYoung, Robert, Mark Flannery, William Lang, and Sorin Sorescu. 2001. The information content of bank exam ratings and subordinated debt prices. *Journal of Money, Credit, and Banking* 33: 900-925.

Diamond, Douglas. 1984. Financial intermediation and delegated monitoring. *Review of Economics Studies* 59: 393–414.

———, and Philip Dybvig. 1983. Bank runs, deposit insurance and liquidity. *Journal of Political Economy* 91: 401–19.

Diamond, Douglas, and Raghuram Rajan. 2001. Liquidity risk, liquidity creation and financial fragility: A theory of banking. *Journal of Political Economy* 109: 287–327.

Duffie, Darrell, Robert Jarrow, Amiyatosh Purnanandam, and Wei Yang. 2003. Market pricing of deposit insurance. *Journal of Financial Services Research* 24 (2/3): 93–119.

Elton, Edwin, Martin Gruber, Deepak Agrawal, and Christopher Mann. 2001. Explaining the spread on corporate bonds. *Journal of Finance* 56: 247–77.

Evanoff, Douglas, and Larry Wall. 2000. Subordinated debt as bank capital: A proposal for regulatory reform. (Federal Reserve Bank of Chicago) *Economic Perspectives* 24 (2): 40–53.

Falkenheim, Michael, and George Pennacchi. 2003. The cost of deposit insurance for privately held banks: A market comparable approach. *Journal of Financial Services Research* 24 (2/3): 121–48.

Federal Deposit Insurance Corporation. 1984. *The First Fifty Years*. Washington, D.C. http://www.fdic.gov/bank/analytical/firstfifty/.

Feldman, Ronald. 1998. When should the FDIC act like a private insurance company? When it comes to pricing, not reserves. Federal Reserve Bank of Minneapolis. *The Region* 12 (3): 43–50.

Flannery, Mark. 1982. Deposit insurance creates a need for bank regulation. Federal Reserve Bank of Philadelphia. *Business Review* Q1: 17–27.

———. 1991. Pricing deposit insurance when the insurer measures bank risk with error. *Journal of Banking and Finance* 15: 975–98.

———. 2005. No pain, no gain? Effecting market discipline via "reverse convertible debentures." In *Capital adequacy beyond Basel: Banking, securities, and insurance*, ed. Hal S. Scott, 171–96. Oxford: Oxford University Press.

Friedman, Milton, and Anna Jacobson Schwartz. 1963. *A monetary history of the United States: 1867–1960*. Princeton, NJ: Princeton University Press.

Gorton, Gary, and George Pennacchi. 1990. Financial intermediaries and liquidity creation. *Journal of Finance* 45: 49–71.

———. 1992. Financial innovation and the provision of liquidity services. In *The reform of federal deposit insurance: disciplining the government and protecting taxpayers*, ed. James R. Barth and R. Dan Brumbaugh, 203–24. New York: Harper Collins.

———. 1993. Money market funds and finance companies: Are they the banks of the future? In *Structural change in banking*, ed. Michael Klausner and Lawrence J. White, 173–214. Homewood, IL: Irwin.

Kashyap, Anil, Raghuram Rajan, and Jeremy Stein. 2008. Rethinking capital regulation. In *Maintaining stability in a changing financial system*. Federal Reserve Bank of Kansas City symposium. http://www.kansascityfed.org/publicat/sympos/2008/KashyapRajanStein.03.12.09.pdf.

Laeven, Luc. 2004. The political economy of deposit insurance. *Journal of Financial Services Research* 26: 201–24.

Marino, James, and Rosalind Bennett. 1999. The consequences of national depositor preference. *FDIC Banking Review* 12 (2): 19–38.

Merton, Robert. 1977. An analytical derivation of the cost of deposit insurance and loan guarantees. *Journal of Banking and Finance* 1: 3–11.

———. 1995. A functional perspective of financial intermediation. *Financial Management* 24: 23–41.

Osterberg, William, and James Thomson. 2003. Depositor preference legislation and failed banks' resolution costs. *Research in Finance* 20: 33–59.

Pennacchi, George. 2000. The effects of setting deposit insurance premiums to target insurance fund reserves. *Journal of Financial Services Research* 17 (1): 153–80.

———. 2005. Risk-based capital standards, deposit insurance, and procyclicality. *Journal of Financial Intermediation* 14: 432–65.

———. 2006. Deposit insurance, bank regulation, and financial system risks. *Journal of Monetary Economics* 53: 1–30.

Stern, Gary, and Ronald Feldman. 2004. *Too big to fail: The hazards of bank bailouts.* Washington, D.C.: Brookings Institution Press.

Stiglitz, Joseph. 1993. Perspectives on the role of government risk-bearing within the financial sector. In *Government risk-bearing,* ed. Mark Sniderman, 109–30. Boston: Kluwer Academic Publishers.

2

Reforming the Pension Benefit Guaranty Corporation

Jeffrey R. Brown and Andrew G. Biggs

The Pension Benefit Guaranty Corporation (PBGC) was established by Congress in 1974 as part of the Employee Retirement Income Security Act (ERISA). The goals of this independent agency are to encourage the continuation and maintenance of voluntary private pension plans, ensure the continued payment of pension benefits, and maintain premiums paid by firms to provide this protection at the lowest possible level.

As noted in its 2008 annual report, the PBGC insures 30,460 pension plans covering nearly 44 million workers. The PBGC currently oversees over 3,900 terminated or likely-to-be-terminated pension plans and pays benefits to around 640,000 retirees. Including covered workers who have not yet retired and participants in multiemployer plans receiving financial assistance, the PBGC is responsible for the current and future pensions of

---

Many of the ideas and some portions of the text in this chapter are drawn from Jeffrey R. Brown, "Guaranteed Trouble: The Economic Effects of the Pension Benefit Guaranty Corporation," *Journal of Economic Perspectives* 22, no. 1 (2008): 177–98 (copyright 2008, American Economic Association; reproduced with permission of the *Journal of Economic Perspectives*). For their helpful discussions of the chapter, the authors wish to thank Brad Belt, Chuck Blahous, Zvi Bodie, Jeremy Bulow, Julia Coronado, Doug Elliott, Doug Holtz-Eakin, Bill Gale, Jim Hines, Olivia Mitchell, George Pennacchi, Andrei Shleifer, Kent Smetters, Jeremy Stein, Tim Taylor, Mark Warshawsky, David Wilcox, and participants in the American Enterprise Institute January 2009 conference on private markets and public insurance.

over 1.3 million people, a figure that has risen from only 500,000 in fiscal year 2000 (PBGC 2008a).

The PBGC does not provide full payment of all terminated pensions. The maximum pension benefit guaranteed by PBGC is set by Congress with annual adjustments. For plans terminating in 2009, pensions for workers claiming benefits at age sixty-five are capped at $54,000 per year for a straight life annuity, with actuarial adjustments for survivor benefits and for earlier or later retirement ages. Retirees whose pensions are overseen by the PBGC may receive benefits up to this maximum, although the guarantee may be further reduced by other statutory and regulatory provisions.[1]

The Pension Benefit Guaranty Corporation is, by statute, supposed to be self-financing. It receives no tax revenue and is not officially backed by the full faith and credit of the U.S. government. The PBGC's funds primarily derive from four sources:

(1) Insurance premiums paid by sponsors of defined-benefit pension plans (and interest and principal derived from accumulated premiums);

(2) Interest and principal derived from assets held by pension plans for which the PBGC serves as trustee;

(3) Recoveries of unfunded pension liabilities and unpaid minimum contributions from the controlled group of the plan sponsor, generally in a bankruptcy proceeding;

(4) Assets from defined-benefit plans under PBGC trusteeship.

While the PBGC is funded through employer premiums, Congress—not the PBGC—has the sole authority to set premiums. For that reason, the PBGC itself had little ability to prevent the significant deterioration of its net financial position over the last decade as record claims accumulated. The PBGC's net asset position peaked at a net surplus of $9.7 billion in fiscal year 2000. But by the end of fiscal year 2008, PBGC's assets of $63.0 billion were outweighed by liabilities of $74.1 billion, leaving a net deficit of $11.1 billion (PBGC 2008a).

Despite its legal status as self-financing, it seems unlikely that Congress would allow the PBGC to become insolvent and thereby reduce or eliminate pension payments to millions of beneficiaries. This implicit taxpayer guarantee of benefits makes it important that policymakers understand the PBGC's structure and the often damaging incentives it creates for sponsors of defined-benefit pension plans. While recent market conditions have played a significant role in the PBGC's financial decline, they do not fully explain the increase in the number of pensions trusteed by the PBGC or in the potential demands on the agency in the future. The fullest explanation requires an understanding of why pension plan sponsors exposed themselves to these financial market fluctuations in the first place.

Much of the responsibility for the poor financial state of the PBGC, as well as the defined-benefit system more generally, lies in the major design flaws of the PBGC pension insurance program as defined in ERISA and the Internal Revenue Code.[2] Specifically, Congress has failed to do three things:

(1) It has not properly priced insurance, thereby encouraging excessive risk taking by plan sponsors;

(2) It has not promoted adequate funding of pension obligations;

(3) It has not required sufficient information disclosure to market participants.

Together, these three flaws have fostered an environment in which many firms do not adequately fund their pension obligations, knowing that in financial distress they can offload their pension liabilities onto the PBGC.

The Congressional Research Service (2007, 1) makes the point clearly: "Although low interest rates and low stock market returns also contributed to the recent losses, the primary threat to the PBGC's financial condition is underfunding in pension plans of weak sponsors. In some cases, plan terminations were preceded by years of low contributions—or no contributions—which significantly increased underfunding." In response to such concerns, President Bush signed into law the Pension Protection Act of 2006 (PPA), which made substantial changes to the PBGC insurance system.[3] Since the enactment of this law, however, deteriorating economic conditions have once again raised the level of concern about the funding status of corporate defined-benefit pension plans. Munnell, Aubry, and Muldoon (2008) report that from October 9, 2007, through October 9, 2008, the value of equities in private-sector defined-benefit pension plans dropped by nearly

$1 trillion. In addition to worsening the funding status of private defined-benefit plans, poor macroeconomic conditions have increased the probability of corporate financial distress. Together, these factors are likely to increase the future burden on the PBGC.

Even if the economy had remained strong, however, there would be reasons for concern about the PBGC. Though the PPA made some progress in improving the PBGC program, it failed to fully correct its three major problems. Absent further reform, substantial problems will continue to plague the private defined-benefit pension system in decades to come. To prevent this deterioration, we argue, Congress should transfer much of the responsibility for defined-benefit pension insurance to compulsory private markets.

It is ironic, but not altogether unexpected, that the government corporation designed to insure the pensions of workers and retirees in financially distressed firms has ended up facing its own long-term financial distress. Given the significant contingent liability posed to taxpayers by the PBGC, reforms to strengthen the agency over time are needed. We propose incremental reforms that would more closely align the incentives of the various stakeholders in the program, and also consider how pensions could be insured through private markets if the PBGC were eliminated outright. Employers and employees will be able to make economically appropriate decisions about compensation only if firms are forced to face the full economic consequences of their pension plan funding decisions. At the very least, then, market signals regarding the adequacy of pension funding should be integrated into the structure of private pension insurance.

Trends in U.S. Corporate Pensions

Defined-benefit (DB) pension plans have dominated the landscape in the United States ever since they were introduced by American Express in 1875 (Seburn 1991). DB plans promise an employee a specified monthly benefit at retirement that is usually based on years of service and earnings. For example, a plan might offer a benefit that is equal to 1.5 percent of average salary during the last three years of employment multiplied by the number of years of service with the employer. Thus an employee with thirty years of service who retires at the plan's normal retirement age would receive a benefit that is 45 percent of that employee's final three-year average salary. There are a myriad of formula variations, but plans must meet specific legal requirements to be "qualified" for favorable tax treatment. Benefits from traditional defined-benefit plans are typically paid as life annuities, meaning that they are paid for as long as the participant lives.

It is well known that the private sector has undertaken a dramatic shift over the past few decades away from DB plans and toward defined contribution (DC) plans. In a DC plan, the employer promises to make a specified contribution, rather than fund a specified benefit. In 401(k) plans, employee participation is voluntary, employees make their own portfolio allocation decisions, and account balances are rarely turned into annuities at retirement. A defined-contribution pension plan promises to pay out only what was contributed, plus the return on the assets in the participant's account. Such plans are not insured by the Pension Benefit Guaranty Corporation.

Munnell and Sunden (2004) summarize the many reasons behind the shift from defined-benefit to defined-contribution plans. These include a preference by employers for certainty regarding what their pension contributions will be in any given year (the DB plan involves increasing or decreasing contributions each year depending on external changes in equity markets and interest rates); and the reluctance of employers to be in the business of managing long-term economic and demographic risk (which a DB plan requires).

While defined-benefit pensions may not be the predominant form of employer-sponsored retirement saving for most younger workers, these plans nevertheless cover tens of millions of current employees and retirees and oversee trillions of dollars in assets and benefit liabilities. How these programs are managed has significant effects on individual retirement preparation as well as potentially large fiscal implications for the PBGC and the taxpayer.

Background on the Pension Benefit Guaranty Corporation

The Pension Benefit Guaranty Corporation is headed by a director who reports to a board consisting of the secretaries of the Commerce, Labor, and

Treasury departments, with the secretary of labor serving as chair (PBGC 2007a). In addition, a seven-member advisory committee appointed by the president is meant to represent the interests of employers, employees, and the general public.

The PBGC runs two programs insuring private-sector defined-benefit pension plans. The single-employer program insures the pensions of 33.8 million workers and retirees in approximately 27,900 pension plans. The multiemployer program insures the benefits of approximately 10.1 million workers in about 1,500 multiemployer plans (PBGC 2008a). A multiemployer plan is a collectively bargained pension plan that covers workers from multiple employers, often in a common industry such as construction. The multiemployer program is funded separately from the single-employer program and operates under different rules. For example, the PBGC makes loans to insolvent multiemployer plans but not to comparable single-employer plans. At the end of fiscal year 2008, the multiemployer program had assets of $1.3 billion and liabilities of $1.8 billion. This chapter focuses on the single-employer program, which is much the larger of the two programs and on which most of the policy focuses.

Most firms that offer defined-benefit pension plans are required to participate in the Pension Benefit Guaranty Corporation single-employer pension insurance program.[4] For a claim to be made against the PBGC, the firm "must prove severe financial distress, for instance, the likelihood that continuing the plan would force the company to shut down" (PBGC 2007b), and the plan must be underfunded—that is, assets must be insufficient to cover liabilities. In such a case, the PBGC will pay guaranteed pension benefits and attempt to recover the underfunding from the controlled group of the plan's sponsor. The PBGC may also choose to terminate a plan without the consent of the employer if losses are likely to increase unreasonably in the future.

When an underfunded pension plan terminates, the Pension Benefit Guaranty Corporation takes responsibility for paying monthly benefits to retirees. In fiscal year 2008, the PBGC paid almost $4.3 billion in benefits to over 640,240 retirees in 3,860 terminated pension plans (PBGC 2008a). Another 634,000 people expect benefits from the PBGC in the future, or are in multiemployer plans receiving financial assistance from the PBGC. The PBGC guarantee is limited: for plans terminating in 2008, the maximum guaranteed benefit paid to participants retiring at age sixty-five is $54,000—although the amount is higher for those retiring later and lower for those retiring earlier. The maximum insurance benefit is established by Congress and is also affected by legal restrictions on PBGC insurance coverage.[5] While the vast majority of participants in plans taken over by the PBGC fall below this guaranteed benefit limit, in some prominent cases, including those of some airline pilots, the guaranteed benefit of insured workers was substantially lower than their promised retirement income. In the case of the pilots, however, much of the potential loss in benefits was made up by nonguaranteed benefits payable under ERISA (the specific provision allocates plans' assets to the benefits of retired participants and those who were eligible to retire three years before the plan terminated).

Sources of PBGC Revenue. As we indicated above, the operations of the Pension Benefit Guaranty Corporation are financed from four sources: insurance premiums paid by sponsors of defined-benefit plans; assets from defined-benefit plans under PBGC trusteeship; asset recovery from bankrupt companies; and investment income on PBGC assets. About two-thirds of PBGC's total income in fiscal year 2008 was derived from investment income (PBGC 2008a).

Absent from this list of income sources is funding from general tax revenue, as there is very little provision in current law for any taxpayer backing of the Pension Benefit Guaranty Corporation.[6] Yet while the PBGC was intended to be self-financing, many analysts believe that there is an implicit political guarantee, such that Congress would likely use taxpayer dollars to bail out the PBGC if pensioners' benefits were at immediate risk.

Congress sets the employer's pension insurance premium. The single-employer premium was initially set in 1974 at $1 per pension participant; it has been increased by Congress on an irregular basis, reaching $30 per participant for plan years beginning on or after January 1, 2006. Since 2007, this basic premium amount has been indexed to wage inflation, and it reached $34 per participant in 2009. In addition to this flat-rate premium, underfunded pension plans pay an additional premium of 0.9 percent of the value of the unfunded vested benefits. During fiscal year 2008, premium income totaled $1.4 billion (PBGC 2008a).

Strikingly, aside from the extra premium paid for being underfunded, PBGC premiums contain no risk adjustment.[7] A financially distressed firm that has invested pension plan assets in a portfolio of risky assets mismatched with the plan's liabilities pays the same annual premium as an AAA-rated firm that has fully immunized its pension liabilities from financial-market fluctuations. The dangerous implications of this pricing model will be discussed in greater detail below.

Historical and Projected Financial Status. The official measure of the PBGC's financial status is the market value of its assets net of its liabilities. The liabilities are calculated using group annuity prices, an approach that is meant to assure "parity between the valuation of liabilities in plans taken over by PBGC and the cost of providing annuities when a company voluntarily terminates a plan, and by law, provides annuities through the purchase of annuities in the marketplace" (PBGC 2007a). In addition to including losses from plans that have already terminated, the PBGC's official liability measure includes "probable" terminations. This means that a plan is included if, consistent with financial accounting standards, the PBGC determines that the plan is likely to terminate. When liabilities exceed assets, the PBGC is said to have a deficit.

In addition, in the footnotes to its financial statements, the PBGC records a figure known as reasonably possible exposure, which represents net underfunding in plans whose sponsors are experiencing financial difficulty. As of the end of fiscal year 2008, the PBGC estimated its exposure to reasonably possible terminations at $47 billion (PBGC 2008a).

The PBGC's single-employer program has been in deficit during most of its existence, as shown in figure 2-1. From 1980 through 1995, the PBGC had a small but persistent deficit each year of less than $5 billion. From 1996 to 2001, with the help of a booming stock market, the program moved into surplus. But as a result of the wave of large bankruptcies from 2001 to 2007 (detailed in table 2-1),[8] the PBGC's net financial position deteriorated to a nearly $23 billion deficit at the end of fiscal year 2005.

Although it recovered somewhat—achieving a $10.7 billion deficit—by the end of 2008, much of the measured recovery is attributable to accounting changes rather than to improvements in the underlying economics. First, provisions in the Pension Protection Act of 2006 resulted in some

FIGURE 2-1
NET FINANCIAL POSITION OF THE PBGC'S SINGLE-EMPLOYER PROGRAM, 1980–2009 ($billions)

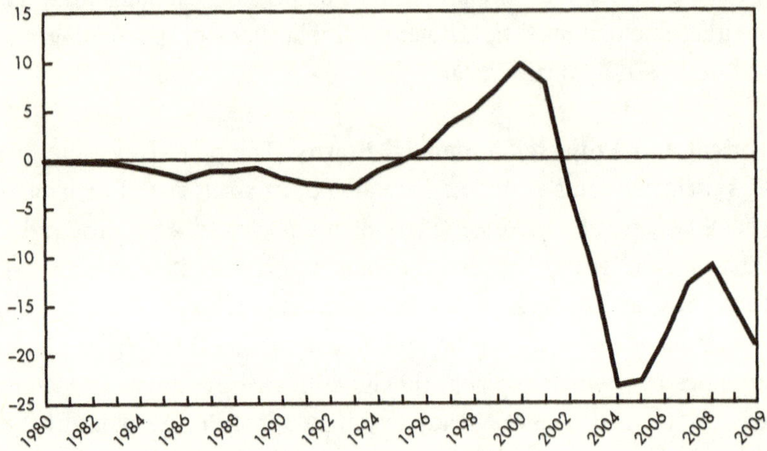

SOURCE: PBGC 2007c supplemented with FY 2008/2009 results.

large airline plan liabilities being taken off the books without any improvement in the real health of the plans. Second, favorable changes in interest rates reduced the present value of future liabilities (PBGC 2008a). There is some debate about what discount rates the PBGC ought to use when valuing its liabilities, especially given the implicit political guarantee that backs up these liabilities. Were the PBGC to discount its existing liabilities using a risk-free rate, as some have recommended, its stated liabilities and its deficit would be significantly higher, and they would not have declined as much over the twelve-month period ending on September 30, 2008, because Treasury rates were more stable over this period.

The PBGC's methods for calculating its liabilities have been the subject of some criticism, and independent analyses have reinforced the general finding that the program is in poor fiscal health. For example, the Congressional Budget Office (2005a) estimated that the present value of the PBGC's future shortfalls (including already sunk costs as well as the present value of

TABLE 2-1
TOP TEN FIRMS PRESENTING PBGC CLAIMS, 1975–2007
(single-employer program, by dollar amount of claim)

Top ten firms	Number of plans	Fiscal year(s) of plan terminations	Claims (by firm)	Vested partici- pants	Per- centage of total claims (1975– 2007)
1. United Airlines	4	2005	$7,503,711,171	122,541	21.5
2. Bethlehem Steel	1	2003	3,654,380,116	91,312	10.5
3. US Airways	4	2003, 2005	2,684,542,754	57,002	7.7
4. LTV Steel*	6	2002, 2003, 2004	2,134,985,884	83,094	6.1
5. Delta Air Lines	1	2006	1,740,482,711	13,028	5.0
6. National Steel	7	2003	1,275,628,286	33,737	3.7
7. Pan American Air	3	1991, 1992	841,082,434	31,999	2.4
8. Trans World Airlines	2	2001	668,377,106	32,275	1.9
9. Weirton Steel	1	2004	640,480,970	9,410	1.8
10. Kaiser Aluminum	7	2004, 2007	602,132,764	18,402	1.7
Top 10 Total	36		$21,745,804,196	492,800	62.2
All Other Total	3,747		13,193,241,357	1,087,787	37.8
TOTAL	3,783		$34,939,045,553	1,508,587	100.0

SOURCE: PBGC 2007c.
NOTE: * = Does not include 1986 termination of a Republic Steel plan sponsored by LTV.

prospective costs minus future premiums paid) totaled $91 billion, using a twenty-year time horizon and including the cost of market risk, which is not reflected in PBGC's annual report or its financial statements. Likewise, the Government Accountability Office (GAO) placed the PBGC on its "high risk" list in July 2003 and, even following the 2006 reforms, has not removed it (GAO 2003, 2007). As GAO said regarding the Pension Protection Act, "Many of these reforms will be phased in gradually, postponing their potentially positive effect on plan funding, while other changes could have the effect of increasing PBGC's financial exposure" (GAO 2007). The fear is that, notwithstanding the PBGC's statutory status as self-financing, Congress will bail it out rather than let it fail.

That the PBGC ended up in financial distress does not come as a surprise. Numerous pension experts had raised warning flags: in 1992, for example, a secretary of labor (and thus former chairman of the PBGC board) compared the PBGC to the insolvent savings and loan associations bailed out in the 1980s, stating in the PBGC's annual report: "One would have to be an ostrich with its head buried in the sand to ignore the warnings and not learn from the analogy of the savings and loan crisis" (cited in Bodie 1996, 83).

In a prescient article, Zvi Bodie (1996) explored "the uncomfortable parallel" of the PBGC to the savings and loan associations, explaining that a sharp decline in stock prices could push defined-benefit pensions into insolvency. In the early part of this decade, and again in recent months, much of Bodie's scenario has come to pass. The U.S. stock market experienced a sharp drop in equity prices that reduced the market value of pension assets. In the early part of the decade, a decline in interest rates increased the present value of future pension liabilities. These events caused widespread underfunding. Several major defaults of underfunded pension plans, primarily in the steel and airline industries, led Congress to increase premiums from $19 per plan participant to $30 per plan participant on the remaining plans in the system.

It is likely that the current financial crisis and accompanying decline in equity prices will continue to increase the number of pension plans taken over by the agency. UBS Investment Research estimates that 236 of the companies listed in the S&P 500 index have pension plans whose liabilities (determined on an accounting basis, not a plan termination basis) exceed their assets, and twenty of the companies had pension assets whose value exceeded the market capitalization of the company itself (Byrnes 2008). The financial crisis has already resulted in a sharp increase in corporate bankruptcies. In addition, recent market declines have taken a toll on the PBGC's own asset holdings. The PBGC director, Charles E. F. Millard, recently testified that the PBGC's investment holdings lost 6.5 percent of their value, or $4.1 billion, in fiscal year 2008 (Millard 2008a).

The net financial position of the Pension Benefit Guaranty Corporation seems likely to deteriorate further in the coming decades, and analysts fear that the PBGC might eventually need an infusion of taxpayer dollars to meet coming obligations. The most recent comparisons have been to Fannie Mae and Freddie Mac, government-sponsored enterprises that were also intended to be self-financing, and that were kept afloat by government intervention. Whether the Pension Benefit Guaranty Corporation remains an appropriate policy response in this setting is a very real question.

Flaws in the Pension Insurance System

Before we outline specific reforms to the PBGC, let us consider in detail some structural flaws in its insurance program. As noted in the introduction, three major flaws have contributed to the program's financial problems: the failure to properly price the insurance protections provided by the PBGC; the inadequacy of pension funding requirements; and the lack of transparency regarding companies' pension financing.

The Failure to Price Pension Insurance Properly. As noted above, PBGC operations are funded not by congressional appropriations but in large part through premiums charged to sponsors of defined-benefit pension plans. Unlike a private insurance company, however, the PBGC does not determine the appropriate premiums to apply to participant firms. Rather, these premiums and the terms by which they are applied are determined by Congress.

PBGC premiums are charged on two different tiers. The first tier is a simple per-participant premium equal to $30 for each individual covered by an insured defined-benefit pension plan. The second tier imposes an additional premium of $9 per every $1,000 of underfunding. This second tier is designed to apply higher premiums to plans that present the largest exposure to the program. However, prior to the Pension Protection Act of 2006, various exemptions written into the law allowed as much as 90 percent of the true amount of underfunding to escape this second-tier premium (Center on Federal Financial Institutions 2005a).

This premium schedule fails to adjust for the probability that the firm will experience financial distress, or for the full extent of underfunding, or for any mismatch in risk characteristics between plan assets and plan liabilities. In fact, the PBGC is prohibited by Congress from charging risk-adjusted premiums. The PBGC's mission statement specifies goals at odds with appropriate risk-based pricing; part of its mission is to "maintain premiums . . . at the lowest level consistent with carrying out its obligations under" ERISA (PBGC 2009). Congress has implemented this mission by keeping average premiums well below their implicit market price, but may not have set premiums appropriately to carry out the PBGC's obligations under the law.

PBGC premiums are on average too low because declines in pension funding typically correlate with periods of equity market downturns, which in turn correspond with periods in which there is an above-average incidence of financial distress by firms and a higher likelihood of a pension plan being turned over to the PBGC. The PBGC's assets, which currently include equity investments, are likely to decline in value at precisely the time they are needed the most. Thus much of the risk being borne by the PBGC is what financial economists refer to as systematic or market risk, which signifies that it cannot be diversified away. Private market insurers charge significant risk premiums to bear nondiversifiable risks. For that reason, the appropriate market price for bearing pension risk will be such that, on average, premiums will significantly exceed the cost of expected losses. Therefore, as Pennacchi (2006) notes in the context of federal deposit insurance, charging a risk-based premium would result in accounting profits for the government on average. That the PBGC has not run persistent accounting profits in its history—in fact, precisely the opposite—suggests that its premiums are too low.

A number of academic studies have attempted to directly calculate the price private markets would charge to provide PBGC-like insurance. Boyce and Ippolito (2002) calculate that the private sector would charge twice as much as the PBGC to provide the same type of insurance, while the Congressional Budget Office (2005b), Lewis and Pennacchi (1999), and VanDerHei (1990) find that the appropriate market-based premium would be even higher, at four to six times current levels. The PBGC is aware of these alternate valuations: until recently, its own Web site acknowledged that "a number of academic and financial institution studies have found that premiums have historically been under-priced by as much as six times the amount necessary to cover actual and expected claims." This reference to alternate valuations has now been deleted, however.[9]

At the same time, these much higher premium levels are those that would be necessary to reflect the risk of the current PBGC system, not an efficiently designed system (Wilcox 2006; Boyce and Ippolito 2002). If sponsors were faced with risk-adjusted premiums and were simultaneously subject to tighter funding rules and portfolio investment restrictions, the premiums could be lower, on average, than those currently charged (Boyce and Ippolito 2002).

The PBGC premium schedule also fails to differentiate between high- and low-risk pension plan sponsors—that is, its insurance premiums are linked to the number of participants and the amount of measured underfunding, which are only imperfect measures of firm creditworthiness. Even in the unlikely event that Congress granted the PBGC the power to explicitly risk-adjust its premiums, implementing this power would be problematic in a political environment. For instance, the government is at a disadvantage in assessing risks and charging premiums based on risk differences (Stiglitz 1993);[10] as a result of pressure from various constituencies, the Pension Protection Act of 2006 retains a naïve approach to insurance pricing that will continue for the foreseeable future.

Inadequate Funding Requirements. Prior to passage of the Pension Protection Act of 2006, the executive director of the PBGC told the U.S. Senate Budget Committee that "the current defined-benefit pension funding rules . . . are in need of a complete overhaul. Current rules are needlessly complex, don't reflect economic reality, and don't ensure that plans become well funded" (Belt 2005). Making such calculations even more complex, many of the assumptions and methods used in the funding calculations for the PBGC differ from those used for tax purposes, which in turn differ from those used in financial statements. As a result, pension accounting measures are not easily translatable to terms familiar to plan participants or financial markets.

There are too many flaws in the PBGC funding rules to provide a complete list here, but we mention a few that existed prior to the Pension Protection Act of 2006. First, in practice, firms were required to fund only 90 percent of their liabilities. Second, the rules for calculating liabilities were subject to considerable discretion, allowing firms to game the system. Third, pension plans were permitted to "smooth" interest rates over four years, which allowed firms to report smaller liabilities than they should have in periods of declining interest rates (Government Accountability Office 2005). Fourth, plans were allowed to use the smoothed "actuarial" value, rather than the market value, of plan assets, with up to a 20 percent deviation from actual market values permitted (Government Accountability Office 2005). Fifth, various contribution credits allowed firms to avoid making cash contributions to their pension plan, even if the plan was underfunded. For example, if a firm contributed more than the minimum required in a given year, this created a "credit balance" that increased each year, with an interest credit chosen by the plan to reflect expected long-run returns on plan assets. Firms were allowed to use these credits in lieu of cash contributions even when the value of plan assets had declined. Sixth, it was possible for changes in plan liabilities due to amendments to the pension plan benefit structure to be amortized over three to seven years, whereas the PBGC's insurance coverage of the new benefits is typically phased in over five years. Finally, sponsors of badly underfunded plans were permitted to increase benefits.

The Pension Protection Act of 2006 addressed some of these shortcomings. For example, the requirement to contribute to a plan is now binding after a phase-in period for plans that are less than 100 percent funded, not 90 percent funded as in the past. The time period for smoothing assets and liabilities was reduced to two years. Several new restrictions were imposed on the use of "credit balances," although the 2006 law fell short of eliminating their use. Further, the 2006 law made it harder to increase benefits when a plan is underfunded.

But the PBGC insurance program continues to operate with significant flaws. Measured assets and liabilities, for instance, still do not reflect market values. A coalition of powerful industry groups successfully fought to retain smoothing techniques, arguing that their elimination would increase "the volatility and unpredictability of the funding rules" (Eickelberg 2005). Furthermore, Congress only limited and did not bar outright the use of various credits by firms to avoid paying contributions.

The Pension Protection Act of 2006 also contained at least one provision that constituted a giant leap backward—the special rules for airlines. Airlines that agree to freeze the accruals in their pension plans are given seventeen years to fund their initial pension deficits. In addition, they may use an 8.85 percent discount rate for valuing their pension liabilities, a figure two to three percentage points higher than the market rates other firms will use (Center on Federal Financial Institutions 2006). The result is that unfunded obligations of as much as $8 billion were taken off the books. The Congressional Research Service (2007, 12) points out the danger in this approach: "Allowing airlines to use an interest rate of 8.85 percent when actual market rates are significantly lower effectively masks the threat that these plans pose to the PBGC. . . . In the event these plans terminate, the losses to the PBGC would not be similarly reduced."

Given the poor financial health of many of the nation's airlines, these and other special provisions for airlines may significantly increase the future liabilities of the PBGC. Perhaps worse, these provisions set a troubling precedent: industries that become financially distressed in the future will doubtless seek similar treatment.

Lack of Transparency. In efficient financial and labor markets, firms would be appropriately rewarded for good behavior or penalized for bad behavior with respect to pension plan funding. For example, financial markets would place a lower value on firms with poorly funded pensions, knowing that these pension obligations will eat into future cash flows. Unfortunately, most of the information needed to make informed decisions about a plan's funding status is not readily available to workers, investors, or other market participants. While pension plan sponsors are required annually to file a Form 5500, which provides detailed information on pension plan assets and liabilities, this information can be up to two and a half years old by the time it is available for public consumption. This point was succinctly and clearly made by PBGC executive director Bradley Belt in 2005, in testimony before the Senate Budget Committee (Belt 2005): "It is exceedingly difficult to make informed business and policy decisions based on such dated information, given the dynamic and volatile nature of markets."

While the PBGC does receive detailed and timely information for a limited number of plans, the statute governing this disclosure prevents the information from being made publicly available. The Pension Protection Act of 2006 did increase requirements for disclosure of pension plan information, including certain actuarial and financial reports, upon request of any plan participant or beneficiary. However, it did not substantially alter the amount or timeliness of information that is made available to the PBGC itself, nor did it allow the more detailed information on underfunded plans to become public. Indeed, the Pension Protection Act reduced the information available to the PBGC, because fewer companies will now be required to file a supplemental form disclosing to the PBGC, a plan's current termination liability.

A Case Study: Bethlehem Steel. To see just how poorly the pension rules can operate in practice, it is instructive to consider the case of Bethlehem Steel. The program flaws specified above made it possible for Bethlehem Steel to report a funding status of 84 percent, despite having a market value of assets that, upon termination, equaled only 45 percent of the market value of the plan's liabilities. More details about this collapse from 1996 through 2002 (taken from Belt 2005) are summarized in table 2-2.

For calculating a plan's liabilities, the Internal Revenue Code requires that firms use a concept called "current liability." By this measure, Bethlehem Steel was only 78 percent funded in 1996, and was therefore required to make deficit reduction contributions as well as pay a variable rate premium on the amount of underfunding. Further, because of its poor funding status, the company was required to send out a written notice to plan participants informing them of the pension's funding status. However, as a result of rising equity markets and the $354 million contribution made during 1996, by 1997 Bethlehem Steel's official funding status had risen to 91 percent, enough to be considered "fully funded" under the minimum funding rules. As such, Bethlehem Steel was no longer required to make deficit reduction contributions, to pay variable rate premiums, or to send out participant notices.

But reality was less rosy than the figures suggested. Because the rise in Bethlehem Steel's funding ratio was due largely to rising equity prices, the plan's funding status was at risk of declining when equity markets declined. During this period Bethlehem Steel's overall financial health was deteriorating, but the PBGC continued (as required by law) to charge the company the same $19 per participant premium that it charged to every other firm. Because it was deemed fully funded and had contribution credit balances, in the three years from 1997 to 1999 the cumulative payments made by Bethlehem Steel to the PBGC totaled less than $75 million. By 2001, Bethlehem Steel's funding ratio had slipped to 84 percent, and its debt rating fell to D. Even so, thanks to the firm's reliance on credit balances from prior contributions, the firm made no additional cash contributions to its plan and no premium payments to the PBGC in 2000 or 2001. When the pension plan was terminated in 2002, it turned out that the assets held by the plan were equal to only 45 percent of its termination liabilities. As a result, the present value of unfunded benefit liabilities totaled $4.3 billion.

TABLE 2-2
BETHLEHEM STEEL PENSION FUNDING, 1996–2002

	1996	1997	1998	1999	2000	2001	2002
Current liability funding ratio ("official" ratio of plan assets to liabilities)	78%	91%	99%	96%	86%	84%	NR
Was company required to make deficit reduction contribution?	Y	N	N	N	N	NR	NR
Was company obligated to send out a participant notice?	Y	Y	N	N	N	N	N
Did company pay a variable rate premium for being under-funded? ($millions)	$15	$17	N	N	N	N	N
Actual contributions to PBGC ($millions)	$354	$32	$31	$8	$0	$0	$0
Debt rating	B+	B+	B/B–	B/B–	B+	D	With-drawn

SOURCE: Belt 2005.
NOTE: NR = Not reported.

The Bethlehem Steel case illustrates all three structural flaws of the pension laws. First, Bethlehem Steel did not have to pay higher premiums, despite the risk it posed. Indeed, the cumulative premiums paid by Bethlehem Steel in the five years prior to bankruptcy totaled less than 2 percent of the amount of ultimate underfunding, despite the firm's increasingly obvious slide toward bankruptcy. Second, the plan was inadequately funded, as evidenced by the $4.3 billion funding shortfall. Yet Bethlehem Steel was not required to make additional contributions in the years prior to bankruptcy. Third, Bethlehem Steel was not even required to notify plan participants of its financial status in the years immediately prior to bankruptcy.

Nor is Bethlehem Steel an isolated case. The US Airways pension plan for its pilots was 94 percent funded according to the minimum funding rules, but when the plan was terminated, it actually was only 33 percent funded on a termination basis, resulting in a $2.5 billion shortfall. Moreover, for six years leading up to the year of termination, US Airways was not subject to a deficit reduction contribution. In these and numerous other cases, the design flaws of the pension laws have become apparent.

Pension Obligations of the U.S. Auto Industry

In recent months, the precarious financial situation of the U.S. automobile industry has become obvious, with both General Motors and Chrysler being forced to accept federal aid and initiate bankruptcy proceedings. (To date, Ford has not accepted federal aid or filed for bankruptcy.) One significant factor in the "Big Three" automakers' financial condition is their pension obligations, which total tens of billions of dollars and are insured by the PBGC. The General Motors pension fund is the largest in America, covering more than 600,000 workers, retirees, and surviving spouses. Ford and Chrysler pensions, while smaller, are still significant in size.

The Big Three automakers face a higher cost structure than their competitors and have been losing market share for decades. Their workforce has shrunk considerably relative to the number of retired autoworkers, whose pensions and health care are financed by the automakers. Approximately 145,000 Americans are directly employed by automakers, but over 600,000 retirees depend on automakers for their pensions.

To date, bankruptcy proceedings have not included shifting Chrysler or General Motors pensions to the PBGC, although the pension for auto parts supplier Delphi—a former subsidiary of General Motors, which had pledged to support its pension—has been taken over by the PBGC at a cost of $6.2 billion. The PBGC has the option, which it has exercised in the past, of arguing to bankruptcy judges that a company can afford to retain its pension and should be forced to do so. In 2007, for instance, PBGC successfully argued that auto parts makers Dana and Federal-Mogul should retain their pension plans as they worked through bankruptcy.[11] In this way the PBGC avoided taking on the pensions of ninety-six thousand employees and retirees. While both General Motors and Chrysler have undergone significant restructuring designed to return the companies to profitability, the likelihood that automaker pensions might eventually be turned over to the PBGC remains high.

It is also probable that additional associated companies such as auto parts producers could enter bankruptcy and look to the PBGC for pension protection. The PBGC does not count auto-sector pensions among its current obligations, although there are media reports that the agency is pressing automakers for a more accurate accounting of their pension assets and liabilities.[12]

In January 2009, then–PBGC director Charles Millard noted in an interview that total underfunding of the Big Three automakers' pension funds could be as high as $41 billion in the event that one or more of them had to terminate their pension plan following a bankruptcy (Stoll 2009); GM's plan was estimated to be underfunded by $20 billion, Chrysler's by $9 billion, and Ford's by around $12 billion. For perspective, the most expensive pension takeover to date—that of United Airlines in 2005—involved underfunding of $9.8 billion (Congressional Research Service 2007). While a PBGC takeover of any of the Big Three pensions would not create cash flow problems for the agency in the short term, these new obligations would add substantially to the almost $11 billion shortfall the agency is already projected to face.

Doubling Down on Risk: The PBGC's New Investment Policy

On February 12, 2008, PBGC's then-director Charles Millard unveiled a new investment policy for the PBGC that will likely exacerbate the volatility of the agency's funding status. The agency would begin shifting its asset portfolio more heavily into equities, with an ultimate goal of reaching 45 percent in equities, 45 percent in fixed income, and 10 percent in alternative investments such as private equity. Millard justified this switch as "taking advantage of the PBGC's long-term investment horizon," and cited a review that "showed the new diversified portfolio would have yielded better results than the old investment policy 98 percent of the time over rolling 20-year periods" (Millard 2008b).

Many leading financial economists have criticized this new investment policy, or at least the flawed logic used to justify it. The fundamental problem with this approach is that it induces a strong negative correlation between the PBGC's liabilities and its assets. In other words, the PBGC's asset values are likely to be low precisely when those assets are needed the most. To see this, start with the basic observation that the PBGC provides insurance against the intersection of two events: a plan sponsor experiencing financial distress and this same plan sponsor having an underfunded pension plan. These two events are both more likely when equity markets are performing poorly, because poor equity-market performance is often associated with stress in the macroeconomy (making it more likely that firms will experience distress), and because most private DB plan sponsors invest their pension assets heavily in equities.

In essence, the new PBGC investment strategy will "double down" on equity markets. As the Congressional Budget Office put it, "The new strategy is likely to produce higher returns, on average, over the long run. . . . [But] by investing a greater share of its assets in risky securities, PBGC is more likely to experience a decline in the value of its portfolio during an economic downturn—the point at which it is most likely to have to assume responsibility for a larger number of underfunded pension plans" (CBO 2008). The Government Accountability Office echoed these concerns in a July 2008 report (GAO 2008). In other words, while the PBGC's proposed investment plan accounts for the correlation of returns between stocks and bonds within its portfolio, the plan does *not* account for the correlation between the PBGC's portfolio returns and the likelihood that PBGC assets will be called on to finance an insolvent pension plan. Just when the PBGC will have to absorb additional unfunded liabilities from failed plans, its own assets will have declined. As Bodie memorably noted, "A company that insures against hurricane damage should not invest its reserves in beachfront properties" (cited in Krueger 2008).

Director Millard's response to these observations? "If sixth-graders in America took finance, I could say to you that, 'As every sixth-grader knows, diversification mitigates risk, and this policy is substantially more diversified, and that is why it has a lower standard deviation'" (Norris 2008). Of course, if sixth-graders in America really did take finance, they would know that the standard deviation of the asset portfolio is not the appropriate measure of risk in this context, because standard deviation completely ignores the fact that the PBGC's liabilities are correlated with the same underlying risk factors as the assets. The best way to reduce the PBGC's risk with regard to the liabilities of terminated plans already on the books is to invest in a portfolio of assets, such as bonds, that have a known payoff with a duration similar to that of the liabilities being backed. For liabilities not yet on the books, which are more likely to be absorbed by the PBGC when equity markets are down, a better way to reduce funding risk would be to take a short position in equities, especially in those industries (such as airlines, steel, and automobiles) that appear most at risk.[13] These steps would produce a broadly defined asset portfolio, inclusive of both PBGC's explicit assets and demands on those assets placed by pension sponsors, with less risk than the investment policy proposed by Director Millard.

If there is an economic case to be made for investing PBGC assets in equities, the PBGC has not yet made it. There are situations in which the federal government may optimally choose to invest some government assets in equities; for example, there may be arguments for investing the Social Security trust funds in equities and/or establishing personal retirement accounts (see e.g., Diamond and Geanakoplos, 2003). But it is important to note that arguments for such investment are independent of whether the investment is done through the PBGC or some other program. Further, the rationale for doing so is entirely different from the rationale articulated by the PBGC.

In July of 2009 the PBGC indicated that it will not move ahead with the proposed shift to a more equity-oriented investment portfolio. This change came about, however, not due to a rethinking of such a portfolio's merits but because of revelations that former director Millard may have had improper contacts with investment firms seeking contracts to manage the PBGC portfolio.[14]

Incremental and Wholesale Reforms to the PBGC

Current law prevents the PBGC from properly pricing the insurance it provides, encourages firms to underfund their pensions, and fails to encourage the transparency regarding pension financing status that would enable workers to bring pressure to bear on employers who fail to manage pension financing responsibly. For these reasons, we propose a number of incremental and wholesale reforms for the PBGC.

This is not to ignore the fact that the PBGC faces billions in sunk costs. Firms that are already financially distressed and hold underfunded plans are likely to bequeath their costs to the PBGC, and with high probability to the taxpayers. As Douglas Holtz-Eakin noted when he was director of the Congressional Budget Office, "Those sunk costs cannot be avoided, and policy decisions can determine only who will bear them" (CBO 2005a, 3). Indeed, for financially distressed firms that have a large deficit relative to their equity value, there is likely no insurance premium that would cover the unfunded liabilities without providing an incentive for the company to immediately declare bankruptcy and dump its liabilities on the insurer.

But thousands of other pension plans are at firms not currently in financial distress, and policymakers should be concerned about the growth of future PBGC liabilities. Even though conventional DB plans are on the decline, many firms are turning to various "hybrid" plans, which combine features of defined benefit and defined contribution. Hybrid plans are legally considered defined-benefit plans and are thus insured by the PBGC, so it would be premature to argue that the PBGC will become obsolete once the old defined-benefit plans have disappeared.

Useful reforms of the laws affecting PBGC can be divided into two categories: those that seek to insert some additional market incentives into PBGC, and those that would eliminate the PBGC in favor of (perhaps mandatory) private insurance for pension plans. We consider incremental reforms first and then examine the potential effects of eliminating the PBGC.

Adding Market Incentives to Government Pension Insurance. A number of parametric reforms could subject pension providers to greater market discipline without altering the basic structure of the PBGC. One approach would further tighten funding rules and implement risk-based pricing. Wilcox (2006) has proposed a number of reforms to safeguard pensions, including restricting pension portfolios to ensure better asset-liability matching. This approach is designed to make the pension promise close to risk free,[15] compensate taxpayers at market rates for insuring the plans, and stop cross-subsidization of high-risk by low-risk sponsors.

A second approach might introduce market pricing and market information to the PBGC. Belt (2006b) proposes that the PBGC be permitted to use private reinsurance markets to lay off some of its exposure or to securitize its assets or revenue streams. In either case, markets would be able to price the pension liabilities taken on by the PBGC. This in turn might promote further reforms by Congress.

A third approach would require that pension benefit promises be given seniority over other liabilities in bankruptcy proceedings. Combined with improved disclosures on pension financing, the subordinate placing of bonds relative to pension liabilities in bankruptcy proceedings would provide bond and equity markets with both the means and the motive to incorporate pension liabilities into the market valuation of the firm. Bondholders, including sophisticated institutional investors, would have a greater incentive to require that pension promises are fully funded, so as to avoid having greater risk imposed on them.

This approach might help to reduce the moral hazard that exists when financially distressed firms reduce cash contributions to their defined-benefit plans.[16] By itself, it would still not make the promise of a defined-benefit plan risk free; from 1981 to 2000, the average default recovery rate from senior secured bonds of all ratings was only just over 50 percent (Hamilton, Gupton, and Berhault 2001). Moreover, the experience of Republic Steel, as described by Bodie and Merton (1993), suggests that elevating the PBGC's status in bankruptcy proceedings might not be sufficient, given the cleverness of plan sponsors in devising ways of stripping assets from the pension fund. Nonetheless, such an approach could bring greater market discipline to bear.

A fourth option would be to alter PBGC policy to protect less than 100 percent of pensions for all employees, even those under the current $54,000 threshold. For instance, the PBGC might guarantee only 90 percent of total pension benefits under the threshold.[17] This policy change would have two effects. First, it would reduce the government's exposure to pension liabilities. Current law dictates that if a company goes bankrupt with a plan that was (for example) only 50 percent funded, the PBGC is liable for 50 percent of pensions under the guarantee threshold. With the policy change illustrated here, the PBGC liability would be reduced by half, as the agency would fund benefits only up to 90 percent of promised levels. Second, and more importantly, this change would cause all employees (not just those with large pensions or highly subsidized early retirement benefits) to have some "skin in the game," and thereby provide incentives for the employees, unions, etc, to be better monitors of pension plan investments and funding status. It would differ from a simple reduction in the threshold, which might reap similar savings to the government, in that every individual with a claim on the pension program would have a stake in maintaining the sponsor's ability to fund the pension. Currently, only around 16 percent of individuals receiving pensions through the PBGC receive any reduction in their payments (PBGC 2006). This implies that many or most working-age individuals have little stake in whether their pension sponsor is able to meet its obligations to the program.

Eliminating the Pension Benefit Guaranty Corporation. An alternative to the incremental reforms outlined above is to eliminate the PBGC outright. From a purely theoretical perspective, there is no reason to assume that private markets could not provide pension insurance similar to that currently provided by the PBGC. As Bodie (1996) notes, while mandating insurance coverage for defined-benefit pensions makes sense, there is no economic rationale for that coverage coming from the federal government. That is to say, there is no obvious market failure which would prevent private insurers from replicating the essential functions of the PBGC. Indeed, the U.S. government's poor record of properly pricing a wide variety of insurance programs—including terrorism risk insurance, flood insurance, and deposit insurance—illustrates just how difficult it is for the government to be an efficient insurance provider.

Instead of providing insurance, the government could simply mandate that firms insure their defined-benefit plans in the private market, much as it mandates insurance coverage in other spheres of the economy. Private insurers would risk-adjust the premiums that they charge to defined-benefit plans. Such an idea is hardly new. While serving as the chief economist for the PBGC, Ippolito (1987, 22) wrote that one way to solve the PBGC's problems would be "to simply eliminate the PBGC." He expounded on this idea further in book form, noting that the government might develop an assigned risk pool to cover the highest-risk companies (Ippolito 1989). Other authors supportive of this approach include Sharpe (1976), Pesando (1982), Smalhout (1993), and Weaver (1997).

There are some legitimate criticisms of this approach. First, as noted earlier, there is the "sunk cost" problem that must be handled. We are not starting the program from scratch, and given the significant pension debt overhang created by the existing program, it may not be possible to get the private market to insure some of the plans that are already substantially underfunded and are sponsored by financially distressed firms. Second, as we have already suggested—and as some of the other chapters in this book suggest as well—it is difficult to sustain an economically sensible insurance program in a political environment. In all likelihood, transferring responsibility from the PBGC to private insurers would not fully insulate the private insurers from the efforts of elected officials to protect certain constituencies through laws and regulations.

Other criticisms of this approach are easier to respond to. Some analysts believe that the PBGC should be viewed as a social insurance program with intentional subsidies to the defined-benefit system, rather than as a federal agency simply acting as a stand-in for market provision of insurance (for example, Salisbury 1996). However, even if one accepts that defined-benefit subsidies are desirable, implementing such a policy with non-risk-adjusted premiums and questionable funding rules makes no sense. Subsidies coupled with risk-adjusted insurance pricing are superior public policy to subsidies *through* non-risk-adjusted insurance pricing.

Others will argue that private-sector insurers cannot insure systematic risk as efficiently as the government, as the insurers themselves are exposed to financial distress if many underfunded defined-benefit plans terminate during an economic downturn. This claim both overstates the government's theoretical advantages in provision of insurance (particularly in light of the practical difficulties government has exhibited in properly pricing a wide range of insurance programs) and ignores the fact that both private insurers and the government have access to a wide range of financial instruments for hedging market risk. Further, unlike some sources of systematic risk that are beyond the control of the insurers, such as terrorism or natural catastrophes, the risk of pension underfunding can be substantially mitigated if private insurers impose tight funding and portfolio restrictions.

Yet another criticism is that the transition to a private insurance system would be difficult for firms with plans that are already substantially underfunded. Indeed, the cost of paying market premiums for some firms might be enough to trigger bankruptcy.[18] It could be argued that if a company depends on a large government subsidy in the form of underpriced pension insurance to prevent bankruptcy, continuing the subsidy is unlikely to constitute an efficient long-run solution. Nonetheless, in light of such transition difficulties, some analysts (for example Wilcox [2006]) argue that it would be desirable to first reform the PBGC further, including imposing portfolio restrictions on plan sponsors.

While the Pension Benefit Guaranty Corporation has protected thousands of workers and retirees who might otherwise have experienced devastating losses to their pensions after their employer declared bankruptcy, it has also created perverse economic incentives for plan sponsors. These grow out of the program's inability to price insurance according to sensible economic principles as well as the failure of pension law either to provide adequate funding incentives or to require adequate information disclosure. Recent legislation has improved the program rules, but the reforms did not go nearly far enough. Three decades of experience with the PBGC, as well as lessons from other federal insurance programs, suggest that a government-run insurance program is ill-suited to the task of imposing market discipline. While replacing the PBGC with mandatory participation in a private insurance market would present new regulatory challenges, the advantages of forcing defined-benefit plans into a competitive insurance market are likely to outweigh these costs.

Conclusion

The Pension Benefit Guaranty Corporation provides insurance for employer-sponsored defined-benefit pensions. However, the cost and terms for premiums applied to plan sponsors are set by Congress, not by the PBGC. As a result, PBGC policies fail to properly price insurance, which encourages plan sponsors to take on excessive risk; discourages adequate funding of pension obligations; and leaves employees, retirees, and market participants without much-needed information. These factors, as much as declines in stock market values, account for the PBGC's multibillion-dollar projected shortfalls. The potential reforms we outline, ranging from incremental changes to the elimination of the PBGC as a whole, would provide markets with better information regarding pension funding and allow markets to impose discipline on pension sponsors who fail to adequately fund their plans.

Notes

1. Retirees and other beneficiaries can also have their vested benefits reduced by the "accrued-at-normal" limitation, which constrains the benefit guarantee to be no larger than the amount provided by a straight life annuity available at the plan's normal retirement age, or by the "phase-in" limitation, which restricts coverage of benefits arising from recent benefit improvements provided through a plan amendment. Readers interested in the details of these provisions can find a useful summary in Pension Benefit Guaranty Corporation (2008b).

2. Another major factor contributing to defined-benefit funding problems is the set of flawed accounting standards that have largely hidden the true economic costs of firms' pension funding and investment decisions. The Financial Accounting Standards Board (FASB) issued new standards in September 2006 to change the method of accounting for pensions on corporate balance sheets. A full analysis of the role of accounting is beyond the scope of the current paper; readers interested in more detail may consult Belt (2006a), Coronado and Sharpe (2003), Gold (2000), and references therein.

3. The Pension Protection Act of 2006 also made significant changes to the rules governing defined-contribution plans, including numerous provisions to encourage automatic enrollment. While these other features of the act may, in the long run, turn out to be far more important to the overall income security of retired workers, a discussion of these changes is beyond the scope of this paper.

4. Church plans, plans of professional corporations with fewer than twenty-five employees, and public plans are not covered under ERISA.

5. For details on these restrictions, and on situations in which more than the guaranteed benefit is paid, see Pension Benefit Guaranty Corporation, "PBGC Announces Maximum Guaranteed Benefit," December 5, 2006, http://www.pbgc.gov/media/news-archive/news-releases/2006/pr07-07.html.

6. A minor exception is that ERISA gave the PBGC a $100 million line of credit with the Treasury, which was utilized to get the agency operational before premium income was collected.

7. In 2005, the Bush administration proposed pension reforms that included risk-adjusted premiums, but this concept was quickly rejected by Congress. The PBGC's counterpart in the United Kingdom, the Pension Protection Fund, assesses risk-adjusted premiums.

8. Table 2-1 presents data on the ten firms making the biggest claims on the PBGC between 1975 and 2007. The top ten claims are primarily from firms in the steel and airlines industries, and nine of the ten firms presented their claims in the years since 2001.

9. As of February 12, 2008, the quotation was at Pension Benefit Guaranty Corporation, "Understanding the Financial Condition of the Pension Insurance Program," http://pbgc.gov/media/key-resources-for-the-press/content/page15247.html#qi2. This page can be accessed at http://web.archive.org.

10. When the Bush administration proposed risk-adjusted premiums in 2005, the proposed risk factors were to come from private-sector sources, not the government's own assessment of risk.

11. See Pension Benefit Guaranty Corporation, "PBGC Hails Continuation of Dana Corp. Pension Plans After Reorganization," February 1, 2008, http://www.pbgc.gov/media/news-archive/news-releases/2008/pr08-17.html.

12. Dow Jones, "PBGC, GM Leaders Negotiate Over Auto Maker's Pension Data," November 18, 2008.

13. In practice, it may not be cost-effective to implement the short strategy, but the main conceptual point—that the PBGC should not hold long positions in these same securities—certainly holds.

14. For instance, see Eric Lipton, "How Firms Wooed a U.S. Agency With Billions to Invest," *New York Times*, July 28, 2009, http://www.nytimes.com/2009/07/29/business/29pensions.html.

15. Some risk, such as that arising from longevity risk, would remain.

16. Coronado and Liang (2006) find that riskier firms make lower cash contributions to their defined-benefit plans and have lower funding ratios, even after controlling for excess cash flow. Consistent with the findings of Rauh (2009), however, they do not find that firms closer to bankruptcy invest more in equities to maximize the value of what is effectively a put option on the PBGC.

17. The UK's Pension Protection Fund does limit the guarantee for nonretired participants. Retirees receive 100 percent.

18. For further discussion of these transition issues, see Center on Federal Financial Institutions (2005b).

References

Belt, Bradley D. 2005. Testimony of Bradley D. Belt, executive director, Pension Benefit Guaranty Corporation, before the Committee on the Budget, U.S. Senate. June 15. http://budget.senate.gov/democratic/testimony/2005/belt_pbgc061505.pdf.

———. 2006a. Through the looking glass: Adventures in pension land. Remarks before the National Association for Business Economics, March 13. www.pbgc.gov/media/news-archive/speeches/sp15669.html.

———. 2006b. Look ahead part IV—Longer-term strategic and structural issues. Memo from the PBGC executive director to the PBGC board of directors, the director of the Office of Management and Budget, and the director of the National Economic Council. May 30.

Bodie, Zvi. 1996. What the Pension Benefit Guaranty Corporation can learn from the Federal Savings and Loan Insurance Corporation. *Journal of Financial Services Research* 10 (1): 83–100.

———, and Robert C. Merton. 1993. Pension benefit guarantees in the United States: A functional analysis. In *The future of pensions in the United States*, ed. Ray Schmitt, 194–234. Philadelphia: Pension Research Council.

Boyce, Steven, and Richard A. Ippolito. 2002. The cost of pension insurance. *Journal of Risk and Insurance* 69 (2): 121–70.

Byrnes, Nanette. 2008. Why pensions are probably safe. *BusinessWeek*, October 23.

Center on Federal Financial Institutions. 2005a. PBGC: Premium hike possibilities. April. http://www.coffi.org/pubs/PBGC%20premium%20hike%20possibilities.pdf.

———. 2005b. PBGC: Policy options. January. http://www.coffi.org/pubs/PBGC%20Policy%20Options%20%20January%206%202005.pdf.

———. 2006. Pension reform: Summary of final 2006 bill. August. http://www.coffi.org/pubs/Pension%20Reform%20Summary%20of%20Final%20Bill.pdf.

Congressional Budget Office. 2005a. CBO testimony. Statement of Douglas Holtz-Eakin, director, before the Committee on the Budget, U.S. Senate. The Pension Benefit Guaranty Corporation: Financial conditions, potential risks, and policy options. June 15. http://www.cbo.gov/ftpdocs/64xx/doc6426/06-15-PBGC.pdf.

———. 2005b. The risk exposure of the Pension Benefit Guaranty Corporation. September. http://www.cbo.gov/ftpdocs/66xx/doc6646/09-15-PBGC.pdf.

———. 2008. Letter from Director Peter R. Orszag to Rep. George Miller, Chairman, Committee on Education and Labor. April 24. http://www.cbo.gov/ftpdocs/91xx/doc9156/04-24-Miller-PBGC_Letter.pdf.

Congressional Research Service. 2007. The financial health of the Pension Benefit Guaranty Corporation (PBGC). March 23. http://assets.opencrs.com/rpts/RL33937_20070323.pdf.

Coronado, Julia Lynn, and Nellie Liang. 2006. The influence of PBGC insurance on pension fund finances. In *Restructuring retirement risks*, ed. David Blitzstein, Olivia S. Mitchell, and Stephen P. Utkus, 88–108. Oxford: Oxford University Press.

Coronado, Julia Lynn, and Steven A. Sharpe. 2003. Did pension plan accounting contribute to a stock market bubble? *Brookings Papers on Economic Activity* 1: 323–71.

Diamond, Peter A., and John Geanakoplos. 2003. Social security investment in equities. *American Economic Review* 93 (4): 1047–74.

Eickelberg, Henry. 2005. Testimony on behalf of the American Benefits Council, American Council of Life Insurers, Business Roundtable, Committee on Investment of Employee Benefit Assets, ERISA Industry Committee, Financial Executives International, National Association of Manufacturers, and US Chamber of Commerce before a hearing of the House Ways and Means Subcommittee on select revenue measures on the administration's proposals for single-employer pension funding reform. March 8. http://www.uschamber.com/NR/rdonlyres/elntgwkffidw32l6naz42qoc54l564ihdjoccbry5nmj433dx4iomkxbkgjovxnz4kgdsygfqz7gipbxzxacqpk74ec/Chamber+Sign-On+Pension+Testimony+--+3-8-05.pdf.

Gold, Jeremy. 2000. Accounting/actuarial bias enables equity investment by defined benefit pension plans. Pension Research Council Working Paper 2001-5.

Government Accountability Office. 2003. Pension Benefit Guaranty Corporation Single-Employer Insurance Program: Long-Term Vulnerabilities Warrant "High Risk" Designation. GAO-03-1050SP. July.

———. 2005. Private pensions: Recent experiences of large defined benefit plans illustrate weaknesses in funding rules. GAO-05-294. May.

———. 2007. High-Risk Series, An Update. GAO-07-310. January.

———. 2008. PBGC assets: Implementation of new investment policy will need stronger board oversight. GAO-08-667. July.

Hamilton, David T., Greg Gupton, and Alexandra Berhault. 2001. Default and recovery rates of corporate bond issuers. Moody's Investor Service.

Ippolito, Richard A. 1987. Pension security: Has ERISA had any effect? *Regulation* 2: 15–22.

———. 1989. *The economics of pension insurance.* Philadelphia: University of Pennsylvania Press.

Krueger, Alan B. 2008. Looking out for the next bailout. Economix blog. December 22. http://economix.blogs.nytimes.com/2008/12/22/looking-out-for-the-next-bailout/#comments.

Lewis, Christopher M., and George G. Pennacchi. 1999. Valuing insurance for defined-benefit plans. In *Advances in futures and options research,* vol. 10, ed. Phelim Boyle, George Pennacchi, and Peer Ritchken. Amsterdam: Elsevier Science.

Millard, Charles E. F. 2008a. Testimony of Charles E. F. Millard, director, Pension Benefit Guaranty Corporation, before the Committee on Education and Labor, United States House of Representatives. October 24. http://www.pbgc.gov/media/news-archive/ testimony/tm16548.html.

———. 2008b. PBGC's new diversified investment policy. *Pensions and Benefits Daily,* March 4.

Munnell, Alicia H., Jean-Pierre Aubry, and Dan Muldoon. 2008. The financial crisis and private defined benefit plans. Boston College Center for Retirement Research Issue Brief no. 8-18. http://crr.bc.edu/images/stories/Briefs/ib_8-18.pdf.

Munnell, Alicia H., and Annika Sunden. 2004. *Coming up short: The challenge of 401(k) plans.* Washington, D.C.: Brookings Institution Press.

Norris, Floyd. 2008. Profit without risk? Not likely. *New York Times.* August 22.

Pension Benefit Guaranty Corporation. 2006. *Pension insurance data book.* http://www.pbgc.gov/docs/2006databook.pdf.

———. 2007a. Who we are. http://www.pbgc.gov/about/about.html.

———. 2007b. Pension Benefit Guaranty Corporation fact sheet: How pension plans end. available at http://www.pbgc.gov/about/termination.html

———. 2007c. *Pension insurance data book.* http://www.pbgc.gov/docs/2007data book.pdf.

———. 2008a. 2008 Annual report. http://www.pbgc.gov/docs/2008_annual_report.pdf.

———. 2008b. *PBGC's Guarantee Limits—An Update.* September. http://www.pbgc.gov/docs/guaranteelimits.pdf.

———. 2009. Mission statement. http://www.pbgc.gov/about/about.html#1.

Pennacchi, George. 2006. Deposit insurance, bank regulation and financial system risks. *Journal of Monetary Economics* 53 (1): 1–30.

Pesando, James E. 1982. Investment risk, bankruptcy risk, and pension reform in Canada. *Journal of Finance* 37 (3): 741–49.

Rauh, Joshua D. 2009. Risk shifting versus risk management: Investment policy in corporate pension plans. *Review of Financial Studies* 22: 2678–2733

Salisbury, Dallas L. 1996. Comments. In *Securing employer-based pensions: An international perspective,* ed. Zvi Bodie, Olivia S. Mitchell, and John A. Turner, 312–16. Philadelphia: Pension Research Council.

Seburn, Patrick W. 1991. Evolution of employer-provided defined benefit pensions. *Monthly Labor Review,* December 1991, 16–23.

Sharpe, William F. 1976. Corporate pension funding policy. *Journal of Financial Economics* 3 (3): 183–93.

Smalhout, James H. 1993. Avoiding the next guaranteed bailout: Reforms for the pension insurance program. *Brookings Review* 11 (2): 12–15.

Stiglitz, Joseph E. 1993. Perspectives on the role of government risk-bearing within the financial sector. In *Government risk-bearing,* ed. Mark S. Sniderman, 109–30. Boston: Kluwer Academic Publishers.

Stoll, John D. 2009. Government agency that protects pensions raises new concerns on U.S. auto makers. *Wall Street Journal.* January 29.

VanDerHei, Jack L. 1990. An empirical analysis of risk-related insurance premiums for the PBGC. *Journal of Risk and Insurance* 57 (2): 240–59.

Weaver, Carolyn L. 1997. Government guarantees of private pension benefits: Current problems and market-based solutions. In *Public policy towards pensions,* ed. Sylvester J. Schieber and John B. Shoven, 131–75. Cambridge, MA: MIT Press.

Wilcox, David W. 2006. Reforming the defined-benefit pension system. *Brookings Papers on Economic Activity* 1: 235–85.

3

Does the Terrorism Insurance Market Still Need Government Support?

Dwight Jaffee and Thomas Russell

Nothing is so permanent as a temporary government program.
—Milton Friedman

The terrorist attacks of September 11, 2001, imposed significant costs on the U.S. economy. Of these costs, some $36 billion was covered by terrorism insurance, and of this some $15 billion (before tax) fell on domestic U.S. insurers and reinsurers. The remainder was covered by overseas reinsurers; Lloyds, Swiss Re, and Munich Re alone incurred losses in excess of $7 billion (Hartwig 2004). Because the magnitude of this U.S. domestic insurance and reinsurance loss was relatively small—some $10 billion after tax in an industry with property/casualty reserves of some $300 billion—U.S. insurers had no difficulty in meeting the claims.

Going forward, however, the losses presented two problems: First, the attacks demonstrated to insurers that their pricing model for terrorism risk was seriously inadequate. Prior to 9/11, and despite previous terrorist attacks on the United States, terrorism insurance was provided as part of the industry's standard "all-risks" property and casualty insurance contract at no additional cost to the buyers. The losses incurred on 9/11, and the specter

The authors wish to thank Jeffrey Brown for helpful comments on the first draft of this paper.

of future attacks, demonstrated an urgent need to revise this pricing policy; but in the absence of prior modeling of this type of risk, there were no guidelines on what the new premiums should be. Second, foreign reinsurers, who bore the brunt of the 9/11 losses, ceased offering this coverage. Because they were unregulated, foreign reinsurers could withdraw from the market as soon as contracts expired, which in many cases was year-end 2001. This absence of foreign reinsurance left domestic U.S. insurers with considerably more terrorism risk than they were prepared to bear.

Hence in November 2001, Insurance Services Office, Inc. (ISO), an industry services provider, filed endorsements that insurers could use to exclude coverage for terrorism in both their commercial property and liability forms (Alleyn 2003). By February 2002, forty-five states had permitted this clause in standard contracts. Although the right to exclude terrorism loss did not mean that an insurer would actually add this clause to the contract, it was clear by early 2002 that, for the foreseeable future, terrorism coverage would either be unavailable or available only at very high premiums. Insurers willing to offer terrorism coverage might well have believed high premiums to be justified by an increase in risk, but coming after years of "free" coverage, such high premiums provoked considerable resistance from buyers.

The stress on this market presented a public policy challenge for Congress and the Bush administration. As 9/11 had shown, a terrorist attack could reduce a high-rise building to rubble in a matter of hours, eliminating at a stroke the bricks and mortar collateral necessary for lending institutions to make commercial loans. These institutions faced the threat that, if terrorism risk insurance were unavailable or prohibitively expensive, the capitalized value of existing commercial structures might decline. This, in turn, would create financial problems for lenders and building owners and would lead to a possible downturn in new construction and employment. Congress therefore began to consider options for government support for reinsurance against terrorism risks.

In November 2002, Congress passed and the president signed the Terrorism Risk Insurance Act of 2002 (TRIA). This was more than fourteen months after the 9/11 attacks, a period in which U.S. construction and mortgage market activity in fact continued at what appeared to be normal levels, given the general slowing that occurred in the overall economy. Nevertheless, the federal government entered (allegedly temporarily) the terrorism reinsurance business. Given the two subsequent renewals of this legislation, which now continues at least until December of 2014, the federal government will be in the terrorism insurance business for a minimum of twelve years.

Three features of the original act are significant:

(1) Government presence in the private terrorism-insurance market was to be temporary, with a stated sunset date of December 2005.[1]

(2) The private insurance market retained responsibility and the financial risk for a substantial part of the lower tier of expected losses.

(3) For the upper tier of losses covered by government reinsurance, there was no risk-based pricing; indeed, no advance premiums were to be paid at all. In the event of a government payout, the U.S. Treasury was required to recoup a specified part of its reinsurance payments by imposing premium surcharges on all covered commercial property and casualty insurance lines, and the Secretary of the Treasury had the option to impose additional charges. The reimbursements and additional charges were to be proportional to the premiums paid on all designated insurance lines and were thus unrelated to the specific risks covered by each company or to claims actually paid to specific policyholders or on specific insurance lines.

In the event, government presence in the industry did not end in December 2005. As the expiration date of TRIA approached, President Bush signed into law the Terrorism Risk Insurance Extension Act of 2005 (TRIEA). This act extended the essential features of TRIA for a further two years. Then on December 26, 2007, with TRIEA about to expire, but with federal subsidized reinsurance now part of the terrorism insurance landscape, President Bush signed the Terrorism Risk Insurance Program Reauthorization Act of 2007 (TRIPRA). This act extended the essential features of TRIA for a further seven years, although the program was no longer characterized as a short-term emergency response. Federally subsidized reinsurance, which began as a temporary life-support system to reactivate the market for private terrorism insurance, had now become a semipermanent industry crutch.

In this chapter we examine two questions: First, seven years after 9/11, is a private terrorism-insurance market viable in the absence of federal support, or (as its early critics feared[2]) does federally subsidized reinsurance now hinder the private industry from standing on its own feet? Second, if a federal program is needed, is the TRIPRA the best way to support the industry? This second question is particularly important in the light of recent government assistance to the financial sector following the subprime mortgage crisis and as set out in the Emergency Economic Stabilization Act of 2008.

The Terrorism Risk Insurance Program Reauthorization Act of 2007

Before we can answer these questions, we need to understand the details of the current legislation. Passed in December 2007, TRIPRA continues the federal government's role in terrorism insurance at least through 2014. The key features of the act are as follows:[3]

- **Scope.** The act covers commercial property and casualty insurance, including excess insurance, workers' compensation, and directors and officers (D&O) insurance. It excludes crop, private mortgage, medical malpractice, financial guarantee, commercial auto, professional liability (other than D&O), surety, burglary and theft, and farm owners' multi-peril insurance. The act excludes reinsurance and flood insurance provided under the National Flood Insurance Program (NFIP), health insurance, and all forms of life insurance.
- **Coverage.** The act now covers losses from both domestic and foreign acts of terrorism and will expire in December 2014. A terrorist event causing more than $100 million in insured losses certified by the secretary of the treasury will trigger the act's provisions.

- **Mandatory offering.** Terrorism coverage must be "made available" on the same conditions under which nonterrorism coverage was previously offered by each insurer (though it may be offered at a different price).

- **Insurer deductibles and copayments.** Each insurer facing a loss must first pay, as a deductible, 20 percent of its previous year's direct earned premium on all covered lines. For losses above this amount, the insurer will be reimbursed by the government for 85 percent of the covered losses.

- **Cap.** The act sets the maximum responsibility for loss payment, limiting the sum of private market and government payments to $100 billion.

- **Recoupment.** The government is required to recoup 133 percent of the first $27.5 billion of payments it makes under the act by imposing a premium surcharge on all eligible commercial property and casualty policies, and it may impose an additional surcharge of up to 3 percent at the discretion of the Secretary of the Treasury.

To assess the current private insurance industry obligations under TRIPRA, it is necessary to know each firm's direct earned premiums for the relevant lines for the previous year. The U.S. Department of the Treasury estimated that the premiums in these lines totaled $182 billion in 2006, giving an industry-wide deductible of $36 billion in 2007, assuming that the loss affects all insurers in proportion to premiums earned (President's Working Group on Financial Markets 2006). One year later the ISO (2008) reported that total direct written premiums for 2007 in all property casualty lines came to $440.8 billion. Approximately 50 percent of these premiums are lines relevant to the terrorism deductible, so applying the current industry deductible rate of 20 percent, we calculate that by 2008 private insurers were liable for at least the first $40 billion of losses, a number significantly in excess of their losses from the 9/11 attack.

To examine the justification for this law, we turn now to the arguments for government intervention in this industry. From an insurance perspective it is helpful to distinguish two forms of terrorist actions, conventional attacks (truck bombs, etc.) and the much more damaging attacks using weapons of mass destruction.

Federal Terrorism Reinsurance (1): Conventional Terrorist Attacks

Government provision of reinsurance for terrorism risks under the TRIA and its extensions was motivated in part by the argument that terrorism risks are "uninsurable" by private firms and markets. This argument typically features two key points, one concerning the uncertainty of the estimated loss and the second the size of that loss. We focus here on the question of the size of the loss.

Estimates for the size of future possible terrorist attacks are available from the American Academy of Actuaries and are shown in table 3-1. Although these are point estimates subject to a large margin of error, one conclusion is clear from this table. The size of loss is dramatically smaller for conventional terrorist attacks than for attacks using weapons of mass destruction, so-called chemical, nuclear, biological, and radiological (CNBR) attacks.

A conventional terrorist attack (such as a truck bomb in Manhattan) would produce devastating losses—but it is difficult to see why losses of the size shown in table 3-1 could not be covered by private insurance markets. For example, as of March 2008, the reserves of the private property/casualty industry in the United States amounted to $515.6 billion (ISO 2008). This figure does not include state fund reserves which support workers' compensation claims. Adding these, the year-end 2007 reserves amounted to $698 billion (A. M. Best 2008). Certainly this number is now lower due to stock market losses in 2008, but it is still adequate to support multiple conventional attacks of the magnitude of 9/11. And of course such attacks do not occur every year. The frequency of terrorist attacks is difficult to predict, but as a benchmark, the ISO/Air model (a widely used industry terrorism risk assessment tool) suggests expected annual losses of $6 billion. Annual losses of this magnitude are manageable by domestic insurers and reinsurers on their own.

TABLE 3-1

ESTIMATED LOSSES FROM TERRORIST ATTACKS ($billions)

Scenario	Line of business	New York City	Washington, D.C.	San Francisco
Large CNBR	**Total**	**778.1**	**196.8**	**171.2**
	Auto	1.0	0.6	0.8
	Commercial property	158.3	31.5	35.5
	Residential property	38.7	12.7	22.6
	Workers' compensation	483.7	126.7	87.5
	General liability	14.4	2.9	3.2
	Group life	82.0	22.5	21.5
Medium CNBR	**Total**	**446.5**	**106.2**	**92.2**
	Auto	0.2	0.1	0.2
	Commercial property	77.8	15.7	17.1
	Residential property	10.3	3.1	6.9
	Workers' compensation	313.2	71.6	50.8
	General liability	7.3	1.5	1.6
	Group life	37.7	14.2	15.6
Truck bomb	**Total**	**11.8**	**5.5**	**8.8**
	Auto	0.0	0.0	0.0
	Commercial property	6.8	2.1	3.9
	Residential property	0.0	0.0	0.0
	Workers' compensation	3.5	2.8	3.9
	General liability	1.2	0.4	0.7
	Group life	0.3	0.2	0.3

SOURCE: American Academy of Actuaries 2006.

Losses might be still more manageable if the TRIA reinsurance subsidies were eliminated. Then, foreign reinsurers might reenter the U.S. conventional terrorism insurance market and further reduce the exposure of the domestic firms. If the responsibility for conventional terrorism losses were returned to the private market, moreover, there would be no need to consider further reforms of this part of the government program. To be sure, some reform proposals have merit on their own terms; these include permitting insurers to establish tax-deductible reserves for terrorism-related loses, encouraging groups of insurers to pool assets for terrorism risks, facilitating the use of catastrophe bonds for terrorism through amendments to the federal tax code, and limiting certain state regulation of property insurance premiums or amending coverage requirements (GAO 2008). But these issues can be taken up independently.

In contrast, the appropriate role for government in insuring CNBR losses raises more complex questions, which are discussed below. Overall, it makes sense to distinguish between conventional terrorism and terrorism involving CBNR. Serious consideration should be given to the following proposal: When the current terrorism insurance legislation ends in 2014, legislators will draw a clear distinction between acts of conventional terrorism and acts of terrorism involving weapons of mass destruction. At that time, responsibility for insurance against acts of conventional terrorism shall be returned fully to the private insurance and reinsurance industry, and all federal subsidies will cease.

This proposal raises the fundamental question of the costs and benefits of government intervention in the terrorism insurance market. Perhaps surprisingly, no systematic analysis has been carried out to answer this question directly. A key reason is that the evaluation of the TRIA programs has been regularly framed by the industry as the choice between government backing of terrorism insurance or no terrorism insurance at all. In 2014, however, it will have been thirteen years since the 9/11 attacks, and it therefore seems appropriate to compare the market as it now operates (i.e., with government involvement) with what the private market for terrorism insurance would be in the absence of government intervention.

The government's expected expenditures under the TRIPRA program were recently computed by the Congressional Budget Office (CBO) in determining the *ex post* premium surcharge that would be necessary to allow the overall program to be designated as unsubsidized (CBO 2007). For this purpose, the CBO estimated the act's expected average annual expenditure to be about $660 million, not a very large number, given that most government programs are computed in billions, not millions. This expenditure is relatively modest because the TRIPRA deductibles are now high enough to allow the industry to retain most of the risk, except for that associated with the very largest events. Furthermore, the government's payments under the act are expected to be recouped by the *ex post* surcharges. Thus it could be argued that TRIPRA imposes no expected financial cost on the government.

TRIPRA does, however, impose a *resource allocation cost* on the economy. This cost arises because the premiums actually paid by policyholders are subsidized in the sense that no *ex ante* payments are made in obtaining the government reinsurance. Furthermore, the *ex post* surcharges are prorated over all policies on the designated lines, so even *ex post,* no risk-based pricing occurs. Thus, TRIPRA provides no incentive to mitigate risks. The results are evident in the continued willingness of firms to build and carry out their businesses from within "trophy" buildings in urban centers. Of course, it could be that the externality benefits of agglomeration warrant such subsidies. Agglomeration benefits, however, have not been emphasized in the congressional debates over the TRIA and its extensions, and so it would appear this legislation does create a resource allocation cost, albeit one whose size is unknown.

It is equally difficult to quantify what might be the continuing benefits of TRIA. There is little doubt that when TRIA was first enacted in 2002, it had the clear benefit of reactivating the U.S. market for terrorism insurance. The sunset provisions in both the 2002 and 2005 acts, however, presumed that the private markets would recover and then carry on without government support. The sequence of renewals, now in place at least until 2014, thus raises the possibility that the TRIA programs have, in fact, crowded out the very private-market activity that they were designed to save. Advocates of TRIA will, of course, respond that there would be no terrorism insurance market at all in the absence of the government support. Unfortunately, there is no way to determine the accuracy of this position as long as TRIA continues to be subsidized and regularly renewed.

This situation suggests a potential change in our proposal to end government support of insurance for conventional terrorist attacks. This change would allow TRIA to be renewed again, but would introduce explicit, actuarially based premiums for the provision of government reinsurance. The primary insurers would be allowed to opt out of the government program and avoid the costs, presumably to participate in more effective private market reinsurance plans. Such "defections" would be a good signal that the government plan was not precluding private market competition. Indeed, the government's premiums could be steadily raised over time, thus creating a smooth transition to a primarily private market for terrorism insurance.

To be clear, these proposals to introduce risk-based pricing or to eliminate TRIA entirely are hardly radical. As we have seen, private insurers are already liable for approximately the first $40 billion of insured losses. A modest 3.5 percent growth rate in premiums would increase this deductible to about $50 billion by 2014. With this much exposure, even as TRIA continues through 2014 for the highest tiers of losses, it seems likely that the primary insurers will demand reinsurance at this lower tier, and we anticipate that this demand could begin to revive the private terrorism reinsurance market even before 2014.

Federal Terrorism Reinsurance (2): CNBR Terrorist Attacks

As can be seen from table 3-1, losses from CNBR attacks are potentially large enough to wipe out all the property/casualty reserves of the U.S. insurance industry. For historical reasons related to their size, CNBR terrorism losses receive special treatment in the TRIA legislation. Specifically, although insurers are required to offer terrorism coverage, they may impose restrictions as long as the same restrictions were already imposed at the time of 9/11 on the standard policies for nonterrorism losses.[4] This means that the covered policies cannot have exclusions, limitations, or conditions specifically for terrorism (as defined by TRIA). However, insurers are allowed to maintain those exclusions commonly placed in property/casualty contracts. Since most policies in the past excluded or limited coverage for CNBR incidents, a continued exclusion for CNBR incidents is permitted.

If an insurer were, instead, to offer coverage against CNBR risks, losses from these risks would be eligible for the government reinsurance protection mandated by TRIA, and they would also be included within the $100 billion limit on total claims. Nevertheless, in the absence of a "make available" requirement on CNBR risks, most insurers have excluded these risks from their property/casualty terrorism policies.

In contrast, most states do not allow CNBR exclusions in their workers' compensation insurance policies.[5] Thus private insurers who offer workers' compensation necessarily have substantial exposure to CNBR risks. For example, some 5.7 percent of total 9/11 losses (approximately $2 billion) was due to workers' compensation claims, and the estimates of the workers' compensation loss from a New York City CNBR incident given in table 3-1 approach half a trillion dollars. Moreover, the benefits payable under workers' compensation are preset by statute. For some injuries likely to be associated with CNBR attacks (for example, burns requiring skin grafting), these individual benefits may exceed $15 million.

Hence CNBR risks, which the industry views as too great to insure under property/casualty contracts, are fully covered in workers' compensation policies. To be sure, not all of this risk is written by the for-profit private sector. In four states and two territories, workers' compensation insurance is provided by a state-run monopoly,[6] and in thirteen other states a not-for-profit state enterprise competes with the private sector.[7] In New York State, the state exposed to the half trillion dollar estimate of table 3-1, the top five writers of workers' comp insurance in 2006 were the State Insurance Fund of New York, a not-for-profit state agency, with 40.4 percent market share; American International Group, Inc., with 18.7 percent; Liberty Mutual Insurance Cos., with 9.1 percent; Hartford Insurance Group, with 4 percent; and Zurich Financial Services North America Group, with 3.6 percent (A. M. Best 2007). Clearly the exposure of the private sector in this state (60 percent) is significant,[8] and for private insurers who write this line, the argument that CNBR risk is uninsurable because of its size and unpredictability apparently does not apply.

This is not to say that insuring CNBR risks through workers' compensation is easy. Risk concentration is a major complicating factor. If an insurer were to write workers' compensation insurance in the District of Columbia (where the death benefit is worth approximately $1.8 million) for a company which lost three hundred employees as a result of a terrorist attack, the total claim would equal $500 million. It would clearly not be prudent for one company to cover all these employees. Many companies have therefore avoided accumulation of geographic risk. Given the obvious value of regional diversification, it might be thought that there would be benefits to the development of an industry pool to share workers' compensation risks.[9] A private market–sponsored study by Towers Perrin (2004), however, concluded that such a pool would do little to add to capacity, and the industry opted instead to rely on the federal program.

Secondly, premium setting that incorporates the risks of a terrorist attack remains as much an art as a science. But if a premium must be quoted, assumptions can be made, and a rate brought forth. Following 9/11, rates were suggested by the National Council on Compensation Insurance (NCCI) for insurers in the states for which they develop rates (NCCI 2002).[10]

In any case, we simply note here that conventional and CNBR terrorism risks are jointly covered by the private sector under the workers' compensation line, whereas the same firms cover only conventional terrorist attacks under their property/casualty policies. For this reason, the most recent enabling legislation (TRIPRA) required the comptroller general to report on the availability and affordability of insurance for CNBR events, the outlook for future coverage, and the capacity of private insurers and state workers' compensation funds to manage these risks; and to make recommendations for government actions to expand CNBR coverage and lower its cost. Since CNBR risk appears to be the most pressing question for policymakers, we devote the remainder of the chapter to it.

Insuring CNBR Risk: Expanding TRIPRA

In its report on the availability of CNBR coverage, the President's Working Group on Financial Markets (2006) adopted a pessimistic note:

> Even with TRIA in place—which covers CNBR terrorist losses but does not mandate that insurers provide it—insurers by and large continue to avoid this risk. . . . There is virtually no CNBR reinsurance available, and the modeling issues both for exposure and probability become even more complicated for CNBR. Given the general reluctance of insurance companies to provide coverage for these types of risks, there may be little potential for future market development.

In fact, one change could be made that would spur this development: extend the "make available" clause in the TRIPRA legislation to include CNBR risk. The House version of the 2007 extension bill contained exactly this provision, but it was dropped in the final version due to industry opposition, much of which was based on the large potential size of a CNBR loss.[11]

In some ways this industry argument appears disingenuous. If CNBR losses were to be added to the "make available" clause, industry losses for a $1 trillion event would still be capped at 20 percent of direct written premiums (say $40 billion) plus 15 percent of the remainder up to $100 billion (say $9 billion), a total of $49 billion before tax.

To be sure, the size of the expected loss would rise if CNBR losses were added to the TRIPRA coverage. Table 3-2 shows the expected loss consequences for the five largest U.S. insurers from an event with a 1 percent likelihood if CNBR risks were added to the "make available" clause under TRIPRA as it now stands.[12] It is assumed that losses are in proportion to written premiums. As can be seen, the expected loss increments are small. There thus seems no reason why CNBR risks should not be added to the TRIPRA "make available" requirement, especially since insurers would be free to spread and price this risk as they see fit. Moreover, in the original House version of what became TRIPRA, special deductibles and copay arrangements were proposed for CNBR risks. For CNBR, an insurer's deductible would have been reduced to 3.5 percent—significantly lower than the "conventional attack" terrorism deductible of 20.0 percent. This deductible would have increased by 0.5 percent for each additional program year. The House bill would also have allowed insurers with less than $50 million in direct earned premiums to opt out of providing the CNBR coverage. With such CNBR-specific deductibles and copayments, this risk would be even easier to manage.

Behavioral issues may be playing a role in the reluctance of the industry to volunteer to take on CNBR risks for terrorism coverage. The availability heuristic, for example, suggests that a suitcase nuclear bomb exploding in Los Angeles may be such a vivid event as to forestall serious consideration of coverage. Tversky and Kahneman (1973) show that when a horrific event is easy to imagine, decision makers tend to overestimate its likelihood. Mueller (2007, 1) provides further evidence of this tendency:

> Even with the September 11 attacks included in the count . . . the number of Americans killed by international terrorism over

TABLE 3-2
MARGINAL EXPECTED CNBR LOSS UNDER TRIPRA ($billions)

	Direct written premiums	Current TRIPRA deductible	Marginal expected loss if CNBR is required
Insurer A	24.8	4.9	0.11
Insurer B	14.6	2.9	0.06
Insurer C	14.4	2.8	0.06
Insurer D	12.7	2.5	0.05
Insurer E	7.5	1.5	0.03

SOURCES: Government Accountability Office 2008, table 1, 23 (for deductibles); authors' calculations (for marginal expected loss).
NOTES: Insurers A–E are five largest U.S. insurers. Calculations are for an event having a 1 percent likelihood.

> the period [1975–2003] is not a great deal more than the number killed by lightning, or by accident-causing deer, or by severe allergic reactions to peanuts over the same period. In almost all years the total number of people worldwide who die at the hands of international terrorists is not much more than the number who drown in bathtubs in the United States—some 300–400.

Our conclusion here is to endorse a provision requiring CNBR coverage either under the existing TRIPRA deductible or *a fortiori* under a revised lower deductible. This is not, however, to endorse the other features of TRIPRA. Most importantly, there is no reason why the taxpayer should be required to subsidize private insurers (and ultimately commercial developers) by providing "free" reinsurance of the upper tier of loss.[13] Revising the act so that the "make available" clause includes CNBR risk would also be an excellent opportunity, as discussed above, to remove the industry subsidy created by the failure to price the risks embedded in the government's reinsurance obligations. Another possible reform that remains within the TRIPRA structure is to renew the program but this time to cover only CNBR risk. Or reform could go one step further: the government could remove all reinsurance and simply cap CNBR losses at $100 billion. Prudent underwriting within this cap would still allow private insurers to handle their pro-rata share of a loss that could not exceed $65 billion on an after-tax basis.

Insuring CNBR Risk: Thinking outside the TRIPRA Box

The basic structure of the government's support program for terrorism insurance was cobbled together in the months following 9/11, when the market was in disarray. No follow-up attack has taken place, and today much calmer market conditions prevail. These conditions are summarized in a recent Government Accountability Office (GAO) report:

> While commercial property terrorism insurance coverage appears to be available nationwide at rates policyholders view as reasonable, certain policyholders may face challenges in obtaining desired amounts of coverage or obtaining coverage at prices they view as reasonable. The policyholders experiencing these challenges were typically those that own large, high-value properties in areas where many large buildings are clustered, particularly in urban areas viewed as at high risk of attack, such as Manhattan, and to a lesser extent certain areas of other major cities, such as Chicago and San Francisco. (GAO 2008, 4)

Although government presence following the 9/11 attacks stabilized the market,[14] (see, e.g., General Accounting Office 2004), it is possible now to ask whether some alternative structure might work better in the long run. In answering this question, it is useful to identify why large infrequent events present such a challenge to private market structures. Here we draw on Jaffee and Russell (1997) and Russell and Jaffee (1998).[15] Suppose a per-firm loss L occurs once every hundred years. A competitive market for insurance would set a premium for this risk of (L/100 + load), and each firm would make a normal rate of return. For simplicity, assume the load is zero. Suppose the event occurs at the end of year 1. The typical insurance firm will have collected L/100 in premiums but will need to pay out L. This shortfall of (99/100)L will be a large amount whenever L is large. When external capital markets function without frictions, this is not a problem. The firm can simply borrow the amount (99/100)L using the stream of future premiums to pay off the loan. It is now widely recognized, however, that external capital markets do not function without frictions, and in particular that, in times of crisis, capital markets may all but shut down.

In the insurance literature this fact is recognized in the work of Winter (1994), Gron (1994), Froot and O'Connell (2008), Froot (2008), and others. In the corporate finance literature, the notion of a "pecking order," with external capital the least available source of funds, is recognized in the work of Myers and Majluf (1984). Indeed, governments around the world showed they understood the inability of solvent lending institutions to raise external capital during times of crisis when, in response to the 2008 financial meltdown, they injected public capital into private banks.

From the perspective of rational pricing, it is not clear why it should be so difficult to raise external capital when it is most needed and most likely to provide the highest rate of return.[16] Adverse selection is clearly an issue (Jaffee and Russell 1976), but it is not easy to see how asymmetric information about likely terrorist attacks can explain the reluctance to advance capital to CNBR insurers following an attack. It may well be that the explanation is behavioral. As Federal Reserve chairman Greenspan (2004) noted,

> When confronted with uncertainty . . . human beings invariably attempt to disengage from medium to long-term commitments in favor of safety and liquidity. . . . The immediate response on the part of the central bank to such financial implosions must be to inject large quantities of liquidity.

In this view, capital market imperfections are critical in understanding the general failure of catastrophe insurance markets, and therefore solutions that seek to restore a viable private market without government intervention must look to the question of how best to provide insurers with an opportunity to recapitalize following a catastrophic loss. The most frequently discussed such proposal involves catastrophe bonds[17] or some other form of insurance-linked securities (ILS). The market for catastrophe-based ILS has grown rapidly. In 1998, $886 million in catastrophe bonds was issued. From the second quarter of 2007 to the first quarter of 2008, issuance grew to $7.5 billion, with a further $4 billion in sidecars, a special investment vehicle which securitizes a portion of an insurer's book of business (Lane Financial 2008).

As the ILS market has grown, however, no securities that directly cover terrorism risk have been issued.[18] Two major obstacles frustrate securitizing this line: First, the rating agencies will not rate terrorism catastrophe bonds because the risk is man-made. The following response from the director of S&P's North American Insurance Ratings Practice is typical: "We won't rate bonds where human actions could constitute a portion of the risk. Who can be comfortable with what a terrorist is capable of?" (*Insurance Journal* 2008). Second, subsidized reinsurance of terrorism risk crowds out private terrorism catastrophe bonds.

Thus even if the market for natural disaster catastrophe bonds grows further, it is not likely that securitization will offer a private market solution to the capitalization requirements of CNBR risks. If private firms are to provide CNBR insurance on an ongoing basis, government will probably need to play some role in the *ex post* recapitalization that a large loss will require. Because of the parallels between this problem and the recent problems of the lending industry arising from the subprime mortgage crisis, we will now examine the recapitalization problem through the lens of a general financial crisis.

Recapitalization: Government as Catalyst

A large loss of capital following a CNBR attack is not a financial crisis as that term is generally understood. Nevertheless, financial crises and insurance catastrophes share many features. (Coincidentally, one distressed financial institution that suffered during the 2008 financial crisis, AIG, was itself a provider of terrorism insurance.)

The subprime mortgage crisis was in part precipitated by a sharp drop in the value of financial assets, particularly assets whose value was tied to the value of housing. Because risk-management models assigned a low probability to a nationwide drop in the value of housing, insufficient capital was set aside against this downturn in the value of housing assets.

A provider of CNBR insurance faces a similarly sharp potential drop in the value of capital assets, not because of a decline in their market price but because of the need to make a payout following an attack. Regardless of the cause, the consequences for a financial institution caught in an asset price collapse and a CNBR insurer who must make a large payout are the same. Both firms must quickly raise large amounts of capital, and do so in an environment in which capital markets show little or no appetite for risk.

If we assume that external capital markets cannot accommodate this demand, then there is an argument for some form of government assistance. This assistance makes sense, however, only if the assisted institution is solvent. This condition would apply to a CNBR insurer having enough capital to pay its claims but needing to recapitalize in order to fund its ongoing business. It could also apply to a financial firm facing a liquidity crisis, which in the view of the Treasury and Federal Reserve is the situation of some firms receiving governmental bailouts following the subprime mortgage crisis. The issue, then, is how a government can best recapitalize a solvent institution.

Lending institutions do differ from insurers in one important respect. When a solvent bank suffers a decline in asset value, it still has assets (loans, investments, etc.) which it can pledge as collateral, albeit at a reduced value if the credit quality is questionable. Historically, a primary role of a central bank has been exactly to furnish bank liquidity against such collateral in periods when market liquidity has dried up. In contrast, a CNBR insurer suffering a large loss may have no financial collateral to offer, having sold all of its financial securities to pay claims. The insurer would have the net present value of its future premium stream, but until the financial crisis of 2008, a firm's profit prospects as an ongoing business entity would not have provided acceptable collateral for a loan from either the Treasury or the Federal Reserve.

The Emergency Economic Stabilization Act of 2008 and the redirection of the Troubled Asset Relief Program (TARP) have now fundamentally altered the government's role in recapitalizing (presumably) solvent financial institutions. By taking an equity position in banks, the U.S. Treasury has made it clear that the traditional Federal Reserve role of lending against high-quality collateral may not be sufficient to jump-start private capital markets into recapitalizing financial institutions which have suffered a decline in the value of their assets. It seems that only the straight injection of public capital can do that, or at least that the Treasury is willing to try this solution under the highly stressed financial conditions of the subprime mortgage crisis.

If this solution is to be tried for the insurance industry, how should it be carried out? We turn to that question in the next section.

Public Capital and CNBR Insurance

In a paper written before the government took on its new role as capital provider to private financial firms, Jaffee and Russell (2008) examined the possibility of a new role for government as the lender of last resort to the insurance industry following major catastrophe losses. Here we will revisit this issue in the light of the government's expanded new role in handling the subprime mortgage crisis. How might a government assist private insurers in raising capital?

Traditional Excess of Loss (XOL) Reinsurance. A traditional insurance solution to the issue of funding catastrophe risks and recapitalizing after losses was originally proposed by Lewis and Murdock (1996, 1999) and Cummins, Lewis, and Phillips (1999). Under their programs, the government would provide XOL reinsurance for all catastrophic losses (including CNBR terrorism) in some range. The Lewis and Murdock scheme suggested the range \$25 billion to \$50 billion. The reinsurance was also based on industry losses, not indemnity contracts for each insurer's book of business. For terrorism catastrophes, it may be very hard for any firm to replicate to a satisfactory degree the "industry" distribution of losses. As a result, there could exist substantial "basis risk," whereby the government's reinsurance would provide a poor hedge against the insurer's actual book of business. For this reason it is useful to look for alternative solutions that may also place the taxpayer at less risk.

Government-Insured CNBR bonds. In a speech discussing methods for encouraging capital to flow into the housing market, Federal Reserve chairman Bernanke (2008) accepted that private capital markets would sometimes be unable to securitize mortgage debt. Drawing on the work of Hancock and Passmore (2008), he outlined several proposals to assist the mortgage securitizers Fannie Mae and Freddie Mac. One proposal is especially worth noting. It would create

> a government bond insurer, analogous to the Federal Deposit Insurance Corporation (FDIC). This new agency would offer, for a premium, government-backed insurance for any form of bond financing used to provide funding to mortgage markets. For example, debt and mortgage-backed securities issued by the (privatized) GSEs as well as mortgage-backed bonds issued by banks would be eligible for the guarantee. That approach would clearly limit the government's exposure while making the benefits of explicit government support available to the market. (Bernanke 2008)[19]

Clearly such solutions have direct applicability to the insurance industry. Following a loss, a CNBR insurer could recapitalize by selling bonds. If these bonds were government insured, then there should be little impediment to recapitalizing the industry, just as Bernanke's approach would stimulate mortgage securitization.[20] This is a minimalist approach to bond financing assistance.

A more activist approach would have the government itself buy the bonds, giving the industry time to find an alternative source of capital. This approach was adopted by the state of Florida to assist the recapitalization of private hurricane insurers in that state. Florida's Senate Bill 1980 created a one-year $250 million capital-buildup incentive program to provide funding in the form of "surplus notes" to new or existing residential property insurers under the following conditions: the insurer must apply to the State Board of Administration and agree to contribute new capital to its surplus at least equal to the surplus note; the amount of the surplus note may not exceed $25 million or 20 percent of total funds available to the program; the surplus note must be repayable to the state, with a twenty-year term, at the ten-year Treasury bond interest rate; the insurer must commit to meeting a 2:1 writing ratio of net written premium to surplus; and the state would become a preferred creditor if the insurer became insolvent.

Government-Provided Equity. Now that the provision of public equity capital to banks and other financial institutions has become an accepted practice, there seems no reason why the same courtesy should not be extended to catastrophe insurers. That is to say, government could announce an *ex ante* policy in which it would take a temporary equity position in any solvent CNBR insurer willing to continue to write CNBR coverage. By removing the threat of bankruptcy, this policy should increase the flow of capital into this line. Such a policy may be even more appropriate for catastrophe insurers than for banks: the problems of the banking industry arose at least in part from bad portfolio decisions, so bailing out banks raises problems of moral hazard; but catastrophe losses are in the main beyond the control of each insurer or the industry.

As the recent capital injection into banks has demonstrated, it is essential to work through many details, lest the plan fail to achieve its specific goals. Nevertheless, a specific suggestion by Mankiw (2008) offers an intriguing general principle:

> Whenever any financial institution attracts new private capital in an arms-length transaction, it can access an equal amount of public capital. The taxpayer would get the same terms as the private investor. The only difference is that government's shares would be nonvoting until the government sold the shares at a later date.
>
> This plan would solve the three problems. The private sector rather than the government would weed out the zombie firms [those likely to fail even with recapitalization]. The private sector rather than the government would set the price. And the private sector rather than the government would exercise corporate control.

The principle of requiring private equity to match any government contribution could easily be applied as well to the recapitalization of a CNBR insurer. One notable feature of capital markets following a catastrophic loss is that some capital flows into the line. As shown in table 3-3, following Hurricane Katrina close to $10 billion in new capital flowed in. Unfortunately the loss in capital was some $50 billion. What a Mankiw-style government program of equity injection would do for CNBR insurers is provide a multiplier for this new capital. There is no reason, for example, why the

TABLE 3-3
POST-KATRINA CAPITAL ADDITIONS ANNOUNCED IN 2007

New Bermuda startups

New entity	Source of capital	Funding in billions
MaRI, Ltd.	Marsh/Ace Ltd (capacity of up to $1 billion in 2007)	$1.000
Artemis	Not available	$1.000
Kiln Re	Kiln	$0.309
Peleus Re	Argo Group	$0.240
Gamut Re	Nephila Re	$0.310
Total Bermuda startups		**$2.859**

Special-purpose reinsurance vehicles (SPRVs)/Sidecars/CAT bonds

New entity	Source of capital	Funding in billions
Merna Re Ltd.	State Farm	$1.181
Residential Re	USAA	$0.600
Emerson Re	CIG/New Castle Re	$0.500
Longpoint Re Ltd.	Travelers	$0.500
Starbound Re II	Renaissance Re	$0.342
Spinnaker Capital	Swiss Re	$0.330
Calabash Re II Ltd.	Ace	$0.250
East Lane Re	Chubb	$0.250
Willow Re	Allstate	$0.250
Fremantle Ltd.	Brit Ins	$0.200
Kepler Re	Hannover Re	$0.200
Puma Re	Bridge Re	$0.183
Blue Wings Ltd.	Allianz	$0.150
Carillon Ltd.	Munich Re	$0.150
Mystic Re II	Liberty Mutual	$0.150
Ajax Re Ltd.	Aspen	$0.100
Nelson Re	Glacier Re	$0.075
Total SPRVs/Sidecars/CAT bonds		**$5.410**

(continued on the next page)

(table 3-3 continued)

Capital additions

Existing entity	Source of capital	Funding in billions
Aeolus Re	Warburg Pincus & Others	$0.500
Total capital additions		**$0.500**

Expected IPOs (target capital amounts)

Existing entity	Funding in billions
Flagstone	$0.175
Validus	$0.200
Greenlight	$0.175
Castlepoint	$0.050
Total potential IPOs	**$0.600**

	Funding in billions
Grand total capital raised post-Katrina	**$9.369**

SOURCE: Natural Catastrophe Solutions That Work 2008.

leverage cannot be higher than a 1:1 ratio. Once private capital markets determine the cost of capital and identify the solvent firms, governments can choose a higher ratio—say, four units of public capital for every unit of private capital—and still have all the benefits of the Mankiw scheme.

Conclusion

Many commentators on TRIA and its extensions have argued that this government scheme has been a success, in that primary conventional terrorism insurance is, with some exceptions, now readily available. In this chapter we have noted two difficulties with this view. First, terrorism reinsurance is still not readily available, and indeed appears to have been crowded out at the highest tiers by the availability of subsidized government reinsurance; and second, insurance against acts of CNBR terrorism, potentially the most worrying form of terrorism because of the damage it could inflict and its strategic value to terrorists, remains largely unobtainable, despite being backstopped by TRIA and it extensions.

To deal with these two problems, we have suggested a dual strategy.

(1) Remove government entirely from reinsurance of acts of conventional terrorism, or at a minimum remove subsidies and embed risk-based premiums, This eliminates the crowding out of the private market that is otherwise inevitable. Private insurance markets are now large enough to handle losses in the range estimated by experts for this kind of attack, and further government presence and subsidies merely delay the reemergence of a private reinsurance market for this line.

(2) Since private capital markets are unlikely by themselves to be able to provide the amounts of capital necessary for insurers to offer credible CNBR coverage, the government must partner with private investors if this line is to be viable. Designers of such a partnership should pay attention to the successes and failures of recent attempts to recapitalize the banking industry following the catastrophic loss in asset value caused by the subprime crisis.

Notes

1. The Terrorism Risk Insurance Act of 2002 states, "The purpose of this title is to establish a temporary Federal program that provides for a transparent system of shared public and private compensation for insured losses resulting from acts of terrorism." *Terrorism Risk Insurance Act of 2002*, Public Law 107-297, *U.S. Statutes at Large* 116 (2002): 2322–2341.

2. See Sen. Phil Gramm,"The Role of the Federal Government in Assuring that Insurance for Terrorist Acts Remains Available to American Consumers," statement before the Senate Commerce, Science and Transportation Committee, 107th Congress, October 10, 2001.

3. This section draws on Russell and Thomas (2007), who provide a full discussion of the details of TRIPRA and a comparison with the initial legislation (TRIA).

4. Terrorism Risk Insurance Act, U.S. Code 15 § 6701 note (2002), § 103(c).

5. In Pennsylvania, workers' compensation statutes explicitly exclude acts of war. Other jurisdictions are silent on this class of risk. Since acts of war may therefore be included in workers' compensation contracts, TRIA and its extensions provide that the federal program includes acts of war as well as acts of terrorism. See Moss (2002) for further discussion.

6. The relevant locales are North Dakota, Ohio, Puerto Rico, the U.S. Virgin Islands, Washington, and Wyoming.

7. These states are Arizona, California, Colorado, Idaho, Maryland, Michigan, Minnesota, Montana, New York, Oklahoma, Oregon, Pennsylvania, and Utah.

8. In California the share of the risk taken by the state enterprise, State Compensation Insurance Fund, fell sharply between 2005 and 2007 (from over 42 percent to 27 percent), and the state is actively campaigning to attract further private capital. Apparently investors in this state are not put off by the fact that their capital is exposed to CNBR risk.

9. In the UK an organization called Pool Re was established to share terrorism risk; the UK government provides funds if insurers cannot otherwise meet their obligations. Details may be found on the Pool Re Web site, http://www.poolre.co.uk/.

10. The NCCI is the workers' compensation rate-making body for thirty-five states (AL, AK, AZ, AR, CO, CT, D.C., FL, GA, HI, ID, IL, IA, KS, KY, LA, ME, MD, MS, MO, MT, NE, NV, NH, NM, OK, OR, RI, SC, SD, TN, UT, VA, and VT). Details of how rates were arrived at are in NCCI (2002).

11. See e.g. American Insurance Association (2007, 6): "The program would function most effectively if it provided an economic framework through which insurers are able to offer coverage enhancements without putting their solvency at risk, at rates that encourage policyholders to purchase coverage. This cannot be accomplished simply by imposing a CNBR 'make available' mandate."

12. The insurers are not named in the report to preserve confidentiality.

13. In its recent report on catastrophe management, the Wharton Risk Management and Decision Processes Center (2008, ii) made risk-based pricing "Principle 1," stating

that "insurance premiums should be based on risk in order to provide signals to individuals as to the hazards they face, and to encourage them to engage in cost effective mitigation measures to reduce their vulnerability to catastrophes."

14. The "take-up rate," or the percentage of commercial-insurance policyholders opting to buy terrorism coverage, has been between 60 percent and 65 percent since 2004.

15. See also Litan (2008).

16. But consider the case of Berkshire Reinsurance, the reinsurance arm of Warren Buffett's Berkshire Hathaway, which in 1997 reinsured the $5 billion–$7.5 billion layer of the California Earthquake Authority (CEA) for four years for a premium of $590 million. In 2005, the CEA (2005) itself estimated the Probable Maximum Loss from a 6.95 magnitude event on the Northridge fault (the January 1994 event was magnitude 6.7) at $4.89 billion. This suggests that at a high enough price, capital is forthcoming. Zeckhauser (2006) provides a fascinating account of other circumstances in which capital is forthcoming when probabilities are unknown and unknowable.

17. For a discussion of these instruments see General Accounting Office (2002).

18. In 2006 the Fédération Internationale de Football Association (FIFA) issued a $260 million all-risk catastrophe bond to protect against cancellation of the 2006 World Soccer Cup in Germany. Terrorism risk was included among the risks insured.

19. A more detailed proposal for government guarantee of mortgage loans was presented by Jaffee (2008) at the same conference.

20. The subprime crisis has also raised the intriguing circumstance under which private-sector bonds fully guaranteed by the U.S. Treasury are trading at substantially higher yields—on the order of two percentage points—than U.S. Treasury bonds with identical cash flow patterns. It appears that, in the crisis atmosphere, some investors are willing to accept a substantially lower yield to obtain a security with the Treasury as the issuer and not just the guarantor.

References

Alleyn, Richard. 2003. The fall and rise of terrorism insurance coverage since September 11, 2001. Robins, Kaplan, Miller, and Ciresi. http://www.rkmc.com/The_Fall_and_Rise_of_Terrorism_Insurance_Coverage_Since_September_11_2001.htm.

American Academy of Actuaries. 2006. Re: President's working group on financial markets: Terrorism risk insurance analysis. http://www.actuary.org/pdf/casualty/ tris_042106.pdf.

American Insurance Association. 2007. Statement of Brian Dowd, Ace Group, on behalf of the American Insurance Association. United States House of Representatives Committee on Financial Services hearing on "Policy options for extending the Terrorism Risk Insurance Act." April 24. http://financialservices.house.gov/financialservices/hearing110/htdowd042407.pdf.

Bernanke, B. 2008. The future of mortgage finance in the United States. Speech at the UC Berkeley/UCLA symposium on the mortgage meltdown, the economy, and public policy, Berkeley, CA, October 30–31. http://www.federalreserve.gov/newsevents/speech/bernanke20081031a.htm.

Best, A. M. 2007. Aggregates and Averages: Property/Casualty—United States and Canada. Oldwick, NJ: A. M. Best.

———. 2008. Aggregates and Averages: Property/Casualty—United States and Canada. Oldwick, NJ: A. M. Best.

California Earthquake Authority. 2005. Analysis of ideas for improving CEA's financial condition. http://www.earthquakeauthority.com/12-15-2005_GB_Attachments%5CAI6D.pdf.

Congressional Budget Office. 2007. Estimated cost of S. 2285, the Terrorism Risk Insurance Revision and Extension Act of 2007, with an amendment transmitted to CBO by the Senate Committee on Banking, Housing, and Urban Affairs on November 14, 2007 (attachment to letter from Peter R. Orzag to Hon. Christopher J. Dodd). November 15. http://www.cbo.gov/ftpdocs/88xx/doc8825/TRIAltrSenBanking-Comm.pdf.

Cummins, J. David, Christopher M. Lewis, and Richard D. Phillips. 1999. Pricing excess-of-loss reinsurance contracts against catastrophic loss. In *The financing of catastrophe risk*, ed. Kenneth A. Froot, 93–148. Chicago: University of Chicago Press.

Froot, K. A. 2008. Market imperfections and catastrophe insurance: Building the case for government intervention. Available at http://info.worldbank.org/etools/docs/library/158277/natdisaster/agenda.html.

———, and P. O'Connell. 2008. On the pricing of intermediated risks: Theory and application to catastrophe reinsurance. *Journal of Banking and Finance* 32 (1): 69–85.

General Accounting Office. 2002. Catastrophe insurance risks: The role of risk-linked securities. GAO-03-195T. http://www.gao.gov/new.items/d03195t.pdf.

———. 2004. Terrorism insurance: Effects of the Terrorism Risk Insurance Act of 2002. GAO-04-806T. http://www.gao.gov/new.items/d04806t.pdf.

Gollier, Christian. 2004. Insurability. In *Encyclopedia of actuarial science*, ed. J. L. Teugels and B. Sundt, 2: 899–903. Chichester, UK: Wiley and Sons.

Government Accountability Office. 2008. Terrorism insurance: Status of efforts by policyholders to obtain coverage. GAO-08-1057. http://www.gao.gov/new.items/d081057.pdf.

Greenspan, A. 2004. Risk and uncertainty in monetary policy. Remarks at the American Economic Association meetings, January 3, San Diego, CA. http://www.federalreserve.gov/BoardDocs/Speeches/2004/20040103/default.htm.

Gron, Anne. 1994. Capacity constraints and cycles in property-casualty insurance markets. *RAND Journal of Economics* 25 (1): 110–27.

Hancock, Dianna, and Wayne Passmore. 2008. Three mortgage innovations for enhancing the American mortgage market and promoting financial stability. Paper presented at the UC Berkeley-UCLA symposium on the mortgage meltdown, the economy, and public policy. Berkeley, CA, October 30–31. Available at http://urbanpolicy.berkeley.edu/mortgagemeltdown.htm.

Hartwig, Robert. 2004. The cost of terrorism: How much can we afford. Insurance Information Institute. http://server.iii.org/yy_obj_data/binary/736854_1_0/tria.pdf.

Insurance Journal. 2008. S&P reports on the "evolving world of property/casualty securitizations." May 2. http://www.insurancejournal.com/news/international/2008/05/02/89626.htm.

Insurance Services Office, Inc. 2008. Insurer financial results: 2007. http://www.iso.com/Research-and-Analyses/Studies-and-Whitepapers/Insurer-Financial-Results-2007.html.

Jaffee, Dwight. 2008. Regulating the investment banks and GSEs after the subprime crisis. Fisher Center for Real Estate & Urban Economics. Fisher Center Working Paper 309Jaffee. http://repositories.cdlib.org/iber/fcreue/fcwp/309Jaffee.

———, and Thomas Russell. 1976. Imperfect information, uncertainty, and credit rationing. *Quarterly Journal of Economics* 90: 651–66.

———. 1997. Catastrophe insurance: Capital markets and uninsurable risks. *Journal of Risk and Insurance* 64 (June): 206–30.

———. 2008. Financing catastrophe insurance: A new proposal. In *Risking house and home: Disasters, cities, public policy*, ed. John M. Quigley and Larry A. Rosenthal, 37–46. Berkeley, CA: Public Policy Press.

Kunreuther H., J. Meszaros, R. Hogarth, and M. Spranca. 1995. Ambiguity and underwriter decision processes. *Journal of Economic Behavior and Organization* 26: 337–52.

Lane Financial. 2008. Beyond convergence, towards integration. Available at http://www.lanefinancialllc.com/content/view/223/1/.

Lewis, Christopher M., and Kevin C. Murdock. 1996. The role of government contracts in discretionary reinsurance markets for natural disasters. *Journal of Risk and Insurance* 63 (4): 567–97.

———. 1999. Alternative means of redistributing catastrophic risk in a national risk management system. In *The financing of catastrophe risk*, ed. Kenneth A. Froot, 51–92. Chicago: University of Chicago Press.

Litan, Robert E. 2008. Preparing for future "Katrinas." Brookings Policy Brief Series # 151. March. http://www.brookings.edu/papers/2006/03business_litan.aspx.

Mankiw, G. 2008. How to recapitalize the financial system. Greg Mankiw's blog. October 8. http://gregmankiw.blogspot.com/2008/10/how-to-recapitalize-financial-system.html.

Moss, David. 2002. *When all else fails: Government as the ultimate risk manager.* Cambridge, MA: Harvard University Press.

Mueller J. 2007. Reacting to terrorism: Probabilities, consequences, and the persistence of fear. Paper prepared for the National Convention of the International Studies Association, February 26–March 4, Chicago. http://psweb.sbs.ohio-state.edu/faculty/jmueller/ISA2007T.PDF.

Myers, Stewart, and Nicholal S. Majluf. 1984. Corporate financing and investment decisions when firms have information that investors do not have. *Journal of Financial Economics* 13 (2): 187–221.

National Catastrophe Solutions That Work. 2008. Post Katrina Capital Additions Announced in 2007. http://www.natcatus.org/Content/New%20Capital%20Post%20Katrina020808.pdf.

National Council on Compensation Insurance. 2002. Filing Memorandum B1383, Appendix A. http://www.ncci.com/media/pdf/ItemB-1383_FULL.pdf.

President's Working Group on Financial Markets. 2006. Terrorism risk insurance. September. http://www.treas.gov/offices/domestic-finance/financial-institution/terrorism-insurance/pdf/report.pdf.

Russell, T., and D. M. Jaffee. 1998. Catastrophe insurance, dynamic premium strategies and the market for capital. In *Alternative approaches to insurance regulation*, ed. Robert W. Klein, 79–98. Kansas City, MO: National Association of Insurance Commissioners.

Russell, T., and J. Thomas. 2007. Government support for the terrorism insurance industry: Where do we go from here? Paper prepared for Searle Center on Law, Regulation, and Economic Growth symposium on insurance markets and regulation, April 15. http://www.law.northwestern.edu/searlecenter/papers/Russell-Thomas_final.pdf.

Towers, Perrin. 2004. Worker's compensation terrorism reinsurance pool feasibility study. http://www.towersperrin.com/tillinghast/publications/reports/WC_Terr_Pool/WC_Terr_Pool_Study.pdf.

Tversky, A., and D. Kahneman. 1973. Availability: A heuristic for judging frequency and probability. *Cognitive Psychology* 5: 207–32.

Wharton Risk Management and Decision Processes Center. 2008. Managing large scale risks in a new era of catastrophes. March. http://opim.wharton.upenn.edu/risk/library/Wharton_LargeScaleRisks_FullReport_2008.pdf.

Winter, Ralph A. 1994. The dynamics of competitive insurance markets. *Journal of Financial Intermediation* 3 (4): 379–415.

Zeckhauser, Richard. 2006. Investing in the unknown and unknowable. *Capitalism and Society* 1, issue 2, article 5. http://www.bepress.com/cas/vol1/iss2/art5.

4

Market and Government Failure in Insuring and Mitigating Natural Catastrophes: How Long-Term Contracts Can Help

Howard C. Kunreuther and Erwann O. Michel-Kerjan

> Insurance plays a vital role in America's economy by helping households and businesses manage risks. . . . When insurance prices reflect underlying economic costs they can encourage a more efficient allocation of resources. Efforts to keep premiums for insurance against catastrophe hazards artificially low, whether through regulation or through subsidized government programs, can encourage excessively risky behavior on the part of those who might be affected by future catastrophes.
>
> —*Economic Report of the President*, 2007[1]

Given the hundreds of billions of dollars in economic losses that catastrophes have caused in the United States since 2001, it is difficult to remember that when Hurricane Hugo hit the country in 1989, it was the first catastrophe to inflict more than $1 billion of insured losses. But times have changed: there have been repeated large-scale natural disasters in the United States in the past few years, the terrorism threat worldwide—including the potential for nuclear attacks—has increased, and in addition to the 2008–2009 financial crisis, we face the possibility of international pandemics and world cyberfailure.

These catastrophes differ from one another in obvious ways, but they have two important features in common: uncertainty and wide variance in losses from one year to the next. Experts and decision makers face challenges in assessing the risks associated with these extreme events, developing strategies for reducing future losses following them, and facilitating the recovery process in their aftermath.

To understand these challenges, let us consider some recent natural disasters. The world has experienced large-scale losses and fatalities due to the increasing concentration of population and activities in high-risk coastal regions. In Southeast Asia, the tsunami in December 2004 killed more than 280,000 people residing in coastal areas. Cyclone Nargis, which made landfall in Myanmar in May 2008, killed an estimated 140,000 people, making it the deadliest natural disaster in the recorded history of the country. The same month, the Great Sichuan Earthquake is estimated to have killed over 85,000, injured 374,000, and left almost five million homeless (Munich Re 2008). Deaths from the Haitian earthquake in 2010 are estimated at 230,000 (*Insurance Journal* 2010).

But even a developed country like the United States, which has both extensive experience with natural catastrophes and the resources to adequately prepare for them, may have inadequate loss-reduction measures in place and may lack the emergency-preparedness capacity to deal with large-scale natural disasters, such as occurred during the 2004 and 2005 hurricane seasons. Hurricane Katrina, which hit Louisiana and Mississippi at the end of August 2005, killed 1,300 people and forced 1.5 million people to evacuate

The authors would like to thank Jeffrey Brown, David Torregrosa, and other participants in "Private Markets and Public Insurance Programs," a conference sponsored by the American Enterprise Institute in January 2009, for helpful comments on a previous version of this paper. This work also benefits from ongoing discussion with congressional staff on the concept of long-term insurance. The authors appreciate editorial assistance from Carol Heller and Anne Himmelfarb. The authors acknowledge support from the Wharton Risk Management and Decision Processes Center (hereafter Wharton Risk Center) and a grant from the Federal Emergency Management Agency, Office of Preparedness Policy, Planning and Analysis, National Preparedness Directorate, U.S. Department of Homeland Security (Grant #2008-GA-T8-K004). The views and opinions expressed are those of the authors and should not be interpreted as representing the United States Government or FEMA.

the affected area—a historic record for the country. Economic losses caused by Katrina are estimated in the range of $150 to $200 billion.

A series of hurricanes in 2008 caused billions of dollars in direct economic losses along the Caribbean basin and in the United States. Hurricane Ike was the most expensive individual event in 2008, with an estimated privately insured loss of $17.6 billion in addition to $2.4 billion in claims paid by the U.S. National Flood Insurance Program for flood surge resulting from Ike (Swiss Re 2009). Based on these figures, Hurricane Ike ranks as the third-worst weather-related disaster in U.S. history, after Hurricane Katrina and Hurricane Andrew, which hit southeast Florida in August 1992.

These recent catastrophes highlight the challenges of mitigating natural disasters and paying for the damage they cause. The question is not *whether* other large-scale catastrophes will occur, but *when* and *how frequent* they will be, and how extensive the damage—and numerous the fatalities—they will cause.

Now is the time to develop and implement economically sound policies and strategies for managing the risk and consequences of future disasters. To do so, it is important to take a long-term view of these issues and avoid the tendency to be myopic and to misperceive risks. A coherent strategy is necessary to ensure sustainable recovery from large-scale disasters and the appropriate future development of hazard-prone areas. But the issues involved in developing such a strategy are complex. They challenge our capacity as a nation to work together despite the different views of stakeholders and legislators about the role and responsibilities of the private and public sectors in dealing with catastrophic risks. But absence of leadership in this area will inevitably lead to unnecessary loss of lives and economic destruction in the devastated regions.

This chapter focuses on the risk of large-scale natural disasters, although we believe that methods for managing these risks have relevance to other types of extreme events, such as terrorism and catastrophic accidents.[2] We begin by discussing the evolution over the past four decades of economic and insured losses due to major catastrophes, as well as the key drivers of this change. We then propose four guiding principles for developing sustainable insurance and mitigation programs. After a discussion of the behavioral biases (notably myopia) that discourage individuals from investing in cost-effective protective measures, we explain how long-term insurance contracts combined with long-term home improvement loans can overcome these biases. We then discuss the National Flood Insurance Program, which is due for renewal or changes in the coming months, as a natural candidate for these contracts. The chapter concludes with a brief summary and suggestions for future research.

A New Era of Catastrophes

The economic and insured losses from great natural catastrophes such as hurricanes, earthquakes, and floods worldwide have increased significantly in recent years, as shown in figure 4-1 (each vertical bar represents the total economic losses, and the darker zone represents the insured portion of it). A comparison of these economic losses over time reveals a huge increase: \$53.6 billion (1950–1959), \$93.3 billion (1960–1969), \$161.7 billion (1970–1979), \$262.9 billion (1980–1989), and \$778.3 billion (1990–1999). Between 2000 and 2008, there were \$620.6 billion in losses, principally a result of the 2004, 2005, and 2008 hurricane seasons.

Catastrophes have had a more devastating impact on insurers since 1990 than in the entire history of insurance before that time. Figure 4-2, which depicts the upward trend in worldwide insured losses from catastrophes between 1970 and 2008,[3] shows that between 1970 and the mid-1980s, annual insured losses from natural disasters (including forest fires) were in the \$3 billion to \$4 billion range. The insured losses from Hurricane Hugo, which made landfall in Charleston, South Carolina, in September 1989, exceeded \$7.9 billion (2008 dollars). There was a radical increase in insured losses in the early 1990s, with Hurricane Andrew in Florida (\$24.6 billion in 2008 dollars) and the Northridge earthquake in California (\$20.3 billion in 2008 dollars). The four hurricanes in Florida in 2004 (Charley, Frances, Ivan, and Jeanne) collectively totaled almost \$35 billion in insured losses. Hurricane Katrina alone cost insurers and reinsurers an estimated \$48 billion, with total losses of \$87 billion paid by private insurers for major natural catastrophes in 2005.[4]

Table 4-1 reveals the twenty-five most costly catastrophes for the insurance sector from 1970 to 2008 (in 2008 dollars). Of these twenty-five major events, fourteen have occurred since 2001, twelve of them in the United States. Hurricane Andrew and the Northridge earthquake were the first two catastrophes that the industry experienced where losses were greater than \$10 billion (designated "super-cats") and caused insurers to reflect on whether risks from natural disasters were still insurable. To assist them in making this

FIGURE 4-1
EVOLUTION OF GREAT NATURAL CATASTROPHES WORLDWIDE, 1950–2008

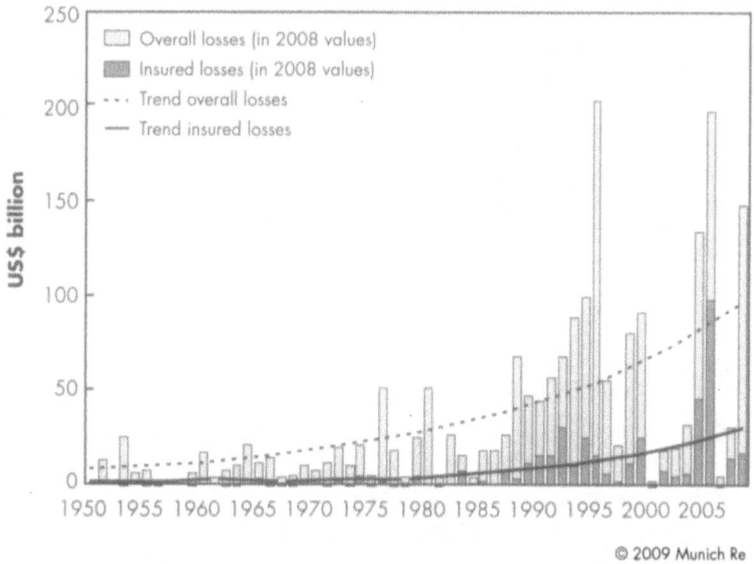

SOURCE: Munich Re 2009a.
NOTE: Dollar amounts are indexed to 2008.

determination, many firms began using catastrophe models to estimate the likelihood of, and consequences to their insured portfolios from, specific disasters in hazard-prone areas (Grossi and Kunreuther 2005). With the exception of the terrorist attacks on September 11, 2001, all twenty-five of the most costly catastrophes were natural disasters.[5] More than 85 percent of these were weather-related events—hurricanes, typhoons, storms, and floods—with nearly three-quarters of the claims in the United States.

Losses resulting from natural catastrophes and man-made disasters in 2006 were far below the losses in 2004 and 2005. Of the $48 billion in catastrophe-related economic losses, $16 billion was covered by insurance ($11 billion for natural disasters and $5 billion for man-made). During the past twenty years, only 1988 and 1997 had insured losses lower than those in 2006. According to Munich Re, there were 950 natural catastrophes in 2007, the most since 1974. They inflicted nearly $27 billion in insured

FIGURE 4-2
WORLDWIDE EVOLUTION OF CATASTROPHE INSURED LOSSES, 1970–2008

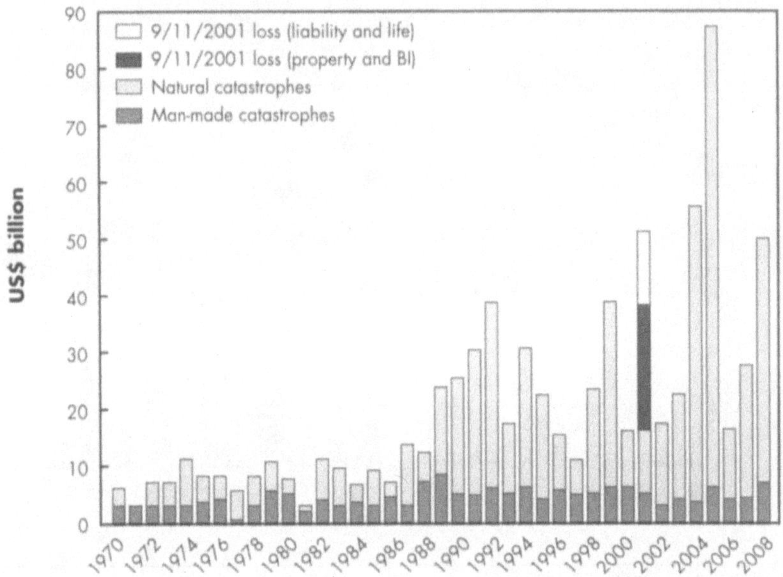

SOURCES: Kunreuther and Michel-Kerjan 2009 with data from Swiss Re 2009 and Insurance Information Institute in New York.
NOTES: All lines, including property and business interruption, in billions of U.S. dollars indexed to 2007, except for 2008, which is current. Man-made catastrophes include major fires and explosions (e.g., in a chemical plant or oil refinery), aviation/rail/shipping-related losses (fires, crashes, collisions), mining accidents, and collapse of infrastructure. BI = business interruption.

losses. Swiss Re estimates that insured losses soared to $52.5 billion for the industry in 2008, making it one of the three costliest years ever. Natural catastrophes accounted for $44.7 billion of these losses, with man-made disasters accounting for the remaining $7.8 billion (Kunreuther and Michel-Kerjan, 2009). In 2009, insured losses due to catastrophes amounted to only $22 billion, due principally to a very benign North Atlantic hurricane season (Munich Re, 2009b).

The occurrence of damaging hurricanes is highly variable and uncertain from year to year. However, it is very likely that in the coming years more

TABLE 4-1
TWENTY-FIVE MOST COSTLY INSURED CATASTROPHES WORLDWIDE, 1970–2008

$Billion	Event	Victims (dead or missing)	Year	Area of primary damage
48.1	Hurricane Katrina	1,836	2005	U.S., Gulf of Mexico, et al.
36.8	9/11 Attacks	3,025	2001	U.S.
24.6	Hurricane Andrew	43	1992	U.S., Bahamas
20.3	Northridge Earthquake	61	1994	U.S.
17.6	Hurricane Ike	348	2008	U.S., Caribbean, et al.
14.6	Hurricane Ivan	124	2004	U.S., Caribbean, et al.
13.8	Hurricane Wilma	35	2005	U.S., Gulf of Mexico, et al.
11.1	Hurricane Rita	34	2005	U.S., Gulf of Mexico, et al.
9.1	Hurricane Charley	24	2004	U.S., Caribbean, et al.
8.9	Typhoon Mireille	51	1991	Japan
7.9	Hurricane Hugo	71	1989	Puerto Rico, U.S., et al.
7.7	Winter Storm Daria	95	1990	France, UK, et al.
7.5	Winter Storm Lothar	110	1999	France, Switzerland, et al.
6.3	Winter Storm Kyrill	54	2007	Germany, UK, NL, France
5.9	Storms and floods	22	1987	France, UK, et al.
5.8	Hurricane Frances	38	2004	U.S., Bahamas
5.2	Winter Storm Vivian	64	1990	Western/Central Europe
5.2	Typhoon Bart	26	1999	Japan
5.0	Hurricane Gustav	153	2008	U.S., Caribbean, et al.
4.7	Hurricane Georges	600	1998	U.S., Caribbean
4.4	Tropical Storm Allison	41	2001	U.S.
4.4	Hurricane Jeanne	3,034	2004	U.S., Caribbean, et al.
4.0	Typhoon Songda	45	2004	Japan, South Korea
3.7	Storms	45	2003	U.S.
3.6	Hurricane Floyd	70	1999	U.S., Bahamas, Colombia

SOURCES: Kunreuther and Michel-Kerjan 2009 with data from Swiss Re 2009 and Insurance Information Institute in New York.
NOTE: Dollar amounts are indexed to 2008.

hurricanes will strike the Atlantic and Gulf coasts. Other parts of the nation will experience severe floods (as occurred in the upper Midwest in 2008) or earthquakes, causing extreme damage to residential and commercial property and infrastructure.

There is a very clear message from these data. Twenty or thirty years ago, large-scale natural disasters were considered to be low-probability events. Today, they not only are causing considerably greater economic losses than in the past but also appear to be occurring at an accelerating pace. It is important to understand more fully the factors influencing these changes in order to design more effective programs for reducing losses from future disasters.

The Question of Attribution. Several elements explain this increase in the cost of disasters in recent years. They include a higher degree of urbanization, an increase in the value at risk and insurance density, and the possible impact of a change in climate. In 1950, approximately 30 percent of the world's population lived in cities. In 2000, about 50 percent of the world's population (6 billion) did. Projections by the United Nations (2008) show that by 2025, that figure will have increased to 60 percent, based on a world population estimate of 8.3 billion people.

In the United States in 2003, 53 percent of the nation's population, or 153 million people, lived in the 673 U.S. coastal counties, an increase of 33 million people since 1980, according to the National Oceanic Atmospheric Administration. And the nation's coastal population is expected to increase by more than 12 million by 2015 (Crossett et al. 2004).[6] Yet coastal counties, excluding Alaska, account for only 17 percent of land area in the United States. In hazard-prone areas, this urbanization and increase in population translate into greater concentration of exposure and hence a higher likelihood of catastrophic losses from future disasters. Given the growing concentration of exposure on the Gulf Coast, another hurricane like Katrina hitting in that area is likely to inflict significant property damage unless strong mitigation measures are put in place.[7]

This new vulnerability is best understood in historical context—that is, compared to the cost of hurricanes in the past. It is possible to calculate the total direct economic cost of the major hurricanes affecting the United States in the past century, adjusted for inflation, population, and wealth normalization. Several studies have estimated what previous hurricanes would have cost had they hit today. The most recent one, by Pielke et al. (2008), normalizes to the year 2005 mainland U.S. hurricane damage for the period 1900–2005.

Drawing on data from Pielke et al. (2008), table 4-2 lists the twenty hurricanes that would have been most costly had they occurred in 2005. The estimate for each is a range based on the two approaches to normalizing losses used by the Pielke study. The table provides the year when the hurricane originally occurred, the states that were the most seriously affected, and the hurricane category on the Saffir-Simpson scale. The data reveal that the hurricane that hit Miami in 1926 would have been almost twice as costly as Hurricane Katrina had it occurred in 2005, and the Galveston hurricane of 1900 would have had total direct economic costs as high as those from Katrina. This means that independent of any possible change in weather patterns, we are very likely to see even more devastating disasters in the coming years because of the ongoing growth in values located in risk-prone areas.

There is another element to consider in explaining the increase in the cost and likelihood of natural disasters: the possible impact of a change in climate. Between 1970 and 2004, storms and floods were responsible for over *90 percent* of the total economic costs of extreme weather–related events worldwide. Storms (hurricanes in the U.S. region, typhoons in Asia, and windstorms in Europe) contributed to over 75 percent of insured losses. In constant prices (2004), insured losses from weather-related events averaged $3 billion annually between 1970 and 1990 and then increased significantly to $16 billion annually between 1990 and 2004 (Association of British Insurers 2005). In 2005, 99.7 percent of all catastrophic losses worldwide were due to weather-related events (Mills and Lecomte 2006).

There have been numerous discussions and scientific debates as to whether the series of major hurricanes that occurred in 2004 and 2005 might be partially attributable to the impact of a change in climate.[8] One of the expected effects of global warming is an increase in hurricane intensity; this increase has been predicted by theory and modeling, and substantiated by empirical data on climate change. Higher ocean temperatures lead to an exponentially higher evaporation rate in the atmosphere, which increases the intensity of cyclones and precipitation. An increase in the number of major hurricanes over a shorter period of time is likely to translate into a greater number hitting the coasts, with a greater likelihood of damage to

TABLE 4-2
TWENTY MOST COSTLY HURRICANES, 1900–2005
(Ranked using 2005 inflation, population, and wealth normalization)

Rank	Hurricane	Year	Category	Cost range in 2005 ($ billions)
1	Miami (Southeast FL/MS/AL)	1926	4	140–157
2	Katrina (LA/MS)	2005	3	81
3	North Texas (Galveston)	1900	4	72–78
4	North Texas (Galveston)	1915	4	57–62
5	Andrew (Southeast FL and LA)	1992	5-3	54–60
6	New England (CT/MA/NY/RI)	1938	3	37–39
7	Southwest Florida	1944	3	35–39
8	Lake Okeechobee (Southeast Florida)	1928	4	32–34
9	Donna (FL-NC/NY)	1960	4-3	29–32
10	Camille (MS/Southeast LA/VA)	1969	5	21–24
11	Betsy (Southeast FL and LA)	1965	3	21–23
12	Wilma	2005	3	21
13	Agnes (FL/CT/NY)	1972	1	17–18
14	Diane (NC)	1955	1	17
15	(Southeast FL/LA/AL/MS)	1947	4-3	15–17
16	Hazel (SC/NC)	1954	4	16–23
17	Charley (Southwest FL)	2004	4	16
18	Carol (CT/NY/RI)	1954	3	15–16
19	Hugo (SC)	1989	4	15–16
20	Ivan (Northwest FL/AL)	2004	3	15

SOURCE: Pielke et al. 2008.

residences and commercial buildings today than in the 1940s—a trend that raises issues about the insurability of weather-related catastrophes.

The combination of increasing urbanization, concentration of value in high-risk areas, and the potential impact of a change in weather patterns raises questions for the insurance industry about how it will provide protection against catastrophic risks in the future. Conventional insurance relies on geographical *and* time diversification, both of which are somewhat compromised by these recent trends. Determining the appropriate roles and responsibilities of the private and public sectors (as a source of financial support or as market regulator) is critical in this regard.

Guiding Principles for Mitigating and Insuring against Catastrophes

The following four guiding principles clarify how the private and public sectors can use the insurance infrastructure to deal more effectively with natural disasters.[9]

Principle 1: Premiums should reflect risk. Insurance premiums should be based on risk in order to provide signals to individuals about the hazards they face and to encourage them to engage in cost-effective mitigation measures that reduce their vulnerability to catastrophes. Risk-based premiums should also reflect the cost of capital that insurers must integrate into their pricing in order to assure adequate return to their investors. The application of principle 1 provides a clear signal of likely damage to those currently residing in hazard-prone areas as well as those considering locating there. Risk-based premiums would also enable insurers to provide discounts to homeowners and businesses that invest in cost-effective mitigation measures. If insurance premiums are not risk-based, insurers are unlikely to offer any premium discounts for those who adopt mitigation measures. In fact, they prefer not to offer coverage to these property owners because it will be a losing proposition in the long run.

Principle 2: Equity and affordability issues should be addressed. Specifically, any special treatment given to homeowners currently residing in hazard-prone areas (e.g., to low-income uninsured or inadequately insured homeowners) should be funded through general public funding and not through insurance premium subsidies. This principle reflects a concern for some residents in high-hazard areas who will be faced with large premium increases if insurers adhere to principle 1. As discussed in the next section, regulations imposed by state insurance commissioners keep premiums in many regions subject to hurricane damage artificially lower than the risk-based level.

Note that principle 2 applies only to individuals who *currently reside* in a hazard-prone area. Those who decide to move to the area in the future should be charged premiums that reflect the risk. If they were provided with financial assistance from public sources to purchase insurance, the resulting public policy would directly encourage development in hazard-prone areas and exacerbate the potential for catastrophic losses from future disasters.

Principle 3: There should be sufficient demand for coverage. The demand by individuals and firms for insurance coverage with risk-based premiums should be sufficiently high so that insurers can cover the fixed costs of introducing a program that provides coverage and that spreads the risk broadly throughout their portfolios. High demand for insurance would also reduce the level of state and federal relief to uninsured or underinsured homeowners in the aftermath of the next disaster.

Principle 4: The likelihood of (re-)insurers' insolvency should be minimized. Insurers and reinsurers should determine how much coverage to offer and what premium to charge against the risk so that the chances of insolvency are below some predefined acceptable threshold. Insurance regulators should play an important role here in assuring that insurers providing coverage in high-risk areas have a solid financial basis for doing so.

The Behavioral Challenges: The Demand for Insurance and Mitigation

How effective is mitigation in reducing exposure to future disaster? In our recent book, we shed some light on this question by analyzing the impact that mitigation would have on reducing losses from hurricanes in four states: Florida, New York, South Carolina, and Texas (Kunreuther and Michel-Kerjan 2009). In our analysis of the impact of mitigation, we consider two extreme cases: one in which no one has invested in mitigation, the other in which everyone has invested in predefined mitigation measures. From the U.S.

hurricane model developed by the catastrophe modeling firm Risk Management Solutions (RMS), losses were calculated assuming an appropriate mitigation measure across the insured portfolio. The mitigation measures were based on various assumptions for the different regions. Thus in Florida, the requirements were those defined by the "Fortified . . . for Safer Living" program of the Institute for Business and Home Safety (IBHS). In New York, South Carolina, and Texas, mitigation meant the application of the latest building codes to the residential structures.[10]

Table 4-3 indicates the differences in losses and savings from adopting mitigation measures for hurricanes with return periods of 100, 250, and 500 years for each of the four states.

The analyses reveal that mitigation has the potential to significantly reduce losses from future hurricanes. The reductions range from 61 percent in Florida for a hundred-year return-period loss to 31 percent in Texas for a five-hundred-year return-period loss. In Florida alone, mitigation reduces losses by $51 billion for a hundred-year event and $83 billion for a five-hundred-year event. These findings are important, given the costly capital needed to cover the tail of the distribution of extreme events. Adoption of mitigation measures on residential structures significantly reduces this tail in each of these four states.

The challenge, however, lies in making sure that residents in hazard-prone areas invest in these mitigation measures. Indeed, recent extreme events have highlighted this challenge, and have led one of us to identify *natural disaster syndrome* as a common phenomenon (Kunreuther 1996). The phenomenon has the following features: homeowners, private businesses, and public-sector organizations fail to voluntarily adopt cost-effective loss-reduction measures. Thus they are highly vulnerable and unprepared should a severe hurricane or other natural disaster occur. But the magnitude of the destruction following a catastrophe often leads governmental agencies to provide disaster relief to victims—even if prior to the event the government claimed that it would not do so. This combination of underinvestment in protection prior to the catastrophic event, together with taxpayer financing of part of the recovery following it, can be critiqued on both efficiency and equity grounds.

There are a range of informal mechanisms that explain natural disaster syndrome. One relates to framing the problem imperfectly: while experts focus on an event's likelihood and consequences in determining risk, several

TABLE 4-3

MONEY SAVED IN REDUCED LOSSES FROM FULL MITIGATION FOR DIFFERENT RETURN PERIODS

State	Unmitigated losses ($billion)	Savings in reduced losses from mitigation ($billion)	Savings in reduced losses from mitigation (percent)
		100-year Event	
FL	$84	$51	61
NY	$6	$2	39
SC	$4	$2	44
TX	$17	$6	34
		250-year Event	
FL	$126	$69	55
NY	$13	$5	37
SC	$7	$3	41
TX	$27	$9	32
		500-year Event	
FL	$160	$83	52
NY	$19	$7	35
SC	$9	$4	39
TX	$37	$12	31

SOURCE: Kunreuther and Michel-Kerjan 2009.

studies show that individuals rarely seek out probability estimates in making decisions. When these data are given to decision makers, they are often not taken into account. In one study, researchers found that only 22 percent of subjects sought out probability information when evaluating several risky managerial decisions (Huber, Wider, and Huber 1997). People have particular difficulty dealing with probabilistic information for small-likelihood events and generally need a context in which to evaluate the likelihood of an event occurring. For example, they have a hard time gauging how concerned to feel about a 1 in 100,000 probability of death without some comparison points. Most people just do not know whether 1 in 100,000 is a large risk or a small risk. In one study, individuals could not distinguish the relative safety of chemical plants whose annual chance of experiencing a catastrophic accident varied from 1 in 10,000 to 1 in 1 million (Kunreuther, Novemsky, and Kahneman 2001).

There is also evidence that firms and residents tend to ignore risks whose subjective odds are seen as falling below some threshold. Prior to a disaster, many individuals perceive its likelihood as sufficiently low that they contend *it will not happen to me* (probability neglect). As a result, they do not feel the need to invest voluntarily in protective measures, such as strengthening their house or buying insurance. After the disaster occurs, however, these same individuals express remorse that they didn't undertake protective measures.

Another reason that individuals do not invest in protective measures is that they are highly myopic and tend to focus only on short-term returns—that is, only on those that occur over the next couple of years. In addition, there is extensive experimental evidence showing that temporal discounting tends to be hyperbolic, so that events in the distant future are disproportionately discounted relative to immediate ones. As an example, people are willing to pay more to hasten the receipt of a cash prize from tomorrow to today than from two days from now to tomorrow (Loewenstein and Prelec 1991). The implication of hyperbolic discounting for mitigation decisions is that residents will be reluctant to invest a tangible fixed sum now to achieve a future benefit; that benefit is instinctively undervalued—and is one that no one hopes ever to see at all. The effect of placing too much weight on immediate considerations is that the upfront costs of mitigation will loom disproportionately large relative to the delayed expected benefits.[11]

There is extensive evidence that residents in hazard-prone areas do not undertake loss-prevention measures voluntarily. A 1974 survey of more than a thousand California homeowners in earthquake-prone areas revealed that only 12 percent of the respondents had adopted any protective measure (Kunreuther et al. 1978). Fifteen years later, there was little change despite increased public awareness of the earthquake hazard. In a 1989 survey of 3,500 homeowners in four California counties at risk from earthquakes, only 5 to 9 percent of the respondents reported adopting any loss reduction measures (Palm et al. 1990). Burby et al. (1988) and Laska (1991) have found a similar reluctance by residents in flood-prone areas to invest in mitigation measures.

In the case of flood damage, Burby (2006) provides compelling evidence that actions taken by the federal government, such as constructing levees, tend to give a false sense of security to residents, who would still be in harm's way should the levee be breached or overtopped. This problem is intensified by local public officials who do not enforce building codes or who fail to restrict development in high-hazard areas. If developers do not design homes resistant to disasters, and individuals do not voluntarily adopt mitigation measures, one can expect large-scale losses following a catastrophic event, as evidenced by the property damage to New Orleans caused by Hurricane Katrina.

Even after the devastating 2004 and 2005 hurricane seasons, a large number of residents in high-risk areas had still not invested in relatively inexpensive loss-reduction measures, nor had they undertaken emergency preparedness measures. A survey of 1,100 adults living along the Atlantic and Gulf coasts conducted in May 2006 revealed that 83 percent had taken no steps to fortify their home, 68 percent had no hurricane survival kit, and 60 percent had no family disaster plan (Goodnough 2006). The failure of many homeowners to voluntarily invest in cost-effective mitigation measures or purchase adequate insurance coverage should not simply be considered irrational. As we have just indicated, people might have their own reasons for not taking these actions until after the next disaster occurs. The way in which these issues could be addressed by our proposal—the development of long-term insurance contracts—is explored below.

A New Concept: The Development of Long-Term Insurance Contracts

To overcome some of the behavioral tendencies described above, it is important to develop an incentive system so individuals will want to invest in risk reduction measures. We propose a move from the standard one-year insurance contracts (for homeowners' insurance and flood insurance for residential properties) to long-term insurance (LTI) as a way of dealing with individuals' tendency to be myopic.[12] Moreover, LTI would also address another problem, the possibility that in hurricane-prone areas, a homeowner's insurance policy (which covers wind damage, but not flood losses) might be subject to unexpected cancellation or very significant premium increases, particularly if there is severe hurricane damage in the near future.

Need for Long-Term Insurance. Short-term insurance policies foster significant social costs. Evidence from recent disasters reveals that consumers who fail to adequately protect their homes, or even insure them at all, create a welfare cost to themselves and a possible cost to all taxpayers in the form of government disaster assistance. Under the current U.S. system, the governor of the affected state(s) can request that the president declare a "major disaster" and offer special assistance if the damage is severe enough. The number of presidential disaster declarations has dramatically increased over the past fifty years: there were 162 over the period 1955–1965, 282 over 1966–1975, 319 over 1986–1995, and 545 over 1996–2005 (Michel-Kerjan 2008).

The development of LTI should encourage individuals to invest in cost-effective mitigation measures. As pointed out above, many homeowners are unwilling to incur the high upfront cost associated with these investments relative to the small premium discount—reflecting the expected reduction in annual insured losses—that they would receive the following year. If an LTI policy were coupled with a long-term home-improvement loan tied to the mortgage, the reduction in insurance premiums would exceed the annual loan payment. The social welfare benefits of LTI coupled with long-term mitigation loans over *N* years could be significant: there will be less damage to property, lower costs to insurers for protecting against catastrophic losses, more secure mortgages, and lower costs to the government for disaster assistance.

Why a Market for Long-Term Insurance Does Not Exist Today. In his seminal work on uncertainty and welfare economics, Kenneth Arrow defined "the absence of marketability for an action which is identifiable, technologically possible and capable of influencing some individuals' welfare . . . as a failure of the existing market to provide a means whereby the services can be both offered and demanded upon the payment of a price" (Arrow 1963, 945). Here we shall discuss several factors which have contributed to the nonmarketability of LTI for protecting homeowners against losses from fire, theft, and large-scale natural disasters. We discuss elements which affect both the supply and demand sides.

Supply Side. Today, political pressure frequently causes insurance rates to be artificially low in hazard-prone areas. The result is that the risks most subject to catastrophic losses also become the most unattractive for insurers to market. A second stumbling block, derived from premium regulation, is that insurers are unclear about how much they will be allowed to charge in the future. Uncertainty regarding costs of capital and changes in risk over time may also deter insurers from providing long-term insurance. In principle, of course, insurers could add a component in their premiums to account for the costs created by these factors. The problem is that the insurance regulator, presumed to be representing consumers' interests, may not allow these costs to be embedded in the approved premiums. A new and less intrusive format for government regulation of insurance markets may be required if the private sector is to be successful in dealing with time-varying risks and capital costs.

Insurers might also be concerned about possible changes in the level of risk over time. For example, global warming could trigger more intense weather-related disasters, and/or local environmental degradation might change the risk landscape in the next several decades. One way to address this concern would be to have renegotiable contracts on a regular basis (e.g., every five years) based on new information validated by the scientific community, in much the same way that there are renegotiable loans with adjustable rates.

Demand Side. Some homeowners, particularly those contemplating an LTI contract, may worry about the financial solvency of their insurer over a long period. Consumers might also fear being overcharged if insurers set premiums that reflect the uncertainty associated with long-term risks. Thus those who have not suffered a loss for ten years but have a twenty-five-year LTI may feel that the premiums are unfairly priced. It is therefore essential that the design of an LTI contract anticipate these concerns and be transparent to the policyholder.

Developing an LTI Policy. To compare the expected benefits of annual vs. LTI contracts, Jaffee, Kunreuther, and Michel-Kerjan (2008) have developed a simple two-period model in a competitive market setting where premiums reflect risk. The authors show that an LTI policy reduces the marketing costs for insurers compared with one-period policies, and also reduces the search costs to consumers if their insurer decides to cancel the policy at the end of period 1. If the policyholder is permitted to cancel an LTI policy at the end of period 1 on learning that the cost of a one-period policy is low enough to justify paying a cancellation cost (*C*), then it is always optimal for the insurer to offer an LTI policy, and for a consumer to purchase one. The insurer will set *C* at a level which enables it to break even on those policies that are canceled before the maturity date.

We should note that in developing any type of LTI policy to be marketed by the private sector, premiums need to reflect risk (principle 1). Permitting insurers to charge prices that enable them to break even will give them incentives to develop new products. Under the current state-regulated arrangements, where many insurance commissioners have limited insurers' ability to charge risk-based premiums in hazard-prone areas, no insurance company would even entertain the possibility of marketing an LTI policy. Insurers would be concerned about the regulator clamping down on them now or in the future regarding what price they could charge, so that a long-term contract would be infeasible from a financial point of view.

A Natural Candidate for Long-Term Insurance: Flood Insurance through the National Flood Insurance Program

Given the existing tension between state insurance regulators and the insurance industry, we feel that it would be best politically to introduce LTI by focusing on flood insurance, which is provided by the federal government here in the United States.[13] The National Flood Insurance Program (NFIP) was created in 1968 because insurers viewed flood risk as uninsurable and refused to cover it. In 2008, the NFIP sold over 5.5 million policies, compared to 2.5 million in 1992; and it covered nearly $1.2 trillion in assets, compared to only $237 billion (nominal) in 1992 (Michel-Kerjan and Kousky forthcoming). Given that the NFIP is up for renewal in Congress, there may be a window for change in the coming months.

It would be useful to consider whether one could make flood insurance policies long-term by tying them to mortgages. Such a program would connect insurance directly to the property, rather than to the homeowner. If a homeowner moved to another location, the flood insurance policy would remain with the property. One might also consider *requiring* everyone in flood-prone areas to take out the insurance, just as those who own a car are required to take out automobile insurance.

Why Have a Long-Term Flood Insurance Policy? A long-term flood insurance program would offer homeowners currently residing in flood-prone areas a fixed rate for a fixed period of time (e.g., five, ten, or twenty years or an adjustable rate based on a risk index re-evaluated regularly). If the homeowner moved away from the area before the end of the policy period, then the insurance policy would automatically be transferred to the new property owner at the same rate. For those homeowners who were being charged subsidized premiums because their homes were constructed before their community joined the NFIP, these prices would be maintained for the length of the policy period. For homeowners living in houses constructed after their community joined the program, premiums would be actuarially based.

From the perspective of the relevant stakeholders—homeowners, FEMA, banks and other financial institutions, and the taxpayer—there are a number of reasons why such long-term flood insurance policies would be a great improvement over the current annual policies. Flood insurance premiums set at a fixed price would provide homeowners with financial stability.

Long-term flood insurance would also assure the spread of risk within the program, since most homeowners in flood-prone areas would be covered. If flood insurance were required for all homeowners residing in hazard-prone areas, then there would be an even larger spread of risk. This type of requirement would provide much-needed financial revenue for the program over time because it would create a much larger policy base than is currently available.

Long-term policies would prevent another practice among homeowners in high-flood-risk areas: the cancellation of policies after a long period without a flood. This practice occurs even where individuals are required to purchase the policy as a condition for obtaining a federally insured mortgage: banks and financial institutions have often failed to enforce this requirement, first because few of them are ever fined if they fail to enforce it, and second because the mortgages are often transferred to banks in non-flood-prone regions of the country, where there is less awareness of either the flood risk or the requirement. Consider the flood in August 1998 that damaged property in northern Vermont. FEMA found that 84 percent of the homeowners in Special Flood Hazard Areas (SFHAs) did not have insurance, even though 45 percent of these individuals were required to purchase this coverage (Tobin and Calfee 2005).

If long-term loans for mitigation were offered by banks, then individuals with long-term flood insurance policies would have a financial incentive to invest in cost-effective risk-reduction measures. To highlight this point, consider the following simple example. Suppose a property owner could invest $1,500 to floodproof his home so as to reduce by $30,000 the water damage from a future flood or hurricane with an annual probability of 1 in 100. The NFIP should be willing to reduce the annual premium by $300 (i.e., 1/100 x $30,000) to reflect the lower expected losses that would occur if a flood or hurricane hit the area in which the policyholder was residing. If the house was expected to last for ten or more years, the net present value of the expected benefit of investing in this measure would exceed the upfront cost at an annual discount rate as high as 15 percent.

Today, many property owners would be reluctant to incur the $1,500 expenditure. If they focused on short-term benefits and underweighted the future, as so many tend to do, they would see that the expected discounted benefits—$300 dollars off the policy next year—are less than the $1,500 upfront costs. In addition, budget constraints could discourage them from investing in the mitigation measure, as could uncertainty about how long they will reside in the house or about whether their premium will be reduced when they renew their policy. There may also be a failure to appreciate the structural interdependencies associated with floods, earthquakes, and other disasters—specifically, the fact that mitigation measures not only reduce the potential losses to one's own property but may alleviate damage to neighboring structures.

If a twenty-year flood insurance policy were tied to the property, then the homeowner could take out a twenty-year home-improvement loan of $1,500 linked to the mortgage at an annual interest rate of 10 percent, resulting in payments of $145 per year. If the insurance premium was reduced by $300, the annual savings to the homeowner would be $155.[14] A bank would have a financial incentive to provide this type of loan, which would help to protect it against a catastrophic loss to the property. The NFIP would have an incentive to offer LTI contracts, which would reduce its potential losses from a major disaster by balancing its portfolio over time. The general public would approve an LTI program, since it lessens the chance that large amounts of their tax dollars will be needed for disaster relief. These new financial products thus benefit everyone involved.

Conclusion

Since the 1990s, we have witnessed a series of large-scale catastrophes that have inflicted historic economic and insured losses. Fourteen of the twenty-five most costly insured catastrophes worldwide between 1970 and 2008 occurred after 2001, and all were natural disasters except for the 9/11 terrorist attacks. The United States has been particularly challenged because twelve of these disasters occurred in this country. The growing concentration of population and structures in high-risk areas, combined with the potential consequences of global warming, are likely to lead to even more devastating catastrophes in the coming years unless cost-effective risk-reduction measures are put in place.

The challenge facing the United States, and many other countries, is how to prevent natural disaster syndrome. The government must encourage residents and businesses to invest in loss-reduction measures and insurance before a disaster so that the government can avoid large-scale disaster relief afterward. The fact remains that even when risk-reduction measures are available and are cost-effective, many people still do not invest in them. In the aftermath of Hurricane Katrina, many victims suffered severe losses from flooding because they had not undertaken loss mitigation and did not have flood insurance to cover the resulting damage to their home. As a result, an unprecedented level of federal disaster assistance was provided to these victims and the affected communities.

There are many reasons why those in harm's way do not undertake protective measures in advance of disaster. Many individuals believe that the event will not happen to them. In the case of New Orleans, some residents may have felt that they were fully protected by flood-control measures such as levees.[15] This mistaken belief has led to increased development in hazard-prone areas without appropriate land-use regulations and well-enforced building codes. In addition, budget constraints and short time horizons may limit people's ability and willingness to invest in hazard-mitigation measures and to purchase insurance. Such a dynamic has been observed in many countries around the world.

We propose a new initiative that could address these issues: long-term insurance contracts coupled with long-term home-improvement loans, which give homeowners an incentive to adopt cost-effective mitigation measures and provide them with stable financial protection over time. Given the potential difficulties of implementing such a program today—insurance regulators in many states do not allow insurers to set premiums that reflect risk—we believe that the NFIP would be a natural first candidate for such a long-term program. With the NFIP up for renewal in the coming months, there may be political will to develop more effective solutions, possibly including long-term contracts like the one we propose.

The quote from the 2007 Economic Report of the President introducing this chapter argues for premiums that reflect underlying economic costs as a means of encouraging efficient allocation of resources. We agree that premiums should reflect risk (principle 1) but also believe that one has to address equity issues, and that the public sector should provide grants to those living in hazard-prone areas who deserve special treatment (principle 2). There is an opportunity for the Obama administration and the U.S. Congress to heed these two principles and take steps now to reduce losses resulting from catastrophic events so we more effectively manage large-scale risks in a new era of catastrophes.

Notes

1. See White House Council of Economic Advisors (2007, 122–23). It is quite remarkable that 2007 was the first year that the *Economic Report of the President* devoted a chapter to catastrophic risk insurance.

2. For a detailed analysis of terrorism insurance, see Kunreuther and Michel-Kerjan (2004), Brown et al. (2004), Wharton Risk Center (2005), Michel-Kerjan and Pedell (2006), and Michel-Kerjan, Raschky, Kunreuther (2009). For a detailed analysis of the question of natural disaster insurance and mitigation in the United States, see Kunreuther and Michel-Kerjan (2009).

3. Munich Re and Swiss Re, the two leading reinsurers in the world, do not use the same definition of catastrophic losses. Natural disasters inflicting insured losses above $38.7 million or total losses above $77.5 million are considered major catastrophes by Swiss Re. Munich Re uses a higher threshold, which explains the differences between figures 4-1 and 4-2. For example, when Munich Re estimated insured loss from natural disasters at about $42 billion in 2004, Swiss Re's estimate was over $52 billion.

4. This figure excludes payment by the U.S. National Flood Insurance Program for damage due to 2005 flooding (over $20 billion in claims).

5. See the chapter by Jaffee and Russell in this volume for a detailed discussion of terrorism insurance markets.

6. Demographic figures for coastal counties vary depending on the definition of such counties. Under a more restrictive definition (such counties as have a coastline bordering the open ocean or associated sheltered water bodies, or contain V zones as defined by the U.S. National Flood Insurance Program), the proportion of population living in such counties is still 30 percent (Crowell et al. 2007).

7. For additional data on the economic impact of future catastrophic hurricanes, see Financial Services Roundtable (2007), especially chapter 2.

8. For more details on the scientific evidence regarding climate change and its impact, see Stern Review (2006).

9. The first two principles are taken from Kunreuther and Michel-Kerjan (2009).

10. We are assuming that because these measures are incorporated in building codes they are cost-effective. In other words, the discounted long-term expected benefits from the mitigation measure over the projected life of the building are greater than its upfront costs. By obtaining detailed cost estimates for specific mitigation measures incorporated in building codes or Florida's "Fortified . . . for Safer Living" program, one could rank their relative cost-effectiveness.

11. For a more detailed discussion of the reasons why individuals do not invest in cost-effective mitigation measures, see Kunreuther, Meyer, and Michel-Kerjan (forthcoming).

12. This section draws heavily on Jaffee, Kunreuther, and Michel-Kerjan (2008).

13. For more details on the National Flood Insurance Program (NFIP), see the chapter by Mark Browne and Martin Halek in this volume.

14. Alternatively, this loan could be incorporated into the mortgage at even a lower interest rate than 10 percent.

15. FEMA clearly thought that the levees would provide this protection. Otherwise they would have designated the Lower Ninth Ward as a flood-prone area, and residents would have been eligible to purchase insurance under the NFIP.

References

Arrow, K. 1963. Uncertainty and the welfare economics of medical care. *American Economic Review* 53 (5): 941–73.

Association of British Insurers. 2005. *Financial risks of climate change*. London. June.

Brown, J. R., J. D. Cummins, C. M. Lewis, and R. Wei. 2004. An empirical analysis of the economic impact of federal terrorism reinsurance. *Journal of Monetary Economics* 51 (5): 861–98.

Burby, R. 2006. Hurricane Katrina and the paradoxes of government disaster policy: Bringing about wise governmental decisions for hazardous areas. *Annals of the American Academy of Political and Social Science* 604: 171–91.

———, S. Bollens, E. Kaiser, D. Mullan, and J. Sheaffer. 1988. *Cities under water: A comparative evaluation of ten cities' efforts to manage floodplain land use*. Boulder, CO: Institute of Behavioral Science, University of Colorado.

Crossett, K. M., T. J. Culliton, P. C. Wiley, and T. R. Goodspeed. 2004. *Population trends along the coastal United States: 1980–2008*. Silver Spring, MD: National Oceanic and Atmospheric Administration.

Crowell, M., S. Edelman, K. Coulton, and S. McAfee. 2007. How many people live in coastal areas? *Journal of Coastal Research* 23 (5): iii–vi.

Financial Services Roundtable. 2007. Blue Ribbon Commission on Mega-catastrophes comprehensive report. http://www.fsround.org/media/pdfs/FINALmegacat4.pdf.

Goodnough, A. 2006. As hurricane season looms, states aim to scare. *New York Times*, May 31.

Grossi, P., and H. Kunreuther, eds. 2005. *Catastrophe modeling: A new approach to managing risk*. New York: Springer.

Huber, O., R. Wider, and O. Huber. 1997. Active information search and complete information presentation in naturalistic risky decision tasks. *Acta Psychologica*. 95: 15–29.

Insurance Journal. 2010. Haiti death toll rises to 230,000; CCRIF, CIMH study future disaster mitigation efforts. February 10. Available at http://www.insurancejournal.com/news/international/2010/02/10/107249.htm (accessed March 2, 2010).

Jaffee, D., H. Kunreuther, and E. Michel-Kerjan. 2008. Long term insurance (LTI) for addressing catastrophic market failure. NBER (National Bureau of Economic Research) Working Paper 14210, Cambridge, MA.

Kunreuther, Howard. 1996. Mitigating disaster losses through insurance. *Journal of Risk and Uncertainty* 12: 171–87.

———, R. Ginsberg, L. Miller, P. Sagi, P. Slovic, B. Borkan, and N. Katz. 1978. *Disaster insurance protection: Public policy lessons*. New York: John Wiley and Sons.

Kunreuther, H., R. J. Meyer, and E. Michel-Kerjan. Forthcoming. Strategies for better protection against catastrophic risks. In *Behavioral Foundations of Policy*, ed. E. Shafir, Princeton, NJ: Princeton University Press.

Kunreuther, H., and E. Michel-Kerjan. 2004. Policy watch: Terrorism risk insurance in the United States. *Journal of Economic Perspectives* 18 (4): 201–14.

———. 2009. *At war with the weather: Managing large-scale risks in a new era of catastrophes*, Cambridge, MA: MIT Press.

Kunreuther, H., N. Novemsky, and D. Kahneman. 2001. Making low probabilities useful. *Journal of Risk and Uncertainty* 23: 103–20.

Laska, S. B. 1991. *Floodproof retrofitting: Homeowner self-protective behavior.* Boulder, CO: Institute of Behavioral Science, University of Colorado.

Loewenstein, G., and D. Prelec. 1991. Negative time preference. *American Economic Review* 81 (2): 347–52.

Michel-Kerjan, E. 2008. Disasters and public policy: Can market lessons help address government failures? Proceedings of the 99th National Tax Association conference, Boston, MA.

———, and C. Kousky. 2009. Come rain or shine: Evidence on flood insurance purchases in Florida. Joint working paper, Wharton School of the University of Pennsylvania and Resources for the Future. http://opim.wharton.upenn.edu/risk/library/WP2009-03-16_EMK,CK_ComeRain.pdf.

Michel-Kerjan, E., and B. Pedell. 2006. How does the corporate world cope with mega-terrorism? Puzzling evidence from terrorism insurance markets. *Journal of Applied Corporate Finance* 18 (4): 61–75.

Michel-Kerjan, E., P. Raschky, and H. Kunreuther. 2009. Corporate demand for property and terrorism insurance in the U.S.: An empirical analysis. Invited paper, annual NBER (National Bureau of Economic Research) Insurance Group Workshop, Cambridge, MA. http://www.nber.org/confer/2009/INSs09/erwann.pdf.

Mills, E., and E. Lecomte. 2006. From risk to opportunity: How insurers can proactively and profitably manage climate change. *Ceres*. August. http://eetd.lbl.gov/emills/pubs/pdf/ceres_report_090106.pdf.

Munich Re. 2008. Catastrophe figures for 2008 confirm that climate agreement is urgently needed. December. http://www.munichre.com/en/press/press_releases/2008/2008_12_29_press_release.aspx.

Munich Re. 2009a. Topics geo: Natural catastrophes 2008, analyses, assessments, positions. February. http://www.munichre.com/publications/302-06022_en.pdf.

Munich Re. 2009b. Few major natural catastrophe losses in 2009: General trend confirmed by large number of weather extremes. Press release. December 29. Munich: Munich Re. Available at http://www.munichre.com/press/press_releases/2009/2009_12_29_press_release.aspx (accessed January 26, 2010).

Palm, R., M. Hodgson, R. D. Blanchard, and D. Lyons. 1990. *Earthquake insurance in California: Environmental policy and individual decision making.* Boulder, CO: Westview Press.

Pielke, R., Jr., J. Gratz, C. Landsea, D. Collins, M. Saunders, and R. Musulin. 2008. Normalized hurricane damage in the United States: 1900–2005. *Natural Hazards Review* 9 (1): 29–42.

Stern Review. 2006. The economics of climate change. H. M. Treasury. December. Available at http://webarchive.nationalarchives.gov.uk/+/http://www.hm-treasury.gov.uk/independent_reviews/stern_review_economics_climate_change/stern_review_report.cfm.

Swiss Re. 2009. Natural catastrophes and man-made disasters in 2008. North America and Asia suffer heavy losses. Sigma, 2/2009. Sigma no. 2/2009. http://www.swissre.com/resources/dd6346004d4e9669ac76eecedd316cf3-sigma2_2009_e.pdf.

Tobin, R., and C. Calfee. 2005. *The national flood insurance program's mandatory purchase requirement: Policies, processes, and stakeholders*. Washington, D.C.: American Institutes for Research.

United Nations. 2008. *World population trends*. New York: UN Population Division, Department of Economic and Social Affairs.

Wharton Risk Management and Decision Processes Center. 2005. *TRIA and beyond: Terrorism risk financing in the U.S.* Philadelphia: Wharton School, University of Pennsylvania.

White House Council of Economic Advisors. 2007. *Economic report of the president. Together with the annual report of the Council of Economic Advisors.* Washington, D.C.

5

Managing Flood Risk: The National Flood Insurance Program and Alternatives

Mark J. Browne and Martin Halek

Since its origin in 1968, the National Flood Insurance Program (NFIP) has made flood insurance available to U.S. homeowners, renters, and business property owners. The NFIP has evolved in an attempt to address the challenges inherent in insuring against catastrophic risk. Recent hurricanes, however, have severely tested the NFIP and demonstrated several flaws in the design of the program. This chapter evaluates the NFIP and offers proposals for improving the financing of losses due to flooding.

In our view, an evaluation of a government program to insure flood risk should take the following five factors into consideration:

(1) Administrative efficiency. Lower administrative costs consume fewer resources and increase the likelihood that individuals will voluntarily purchase insurance.

(2) The amount of risk transferred. It is important that any insurance program be designed to transfer the optimal amount of risk. If there is too little risk transfer, then society forgoes the welfare gains that result from the efficient allocation of risk. On the other hand, too much risk transfer leads to moral hazard.

(3) Control of moral hazard. It is well understood that having insurance can reduce incentives for loss mitigation and therefore can result in a greater likelihood of losses. One way to minimize moral hazard is to ensure that the party best able to control the risk bears the risk. Although an individual property owner cannot usually control the occurrence of a flood, he can influence the resulting damage via decisions about loss-control measures. In the case of floods, arguably the most important loss-control decision is where to build. It is important to ensure that when these decisions are made, the full social costs of flood risk are taken into account.

(4) Consideration of all parties. Assessing the full social costs of flood risk involves taking into account any externalities that flood risk imposes on other parties. For example, one developer's decision to build in a particular area (say, a wetland) may positively or negatively influence the likelihood that other property owners are subject to future flood losses. In the presence of such externalities, some form of government intervention (for example, Pigouvian taxes or quantity regulation) may be appropriate in order to ensure the optimal mix of insurance and mitigation.

(5) Premium determination. The premiums charged by a flood insurance program should reflect the full social costs of the risk being insured. They should be fully risk-based to align private decision making with desired societal outcomes. Subsidized insurance premiums encourage inefficient levels of development and reduced levels of loss control by masking the true cost of flood risk. Accurate, cost-based insurance premiums allow individuals to effectively compare alternative development opportunities, because they are explicit estimates of the cost of risk (Kunreuther and Pauly 2006). Premiums based on the true cost of a risk inform decision makers not only as they evaluate development decisions, but also as they evaluate different means for mitigating the risk and financing the risk.

The NFIP falls short of an ideal program for risk transfer. Although the NFIP was never designed to handle a storm as powerful as Hurricane Katrina, Katrina nonetheless provides a stark example of the program's shortcomings. First, the NFIP participation rates were low among those who suffered losses from Katrina, leaving significant financial losses either uncompensated or inefficiently borne by third parties, including taxpayers and charities. Beyond the $25 billion in NFIP claims, victims of Hurricane Katrina also received an estimated $15 billion in government aid, much of which was used to rebuild damaged property or to relocate households (Drew and Treaster 2006). One of the reasons that so few property owners were insured may be that many of them felt (correctly, in retrospect) that they would be able to receive flood-loss compensation from the federal government whether or not they were insured.[1] This is a classic example of the "Samaritan's Dilemma"—individuals make the rational but socially sub-optimal decision to forgo insurance in order to take advantage of *ex post* government assistance. This phenomenon has been noted in prior research on insurance programs, including flood insurance.[2]

The damages that resulted from Katrina also demonstrated that the flood coverage limits on flood insurance policies were insufficient in many cases. The average claim paid from the NFIP for flood loss was $96,016, an amount significantly below the maximum amount of coverage available for residential or business properties.[3] Moreover, Hurricane Katrina demonstrated that the NFIP was not an administratively efficient program. The legal battles that followed Hurricane Katrina showed both the public's ignorance regarding property insurance coverage (for example, many did not understand that a standard homeowners' policy does not cover flood damage) and the difficulties associated with distinguishing wind damage from flood damage.

In this chapter, we discuss the challenges of providing catastrophic insurance and make recommendations for addressing these challenges. Our suggestions amount to a fundamental overhaul of the NFIP. The chapter is organized as follows. First, we consider why the government has taken an active role in insuring flood risk, when many other property risks are insured through private markets or are not insured at all. Second, we briefly review how the United States has historically managed flood risk, including the creation of the NFIP in 1968 and its subsequent evolution. We then discuss the challenges of providing insurance for a catastrophic risk and the particular challenges when the federal government is the primary insurer. Finally, we offer several alternative approaches to managing flood risk that avoid some of the NFIP's shortcomings.

The Rationale for Government Insurance of Flood Peril

Governments choose how—and whether—to finance property losses. They can transfer the risk to an insurer through private market transactions, transfer the risk to the taxpayer through a government insurance plan, or not transfer the risk at all. Losses due to fire, lightning, windstorms, and theft are typically insured in private markets in the United States. Losses from war and earthquakes are often left uninsured. In contrast, the government offers explicit insurance programs in the case of terrorism and floods. Of course, as noted in other chapters of this book and elsewhere, the U.S. government also provides insurance against a wide range of other risks, including risks to bank deposits, pensions, crops, employment, and health.

The private market for risk transfer has several distinct advantages over government involvement and over leaving risks uninsured. Arguably the most important is the significant competition between insurers that results in innovation in policy forms, service, and pricing. Another important advantage is that competitive private markets internalize the cost of risk. That is, rather than shifting the risk to third parties, they ensure through appropriate premiums that those who have exposed themselves to risk (by owning property) bear that risk.[4] In contrast, programs that transfer risk to the government are monopolistic and prone to political machinations; they often place the costs of the risk on those not in a position to accrue its benefits. Private insurers also have a clear incentive to couple the potential benefits and potential costs of the risk in order to reduce moral hazard.

Flood peril lacks several characteristics of risks that are commonly insured by private market insurers. Such risks tend to be numerous and homogenous; thus automobiles are commonly insured against the collision peril, and homes are commonly insured against fire. Such risks tend to involve losses that are determinable and quantifiable, and whose likelihood can be calculated so that the risk can be priced. They tend also to be accidental—i.e., the loss is fortuitous and not easily influenced by the insured—and to exhibit information symmetry, with both the insurer and the insured having access to the same information about the likelihood of loss and likely amount of loss. Finally, such risks tend to be independent—the event that triggers the loss does not cause losses to other similar exposures—and unpredictable, since in the case of a predictable loss, the transaction costs created in transferring the risk are greater than the value derived by the potential insured from the transfer.

In the case of flood peril, several of these desirable features (that losses be calculable, exhibit symmetric information, be independent and unpredictable) do not apply. The loss distribution, for example, is difficult to calculate. Some flood losses are expected to occur once every hundred years, others once every five hundred years, and others once every thousand years. Given these significant time spans, sufficient data to make accurate pricing estimates are lacking (although advances in science and technology hold out the promise of greater pricing accuracy for highly infrequent floods). At the other extreme, some areas flood so regularly that that there is little uncertainty in the occurrence of a loss. Here, the administrative costs of an insurance program may be too high relative to the gains from risk transfer to make such a program economically efficient. Of course, both of these attributes—either too much uncertainty or not enough—present problems for both private and public insurance programs.

Information problems would also interfere with a potential private market for flood insurance. Research suggests that many individuals have a limited understanding of flood risk. Kunreuther (1984) hypothesizes that property owners do not purchase flood insurance, because they underestimate the probability of loss. This is consistent with findings in Kunreuther (1978), which indicate that the likelihood of an individual purchasing insurance against natural disasters is positively related to his having suffered a prior loss as a consequence of a natural disaster. Chivers and Flores (2002) report that most of those they surveyed were unaware of the risk flood posed to property they were purchasing prior to the closing on the property. Browne and Hoyt (2000) find that flood insurance purchases increase following flood losses. They suggest that more individuals might purchase flood insurance if public service announcements educated the public about flood risk. If individuals underestimate the likelihood of flood loss, as the research suggests they do, many will not purchase flood insurance, because they will view the cost as too high relative to the risk. While these information problems suggest that flood insurance is unsuited to private markets, it is not obvious that a publicly provided insurance program would be able to overcome them.

A final reason why insuring flood risk privately poses problems is that the risk is not independent across the population. The law of large numbers, which is the statistical basis for insurance pooling, is premised on the assumption that risks are independent. However, when a flood occurs, it typically inflicts widespread damage to entire communities. Insolvency risk increases as the correlation increases within an insurer's pool of business, all else equal. Thus the premiums that must be charged in a competitive market must be greater to reflect the correlated nature of this risk. In theory, insurers could come close to creating a pool of independent flood risks if the risks were sufficiently dispersed geographically. Reinsurance markets are beneficial in this regard, as they allow for the pooling of flood risks worldwide. Nonetheless, given the fixed costs of insuring in a particular geographic area, there are practical limitations on the amount of geographic diversification available to most insurers.

As a result of these limitations, flood risk, like other natural disaster perils, is difficult to insure in the private market. Of course, these same limitations make it difficult for the government to insure it as well. Indeed, the history of the NFIP indicates that demand for flood coverage is not substantial even when it is provided by the government at a rate below the fair market cost of coverage, suggesting that there are limitations on the demand side that might limit a private market even in a world where supply problems did not exist. It is not clear which of the possible reasons for this lack of demand are most important. In part, behavioral limitations (for example, myopia or underestimating the probability of loss) may create the lack of demand. It may also be a result of the Samaritan's Dilemma.

In spite of these difficulties, the federal government has over the years expanded its role in supplying flood insurance. Yet overall, as the next section suggests, changes to the program have been relatively minor and have altered neither the essential scope of the program nor the government's general approach to financing flood risk for individuals or businesses. As we will show, this approach is a flawed one.

History and Development of the National Flood Insurance Program

Prior to the establishment of the NFIP, the government's strategies for managing flood risk consisted of *ex ante* loss control and *ex post* loss financing. Beginning in the 1800s, the government initiated various flood control projects, such as the construction of dams and levees, which arguably encouraged development in flood zones. The Swamp Land Act of 1849 and the Swamp Land Act of 1850 transferred federal swamp and overflow land along the lower Mississippi River to states, contingent on states using sales revenue from these lands to construct levees and drainage channels. By 1890, the entire lower Mississippi Valley was divided into state and local levee districts.

Historically, the government provided *ex post* financial disaster relief to those victimized by flood. In 1934, as part of the New Deal, Congress passed Public Law 73-160, which made $5 million in low-interest loans available to victims of all natural disasters. The Disaster Relief Act of 1950 (PL 81-875) created the first permanent system for disaster relief (including flood relief) whereby states could formally request that the president declare a major disaster. Once the federal government declared a disaster, it then provided disaster assistance that supplemented that of state and local governments. This act was significant in establishing a guaranteed framework for federal disaster assistance after the fact.[5]

While these public flood risk–management strategies were well intentioned, they did little to ease the ultimate financial burden of most flood victims. Nor could property owners at risk of flood damage turn to the private sector: private insurance companies tended not to sell flood insurance because the catastrophic nature of flood risk, and the resulting difficulty of developing actuarial rates that reflected the risk, made establishing a sustainable pricing structure difficult. During the 1920s, several dozen fire insurers sold flood insurance, but after severe river flooding in many parts of the country in 1927 and 1928, these insurers withdrew from the market. From the late 1920s until today, flood insurance has not been considered profitable (Congressional Research Service 2005).

National Flood Insurance Act of 1968. In 1951 President Harry Truman proposed a flood disaster insurance program that called for private insurers to issue flood insurance, with the federal government acting as a reinsurer. In 1956, President Dwight D. Eisenhower signed the Federal Flood Insurance Act (PL 84-1016), which established a five-year, $3 billion federal flood insurance and reinsurance program.[6] However, not a single policy was written under either of these programs, as Congress pointed to a lack of any technical study that would help to determine the costs of starting a federal flood insurance program (Congressional Research Service 2005).

A series of natural disasters in the early 1960s renewed interest in creating a federal disaster insurance program. Congress ultimately passed the National Flood Insurance Act of 1968, which created the NFIP and the Federal Insurance Administration (FIA). The initial goals of the NFIP were threefold: to reduce the nation's flood risk through appropriate floodplain management, to improve flood hazard data and risk assessment by mapping the nation's floodplains; and to provide direct, affordable flood insurance to both individuals (residential homeowners) and businesses (nonresidential property owners) in flood-prone communities that adopted and enforced measures designed to reduce the consequences of flooding.[7]

A locality was considered a flood-prone community when the FIA determined that a significant flood hazard existed. The establishment of flood insurance premiums, however, required studies to estimate the actuarial risk of flood. Once these studies were completed, a Flood Insurance Rate Map (FIRM) was published; it provided detailed information on flood hazards in the community and offered a basis for calculating premiums. After the review process for the FIRM was completed, a community was considered a regular participant in the NFIP.[8] Notably, participation allowed existing property owners in high-risk flood areas—later named special flood hazard areas (SFHAs)—to obtain subsidized flood insurance. Owners of structures built in floodplains after the act's passage would pay actuarial, nonsubsidized premiums for insurance through the NFIP (American Institutes for Research et al. 2002).

NFIP funding was created through the National Flood Insurance Fund, into which collected premiums were to be deposited.[9] The NFIP was intended to be self-supporting for the average historical loss year. This meant that flood losses, operating expenses, and administrative expenses were to be paid solely through premiums collected for policies sold, and not by additional taxpayer dollars.[10] In the event that flood losses were excessive, the

NFIP could initially borrow $1 billion from the Department of the Treasury with a promise to repay with interest (Hartwig and Wilkinson 2005).

The St. Germain Amendment to the original 1968 act, passed in December 1969, instituted the NFIP Emergency Program. Here, the necessary completion of actuarial studies was waived so that otherwise eligible communities could become almost immediate "emergency" participants in the NFIP (Power and Shows 1979). The Emergency Program provided a maximum amount (first layer) of flood protection at federally subsidized, uniform rates, regardless of flood risk. The Emergency Program remains in effect today.

Flood Disaster Protection Act of 1973. It gradually became evident that offering flood insurance, even at subsidized rates for existing properties, did not provide sufficient incentive for communities to join the NFIP or for individuals to purchase flood insurance. As of January 1970, only four communities had joined the NFIP, only sixteen flood insurance policies had been sold, and only $392,000 of coverage was in force (American Institutes for Research et al. 2002). To provide stronger incentives, Congress passed the Flood Disaster Protection Act of 1973, which established a mandatory purchase requirement (MPR).[11] Specifically, for communities participating in the NFIP, property owners in high-risk flood areas (SFHAs) whose mortgages were from a federally insured, regulated, or supervised lending institution were now required to purchase flood insurance, at least to the extent of the loan.[12] The 1973 act also mandated that after July 1, 1975, no federal agency could provide financial assistance for purchase or construction of property in an identified flood-prone area unless the property was covered by the NFIP. Finally, the act encouraged communities to adopt and enforce loss-control measures (for example, appropriate land use) to reduce the probability of flood losses.

Flood Insurance Reform Act of 2004. The Flood Insurance Reform Act of 2004 (PL 108-264) sought to reduce repetitive loss to the same property. (When first introduced in the House of Representatives, it was called the Two Floods and You Are Out of the Taxpayers' Pocket Act of 2003.) It was estimated that ten thousand properties had experienced several losses that cumulatively exceeded building values (and the values of the flood policies); these losses cost taxpayers some $200 million annually. Most of these repetitive-loss properties were eligible for subsidized flood insurance because they were built before the 1974 implementation of NFIP's original floodplain management standards. The 2004 act contained reforms designed to more equitably distribute the cost of flood insurance premiums by reducing the number of policyholders who filed repeated flood damage claims.[13]

Flood Insurance Reform and Modernization Act of 2008. The Flood Insurance Reform and Modernization Act of 2008 passed both houses of Congress. Under the version passed by the House, the NFIP's maximum coverage limits were increased for the first time since 1994, from current ceilings of $250,000 for residential properties and $500,000 for commercial properties, to $335,000 and $670,000, respectively. The coverage limit on contents rose to $135,000 from $100,000. Coverage for additional living expenses, business interruption, and finished basements was also introduced.

Other notable provisions of the bill include (1) extending the NFIP through fiscal year 2013; (2) allowing the Federal Emergency Management Agency (FEMA) to increase flood policy rates by 15 percent a year, up from 10 percent; (2) increasing the NFIP's borrowing authority to $20.8 billion; (3) raising civil penalties on federally regulated lenders who fail to enforce the MPR of flood insurance for mortgage holders; (4) increasing program participation incentives; and (5) encouraging revisions of dated flood maps. In short, the 2008 act was intended to protect the integrity of the NFIP by fully funding existing legal obligations and continuing to provide incentives for communities to participate.

THE NFIP Today. The NFIP is officially administered by FEMA, which is part of the U.S. Department of Homeland Security (DHS). At the end of 2007, more than twenty thousand communities were participating in the NFIP, and more than 5.65 million flood policies were providing coverage for over $1.14 trillion in property.[14] In 2007, the average amount of flood coverage provided was $201,598 per policy, the average annual premium paid was $505 per policy, and the average flood claim paid by the NFIP was $24,579 (U.S. Department of Homeland Security 2008). A recent poll by the Insurance Information Institute found that 17 percent of homeowners have a flood insurance policy.[15]

TABLE 5-1
AVAILABLE DOLLAR LIMITS OF COVERAGE FOR EXISTING AND NEW CONSTRUCTION UNDER THE NFIP AS OF MAY 1, 2008

	Emergency program (first layer)	Regular program: Basic insurance limits	Regular program: Additional insurance limits	Total
Building coverage				
Single family	$35,000	$50,000	$200,000	$250,000
2–4 family	$35,000	$50,000	$200,000	$250,000
Other residential	$100,000	$150,000	$100,000	$250,000
Nonresidential/Small business	$100,000	$150,000	$350,000	$500,000
Contents coverage				
Residential	$10,000	$20,000	$80,000	$100,000
Nonresidential/Small business	$100,000	$130,000	$370,000	$500,000

SOURCE: Government Accountability Office 2008.
NOTE: Alaska, Hawaii, Guam, and the U.S. Virgin Islands have different amounts of coverage for the first and second layers of coverage; however, their total limit is also $250,000. The Emergency Flood Insurance Program is intended to provide a first-layer amount of insurance on all insurable structures before the effective date of the initial FIRM.

Two separate flood programs continue to be administered by the NFIP: the Emergency Program and the Regular Program. Table 5-1 shows the current flood coverage limits available under both of these programs for building and contents. The proposed increase in coverage limits under the 2008 FIRM Act would better reflect the current value of homes. For example, average and median sale prices of new residential homes sold in the United States were $313,600 and $247,900 in 2007, respectively, compared to $158,700 and $133,900 in 1995, respectively (U.S. Census Bureau 2008). Of course, these values vary by geographic location, as shown in table 5-2. Moreover, the average and median sale prices of existing single-family homes in the United States rose from $141,500 and $117,000 in 1995, respectively, to $266,200 and $217,900 in 2007, respectively. If an objective

TABLE 5-2

AVERAGE AND MEDIAN SALES PRICES OF SINGLE-FAMILY HOMES

Panel A
New homes

Geographic region	1995 Average	1995 Median	2007 Average	2007 Median
United States	$158,700	$133,900	$313,600	$247,900
Northeast	$216,600	$180,000	$437,700	$320,200
Midwest	$157,200	$134,000	$256,800	$208,600
South	$142,000	$124,500	$269,800	$217,700
West	$169,800	$141,000	$403,700	$330,900

Panel B
Existing homes

Geographic region	1995 Average	1995 Median	2007 Average	2007 Median
United States	$141,500	$117,000	$266,200	$217,900
Northeast	$164,200	$146,500	$313,300	$288,100
Midwest	$115,100	$96,500	$196,100	$161,400
South	$122,500	$99,200	$225,900	$178,800
West	$182,000	$153,600	$372,500	$342,500

SOURCE: National Association of Realtors 2008.

of the NFIP is to provide adequate flood coverage for both new and existing homes across the United States, current coverage limits should be increased.

Some Current Problems in the NFIP

Currently, the NFIP is plagued by a number of problems. Not only does it improperly price flood insurance; it also fails to address some of the key considerations for a public insurance program that we outlined at the beginning of the chapter.

NFIP's Inadequate Pricing of Flood Coverage. In the aggregate, the NFIP collected $2.85 billion in annual premiums in 2007 and paid out $5.23 million in losses.[16] Table 5-3 shows that in most years since 1978, annual premiums collected by the NFIP exceeded annual losses paid out. Over this period, the NFIP has paid average annual claims of $1.16 billion while collecting average annual premiums of $1.10 billion. It is wrong to conclude, however, that insurance pricing under NFIP is adequate. In fact, the current NFIP pricing mechanism violates many insurance pricing principles.

First, consider how a private insurance company would go about establishing a price for flood insurance coverage.[17] The catastrophic nature of the flood peril would make it impossible for insurers to reserve adequately for floods in a given geographic area. Hence, flood risk would have to be viewed as an intertemporal risk as opposed to a purely cross-sectional risk. It is possible to transform flood risk into a cross-sectional risk if the insurer can pool a sufficiently large number of independent risks (which would reduce the risk according to the law of large numbers). Fundamental insurance pricing shows that as the size of the risk pool increases, the expected loss of each pool member approaches the pure premium more certainly as the standard deviation of each pool member's loss amount decreases. Conversely, the smaller the risk pool, the larger the risk loading (an administrative cost that accounts for the uncertainty in predicting the pool's future losses) that an insurer operating in a competitive market will have to charge. Given the catastrophic nature of flood risk, if the insurer were unable to construct a sufficiently large risk pool, the risk loading would become large. As the risk loading rises, the demand for insurance will likely fall as the desirability of insurance becomes less attractive in the eyes of a potential insurance purchaser.[18]

But the NFIP follows a different path in establishing insurance prices, a path that ultimately leads to subsidized rates on one-fourth of its policies. Specifically, the NFIP has established a two-tier rate classification consisting of "full risk" rates and "subsidized" rates. About 75 percent of NFIP policies are based on full-risk rates, which are considered actuarial rates. Here, the NFIP

TABLE 5-3

NATIONAL FLOOD INSURANCE PROGRAM STATISTICS

Calendar year	Premium	Number of policies in force	Number of losses paid	Loss dollars paid out	Amount of coverage provided	Loss ratio
1978	$111,250,585	1,446,354	29,122	$147,719,253	$50,500,956	1.33
1979	$141,535,832	1,843,441	70,613	$483,281,219	$74,375,240	3.41
1980	$159,009,583	2,103,851	41,918	$230,414,295	$99,259,942	1.45
1981	$256,798,488	1,915,065	23,261	$127,118,031	$102,059,859	0.50
1982	$354,842,356	1,900,544	32,831	$198,295,820	$107,296,802	0.56
1983	$384,225,425	1,981,122	51,584	$439,454,937	$117,834,255	1.14
1984	$420,530,032	1,926,388	27,688	$254,642,874	$124,421,281	0.61
1985	$452,466,332	2,016,785	38,676	$368,238,794	$139,948,260	0.81
1986	$518,226,957	2,119,039	13,789	$126,388,812	$155,717,168	0.24
1987	$566,391,536	2,115,183	13,399	$105,422,538	$165,053,402	0.19
1988	$589,453,163	2,149,153	7,758	$51,022,523	$175,764,175	0.09
1989	$632,204,396	2,292,947	36,247	$661,668,435	$265,218,590	1.05
1990	$672,791,834	2,477,861	14,766	$167,919,559	$213,588,265	0.25
1991	$737,078,033	2,532,713	28,554	$353,684,967	$223,098,548	0.48
1992	$800,973,357	2,623,406	44,651	$710,247,980	$236,844,980	0.89
1993	$890,425,274	2,828,558	36,044	$659,069,808	$267,870,761	0.74
1994	$1,003,850,875	3,040,198	21,584	$411,079,605	$295,935,328	0.41

1995	$1,140,808,119	3,476,829	62,441	$1,295,581,467	$349,137,768	1.14
1996	$1,275,176,752	3,693,076	52,679	$828,040,301	$400,681,650	0.65
1997	$1,509,787,517	4,102,416	30,338	$519,505,659	$462,606,433	0.34
1998	$1,668,246,681	4,235,138	57,350	$886,305,129	$497,621,083	0.53
1999	$1,719,652,696	4,329,985	47,245	$754,965,083	$534,117,781	0.44
2000	$1,723,824,570	4,369,087	16,361	$251,719,208	$567,568,653	0.15
2001	$1,740,331,079	4,458,470	43,562	$1,276,963,290	$611,918,920	0.73
2002	$1,802,277,937	4,519,799	25,287	$433,603,879	$653,776,126	0.24
2003	$1,897,687,479	4,565,491	36,716	$778,793,929	$691,786,140	0.41
2004	$2,040,828,486	4,667,446	55,669	$2,214,303,484	$765,205,681	1.09
2005	$2,241,264,140	4,962,011	210,893	$17,575,117,955	$876,679,658	7.84
2006	$2,604,844,133	5,514,895	24,457	$632,688,511	$1,054,087,148	0.24
2007	$2,854,071,096	5,653,949	21,287	$523,219,557	$1,139,822,517	0.18
Total	$32,910,854,743		1,216,770	$33,466,476,902		
Average	$1,097,028,491	3,195,373	40,559	$1,115,549,230	$380,659,912	1.02

SOURCE: U.S. Department of Homeland Security 2008.

uses a model based on outdated flood probability estimates from the 1970s and 1980s. The full-risk rate is calculated by determining expected losses and adding expected loss adjustments and other operating expenses (that is, by risk loading). The other 25 percent of NFIP policies are based on subsidized rates that ultimately generate premiums sufficient to cover only 35 to 40 percent of the full risk. In other words, these policies receive 60 to 65 percent subsidization from the NFIP. Here, the NFIP subtracts the aggregate expected full-risk premium from some average historical loss-year target. The average historical loss-year target set by the NFIP limits the impact of major past catastrophes by ignoring them outright or by considering only a small portion of the losses they generated (Government Accountability Office 2008). Moreover, these subsidized polices tend to cover high-risk properties. Finally, the NFIP does not require owners of properties remapped into higher-risk areas to pay rates based on these new high-risk designations, but rather allows them to pay premiums based on previous rates. This policy of grandfathering further contributes to the financial problems of the NFIP.

Given this mechanism for establishing premiums, it is not surprising that the NFIP continues to be underfunded on an annual basis. The current NFIP flood insurance premiums are attractive for potential insureds, but they do not accurately reflect the true risk of flood and cannot be considered acceptable under any insurance pricing standard. Further, by providing insurance for less than competitive market rates, the NFIP may be encouraging development in high-flood-risk areas, while simultaneously discouraging loss control. Ironically, then, the NFIP program may itself contribute to increasing the very losses it was designed to insure.

Other Inadequacies. Because the private sector has historically had difficulties in providing flood insurance, it might be argued in defense of the NFIP that it manages to insure many who might otherwise remain uninsured. But how should the NFIP be judged overall as an approach to the risk posed by the flood peril? To answer this question, let us return to the five criteria, listed at the start of the chapter, that go into evaluating a government program to insure flood risk.

(1) Administrative efficiency. To the best of our knowledge, there is no study that assesses the administrative efficiency of the NFIP.

On the positive side, the program offers few options to insureds, a practice which tends to keep administrative costs low. On the other hand, the program does not integrate well with homeowners' insurance purchased against other perils. This failing increases the costs of issuing coverage and adjudicating claims.

(2) The amount of risk transferred. The NFIP allows property owners to transfer at least some flood risk to the government by paying a fixed premium. In the absence of any NFIP policy limits, property owners would have the ability to transfer as much flood risk as they desired to the government, so long as they are willing to pay the established premium. An interesting but unresolved question is whether offering a subsidized but limited government program crowds out more complete insurance from private providers.

(3) Control of moral hazard. The NFIP attempts to control moral hazard by establishing and enforcing floodplain management ordinances. However, these ordinances may create a false sense of security in property owners, who may simply comply with the potentially outdated ordinances and assume their risk is thus very limited. The NFIP must ensure that these ordinances (and building codes) are sufficient. The more important issue is that the NFIP distorts optimal decisions about where to live. A property owner can minimize flood risk by choosing to live where flood risk is small; if he chooses instead to live in a flood-risk area, he should bear the risk. But the NFIP prevents efficient decision making by making flood insurance compulsory in some cases and by offering non-risk-adjusted insurance.

(4) Consideration of all parties. Because of the pricing methods utilized by the NFIP, taxpayers continue to subsidize the financial shortfalls created by the NFIP's underpricing. Legislative changes—for example, increased land-use restrictions in high-risk flood areas to protect taxpayers from having to further subsidize property owners—have addressed some other concerns about outside parties.

(5) Premium determination. As noted above, the premiums charged by the NFIP are not strictly risk based. This leads to significant loss-control inefficiencies and uninformed decision making regarding flood insurance purchases.

Despite the existence of the NFIP and the risk transfer that it does facilitate, taxpayers continue to get soaked by flood losses. Since the population in coastal areas continues to increase, and since flood insurance is both underpriced and often not purchased at all, the federal government's exposure to flood risk remains substantial.[19] Reform is needed both to decrease the government's exposure to loss following floods and to establish premium levels for insurance commensurate with the risk being insured. These two goals, which in essence seek for more insurance to be purchased at a higher price, are in conflict with one another. In the following section, we discuss alternative ways of handling flood peril that avoid this conundrum.

Alternative Means to Handle the Flood Peril

The NFIP has been the primary provider and financer of flood insurance in the United States since 1968. As indicated earlier, the program remains essentially the same today as when it was first established, some minor changes notwithstanding. Although academics and government officials have pointed out deficiencies in its risk-bearing mechanism, no alternative mechanism has seemed a plausible replacement. In this section we look at some private market mechanisms that hold out promise for the transfer of flood risk—options and futures contracts; bond instruments whose interest rates are linked to the occurrence of natural catastrophes; contract-embedded risk transfer in mortgage contracts; private flood insurance placed by lenders on behalf of mortgagees in compliance with mortgage requirements imposed on federally regulated lenders; and both voluntary and forced-placed private flood insurance provided by traditional property insurance companies.

Options and Futures Contracts and Bonds. Innovation in the financial markets has resulted in the development of unconventional risk-transfer contracts. These contracts, which are not insurance contracts per se, tap into the greater capacity of the financial markets to bear risk. In 1992 the Chicago Board of Trade (CBOT) began trading derivative contracts whose payoffs were contingent on the occurrence and magnitude of losses following natural catastrophes. The instruments were traded for seven years and then removed from the market due to insufficient demand. The instruments were clearly not intended for individual property owners, but rather for commercial enterprises, such as primary insurers, who were seeking to hedge their exposure to catastrophe-related losses. (For a review of various catastrophe securities, see Sheehan [2003].)

Unlike reinsurance, which may target a specific risk (facultative reinsurance) or a specified portfolio of risks (treaty reinsurance), the payoff on the catastrophe options contracts traded on the CBOT was linked to an index of losses occurring across a specified region during a specified period of time.[20] For an insurer purchasing such an instrument, the protection against fluctuations in its own insurance portfolio afforded by the options contract depended on the degree to which the diversification of the insurer's pool of risks matched the loss index underlying the contract. The degree of correlation between an insurer's risk pool and the index of the options contract is called basis risk. The greater (lower) the correlation, the more (less) protection the contract provided. Other things equal, the greater the basis risk, the less valuable an options contract is to an insurer. Accounting for the paucity of demand for the CBOT catastrophe options is beyond the scope of this chapter (though see White [2001] for a discussion of the options in general); but we can say here that significant basis risk made the contracts less attractive to many potential buyers, including insurers, who had other means of hedging their risk. Doherty (1997) notes that a reinsurance policy provides an alternative and in some ways more attractive hedge for an insurer bearing flood risk. By providing coverage on specifically defined risks, reinsurance eliminates basis risk.

The CBOT options contracts were among the first noninsurance financial instruments aimed at tapping into the greater capacity of the financial markets to bear catastrophic losses. An increasing number of securities have been developed since their introduction. Of greater significance than the CBOT options and of proven viability are catastrophe (CAT) bonds, which Swiss Re (2006) reports grew significantly in volume from 1998 to 2006.

According to Swiss Re, the outstanding volume on these bonds was $7.7 billion at the end of 2006—meaning that insurers who issued the bonds had access to $7.7 billion to pay for catastrophe-related claims. CAT bonds account for the largest share of any form of risk securitization. With a CAT bond, a special-purpose vehicle (SPV)—a legal entity established to sit between the seller of the risk, often a primary insurer, and the purchaser of the bond—contracts both with the cedant (primary insurer) to provide reinsurance and with the investors to borrow money to be repaid on a contingent schedule. Depending upon the structure of the CAT bond, the investors may have at risk the interest payments on the debt, the principal, or both. The established interest rate payable on the bond reflects the risk of the instrument and may be viewed as an objective risk measure.

Industry loss warranties (ILWs), another alternative risk-transfer instrument with the potential to transfer flood risk, are written very similarly to ordinary reinsurance policies. An ILW contract results in the transfer of risk from one party, usually a primary insurer, to a second party. However, unlike a reinsurance policy, an ILW specifies a payoff amount in the event of a loss that is linked to an industry loss index. For the ceding company, the ILW introduces basis risk to the extent that the cedant's risk-pool profile deviates from the profile underlying the specified industry loss index. ILWs are often sold with letters of credit from large commercial banks that secure the agreement. This practice allows unrated reinsurers owned by hedge funds to compete successfully for this business.

Another alternative risk-transfer arrangement relevant to the transfer of flood risk is a contingent capital agreement, which allows the purchaser (for example, a primary insurer) to issue and sell securities to a second party at a predetermined price for a set period of time, if a specified contingent event occurs. The securities may be equity, debt, or some combination. These agreements transfer risk associated with the contingent event to the second party, who need not be a reinsurer.

Reinsurance and noninsurance risk-transfer contracts permit private market transfer of flood risk to parties willing to bear the risk for an agreed-upon price. ILWs, CAT bonds, and other financial instruments that permit the transfer of flood risk to the capital markets are relatively new innovations which were not available when the NFIP was created. The pricing of these contracts reflects the assessment of the risk by the parties to the contracts.

Since the implementation of the NFIP in 1968, significant advances in meteorology and computer technology have allowed for increasingly sophisticated pricing of catastrophic risks, including floods. The advances in science also allow for increasingly accurate pricing of the risks transferred through these financial contracts, and have contributed to their growth.

Contract-Embedded Risk Transfer. The typical mortgage on a house stipulates that the house serves as collateral on the loan. If the borrower fails to make promised mortgage payments and the loan goes into default, the bank has the right to foreclose on the property. In the normal course of events, this is a highly undesirable outcome from the viewpoint of the homeowner, as the use of the home will be lost, the equity built up in the home may be lost, and the individual's credit rating will suffer. Following a major flood loss (and in the absence of flood insurance), however, the homeowner may prefer this outcome to making mortgage payments on a property that is possibly worth less than the amount of the mortgage. The right of the homeowner to quit making mortgage payments and surrender the property to the bank is equivalent to a put option. Exercising this option following a flood loss shifts the excess of the flood loss over the homeowner's equity to the bank. Thus, in situations where homeowners have little equity in their houses, the banks are indirectly exposed to significant potential flood losses.

The findings of Lawless (2005) are consistent with property owners exercising their put options following a disaster, whether by necessity or choice; the study looks at eighteen hurricanes between 1980 and 2004 and finds that bankruptcy filings increased significantly twelve to thirty-six months after a major hurricane. Similarly, Overby (2007) finds that mortgage default rates significantly accelerated in New Orleans following Hurricane Katrina. Further, she finds that the uptick in the rate of foreclosures that would have been expected to accompany the increase in mortgage defaults was actually suppressed by secondary market responses, including the decision by Fannie Mae and Freddie Mac to suspend mortgage payment requirements for three months immediately after Katrina. Fannie Mae and Freddie Mac also established a moratorium on foreclosures that extended until August 31, 2006, a year after Katrina. Overby's data indicate that foreclosures arising out of a post-Katrina default increased significantly between May and August of 2006.

To address the flood risk they face, banks could purchase insurance or transfer the risk through an alternative risk-transfer contract, such as a CAT bond, to another party. Another possibility, at least in theory, for funding this risk would be for banks to charge a higher interest rate on mortgages in areas exposed to the flood peril. The interest rate would reflect all characteristics which would reasonably be expected to impact the likelihood of default from a flood loss, such as the amount of equity the homeowner holds in the property and the risk-control measures built into the structure itself.

Private Insurance Market Contracts. Prior to the creation of the NFIP, the private insurance market facilitated the transfer of flood risk, and today property owners may obtain additional flood insurance, in excess of the limits provided by the NFIP, through the private market. In addition, some lenders are required by the mandates surrounding federally backed mortgages to obtain private market insurance. The Federal Disaster Protection Act of 1973 requires homeowners living in an area at high risk of flood and having a mortgage from a federally backed lender to purchase flood insurance, and the same requirement applies to homeowners whose loans are sold to a government-sponsored enterprise, such as Fannie Mae or Freddie Mac. The act does not require that the insurance be purchased from the NFIP, although it usually is. If coverage is obtained from another source, the coverage must meet or exceed that provided by the NFIP.

Dixon et al. (2007a, b) estimate that there are roughly fifty thousand to seventy-five thousand flood insurance policies voluntarily purchased in the private market each year. Advantages to coverage through the private market rather than the NFIP include higher available coverage limits and flood coverage enhancements. For instance, the NFIP policy provides actual cash-value coverage, whereas private market coverage often provides replacement-cost coverage. Private market coverage typically insures carpets, wallpaper, and personal items in a basement, whereas NFIP coverage does not; and private coverage applies to mudslides, while NFIP coverage does not.

Private market flood insurance is typically designed for owners of homes worth more than the NFIP policy limit. In 2006, Chubb Insurance Company introduced a private market flood insurance policy that could be purchased with a limit up to $15 million (Chubb 2006). (Recall that the NFIP limit on an insured residential home is currently $250,000.) Private insurance coverage may be written in a number of different ways, including as a supplement to NFIP coverage, as a stand-alone policy, or as an endorsement to a homeowner's insurance policy (Silverman 2005). The insurers that do sell private flood insurance—including AIG, Fireman's Fund, and Lloyds of London as well as Chubb—often provide coverage in high-flood-risk areas. Since these policies are not subsidized, the premiums reflect the insurers' true estimates of the cost of this risk.

The vast majority of flood insurance purchased in the private market is lender-placed coverage, including lender forced-placed coverage, which is purchased by a lender on behalf of a borrower, typically when the borrower does not satisfy a loan condition stipulating that coverage be maintained.[21] The borrower repays the lender for the cost of the coverage typically through higher mortgage payments. Dixon et al. (2007a) estimate that there are between 130,000 and 190,000 lender forced-placed flood insurance policies with private insurers at any one time.[22] In a separate report, Dixon et al. (2006) find that 75 percent to 80 percent of homes subject to the mandatory flood insurance purchase requirement, which is the impetus for forced placements, are indeed insured. In contrast, they find that only about 20 percent of homes not subject to forced placement are insured against flood. (Approximately 45 percent of all homes in special flood hazard areas are not subject to forced placement.) Thus while not all homes subject to the mandatory purchase requirement are insured, the requirement is associated with a significantly higher rate of flood coverage than exists for homes not subject to it, and has led to the development of a market for private flood insurance. The estimate by Dixon et al. (2006) of the size of the private flood insurance market suggests that it accounts for 6 percent of the total flood-risk coverage of condominium owners and homeowners.

Of the two segments of the private insurance market—the truly voluntary market and the lender forced-placed market—the first segment satisfies many of the criteria specified earlier for optimal risk transfer: the premiums reflect the risk, the cost of the risk is borne by the party best able to mitigate the risk, the administration of the policy is efficient, individuals are not forced to participate in the program, and the financing of the risk does not impose a negative externality on others. However, the amount of flood risk that is transferred in the private market through voluntary transactions is a relatively small piece of the total risk faced by homeowners and condominium owners; the percentage of those insured voluntarily in the private market is less than 1 percent of those facing flood risk.[23] There are roughly five million policies sold by the NFIP annually.

Going Forward

The NFIP is a less than perfect mechanism for protecting homeowners against the personal and financial devastation caused by severe flooding. Many at risk simply choose not to purchase coverage. This creates an economic distortion to the degree that the risk is borne by others, including taxpayers, family members, and friends. Moreover, the price charged by the NFIP does not completely reflect the cost of the risk. As a result, individuals are likely to make less than optimal tradeoffs between purchasing insurance and investing in other risk-management strategies, including loss prevention and loss reduction (Dehring and Halek 2008). The NFIP is for all practical purposes a monopoly insurer that does not face competitive market pressures to innovate, provide superior service, or meet the needs of customers, many of whom find available coverage limits insufficient. Although research has demonstrated that greater awareness of flood risk leads to greater demand for flood insurance, NFIP does very little to market its products compared to private insurers.

If the United States continues to provide aid to needy homeowners following floods, it is essential that the NFIP be restructured to encourage or require homeowners to fund the potential loss *ex ante* through appropriate risk-adjusted premiums. Doing so will protect other U.S. taxpayers from bearing the cost of aid.

It is also important to recognize that the government has no advantage over the private market in overcoming uncertainty about the loss distribution where floods are concerned. Indeed, as we have indicated, private flood insurance is currently sold by some insurers in the United States, expanding flood insurance availability beyond that provided by the NFIP. Flood risk is increasingly being passed between parties in the financial markets with a variety of different contracts.

A goal of any federal flood program should be complete coverage of flood peril at a price that reflects the risks. To achieve this goal, the federal government could in theory require that all property owners purchase flood insurance in the private market. Mandating private coverage would overcome the individually rational but socially inefficient failure to purchase insurance (the Samaritan's Dilemma), and would also help alleviate any adverse selection problems that might occur in a purely voluntary market. Whether or not insurance industry capacity would expand sufficiently to absorb this requirement is an open question, but there is reason to believe that it might. Following major losses, including Hurricane Andrew and 9/11, new capital came quickly into the industry. The opportunity to provide flood coverage may result in a similar influx of capital.

A slower approach would be to raise NFIP rates. Once the rates reached a level that accurately priced the risk and covered the costs of the program, private insurers would likely enter the market. With financial instruments available to access the capital markets, insurers and reinsurers would likely transfer the risk to those markets, where it would be further spread to willing investors. Significantly, when the NFIP was implemented, this opportunity was not available to insurers. As mentioned above, advances in computer modeling and understanding of the science behind floods increase the accuracy of pricing and the ability of flood risk to be passed to the private market.

If the government is unwilling to mandate flood coverage, an alternative means for expanding flood coverage at an appropriate price would be to place the risk on the banks providing mortgages in flood-prone areas. This could be accomplished through legislation stipulating that, following a flood of a particular size in a specified area, the outstanding balance on all mortgages in the affected area would be considered paid in full. The loss arising from the unpaid value of the mortgages would revert to the credit markets—the banks that underwrote the loans or those that bought the loans from the banks in a secondary transaction. Lenders faced with this risk would price it into the interest rate charged for a mortgage.[24] Alternatively, the banks could require private flood insurance before issuing a mortgage.

An important advantage of this approach is that financial markets have significantly greater capacity than the property and casualty insurance industry. There are several reasons to believe that the financial markets would charge a lower premium for bearing flood risk than the insurance market. First, because flood risk is unlikely to be correlated with market risk, adding flood risk to a portfolio would offer the benefit of diversification, in exchange for which market participants might be willing to charge a lower price for bearing the risk. Second, the financial markets are able to disperse risk broadly (unlike insurers, who aggregate risk), so the risk premium need not be as large. Insurance is an ideal tool for risk transfer when the insured risks are homogenous and independent. But flood risks within a geographic area are highly correlated, thereby limiting the ability of insurers to reduce risk through pooling.

Requiring banks to bear the flood risk associated with outstanding mortgage balances would clearly drive up the cost of home ownership for homes located in high-risk flood areas, but this may be a socially desirable outcome because it ensures that development in risk-prone areas be undertaken only when the benefits of doing so outweigh the total social costs. If this proposal were implemented, administrative costs would admittedly rise, as the loan process would be more cumbersome and expensive in areas subject to flood. Bank underwriting of the risk would require a determination of risk remediation measures at the home: pilings, distance from water, etc. This would presumably be an additional duty performed by a home inspector, thus raising the overall cost associated with real estate transactions.

The important point is that many of the criteria for an ideal risk-transfer program would be satisfied by this proposal. The cost of the risk would be borne by the individual deriving the benefit of the risk, the homeowner. The cost would be fairly priced, as long as the mortgage market is competitive. Administrative costs, while not negligible, would be reasonable relative to the size of the risk. An important drawback to this approach is that it is applicable only to the value of unpaid mortgages.

The history of the National Flood Insurance Program is a story of incremental change, which has tended to occur after floods that demonstrate shortcomings in the program. Since its inception, the program has expanded coverage limits, the range of homes eligible for coverage, and requirements compelling homeowners to purchase coverage. But the time for more fundamental change—made possible by advances in computer technology, meteorology, and finance—is the present; another catastrophic flood will only reveal once again the inadequacies of the NFIP's current approach.

Notes

1. While it is estimated that about half of the victims of Katrina who suffered a property loss had some flood insurance, this number includes damaged properties that were located outside of pre-determined flood zones. The percentage of insured households that were located in actual flood insurance zones in New Orleans proper was about 65 percent, according to Drew and Treaster (2006). Thus, many property owners in known high-risk flood areas either chose not to purchase flood insurance or failed to purchase required flood insurance.

2. Browne and Hoyt (2000) refer to the failure to fund one's exposure to risk because of an expectation of charity from others, in this case the federal government, as a "charity hazard," which is a close cousin to moral hazard.

3. Insurance Information Institute, "Flood Insurance," http://www.iii.org/media/facts/statsbyissue/flood/.

4. Though note that regulation of some insurance markets results in the costs of risk transfer not fully reflecting the true cost of the risk, and that some private insurance markets may not have appropriate incentives to fully account for externalities on other parties.

5. Examples of other federal disaster relief acts include the 1965 Southeast Hurricane Disaster Relief Act (PL 89-339), the Disaster Relief Act of 1970 (PL 91-606), the 1988 Robert T. Stafford Disaster Relief and Emergency Assistance Act (PL 100-707), and the 2000 Disaster Mitigation and Cost Recovery Act (PL 106-390).

6. For a complete history of the NFIP, see American Institutes for Research et al. (2002).

7. Here, the term "affordable" simply implies an amount that a consumer would be willing to pay to acquire flood insurance. Premiums may be capped and ignore or limit any risk adjustment. An economic definition of an "affordable" premium is different, in that it considers all risk adjustments needed for efficient outcomes. NFIP premium determination is discussed in a later section.

8. The time period for establishing a flood insurance program in a community was one to three years.

9. The National Flood Insurance Fund was established in the Department of the Treasury by the 1968 act.

10. By statute, NFIP pricing was not to be actuarially fair. Premium rates for most properties were intended to fully reflect the risk of flooding on an actuarial basis, but the rates for the remaining properties were subsidized as mandated by statute. Hence, risk loading or risk premiums were excluded from pricing. Note also that fiscal year 1986 was the first year that no taxpayer funds were required to meet NFIP flood insurance expenses. Prior to 1986, NFIP administrative expenses, surveys, and studies were financed through congressional appropriations. American Institutes for Research et al. 2002.

11. The incentives worked: by January 1974, 2,850 communities had joined the NFIP, and approximately 312,000 policyholders had $5.5 billion in NFIP flood coverage. By April 1978, 15,898 of 18,826 officially identified flood-prone communities had

joined the NFIP. About 13,000 of these communities were in the Emergency Program, and the other 2,800 were in the Regular Program. American Institutes for Research et al. 2002.

12. The federal financial regulatory agencies affected by the 1973 act were the Office of the Comptroller of the Currency, the Federal Deposit Insurance Corporation, the Office of Thrift Supervision, the National Credit Union Administration, and the Board of Governors of the Federal Reserve System (U.S. Department of the Treasury 1999). Loans on homes in SFHAs sold to government-sponsored enterprises such as the Federal National Mortgage Association (Fannie Mae) and Federal Home Loan Mortgage Corporation (Freddie Mac) were also subject to the MPR. Later, the National Flood Insurance Reform Act of 1994 (PL 103-325) strengthened the MPR by directing federal agencies to create general flood regulations for all lending institutions and lending services subject to their supervision.

13. For example, under a pilot program outlined in this 2004 act, owners of repetitive-loss properties would accept flood-loss mitigation assistance from state and local governments (such as property elevation, relocation, floodproofing, or a complete buy-out of the property), or incur flood insurance premium increases of up to 150 percent.

14. Approximately 5 million of the 5.65 million flood policies were residential policies. An NFIP residential flood insurance policy covers one to three unit structures as well as condominiums.

15. Insurance Information Institute, "Flood Insurance," http://www.iii.org/media/facts/statsbyissue/flood/.

16. The average rate charged was $0.25 per $100 of coverage in 2007.

17. To our knowledge, private insurers do not compete directly with the NFIP in writing flood coverage.

18. For a detailed discussion of why private insurers are not willing to provide insurance against catastrophic events, see Jaffee and Russell (1997).

19. One estimate of residential and coastal property exposures in Florida alone stands at $2 trillion, a number that will certainly increase as coastal growth continues.

20. The index did not include losses that were insured by the NFIP.

21. The lender could place the coverage with the NFIP under its Mortgage Portfolio Protection Program (MPPP). Most lender-placed coverage, however, is obtained in the private market. Private insurers typically provide more extensive coverage and administrative features that are preferred by lenders. See Dixon et al. (2007a) for a detailed discussion and comparison of private-placed coverage and the MPPP policy.

22. Their estimate is based on a survey of market participants, including insurance companies, lenders, and trackers (hired by lenders to track compliance with mortgage requirements).

23. There are approximately fifty thousand to seventy-five thousand voluntarily placed private market policies. There are roughly five million NFIP policies in place, and the NFIP penetration rate is about 50 percent.

24. This approach is similar to a bottomry bond.

References

American Institutes for Research, Pacific Institute for Research and Evaluation, and Deloitte and Touche LLP. 2002. *A chronology of major events affecting the national flood insurance program.* Washington, D.C.: American Institutes for Research. October. http://www.dhs.gov/xlibrary/assets/privacy/privacy_pia_mip_apnd_h.pdf.

Browne, Mark J., and Robert E. Hoyt. 2000. The demand for flood insurance: Empirical evidence. *Journal of Risk and Uncertainty* 20 (3): 291–306.

Chivers, James, and Nicholas E. Flores. 2002. Market failure in information: The national flood insurance program. *Land Economics* 78 (4): 515–21.

Chubb Group of Insurance Companies. 2006. New flood insurance policy provides up to $15 million in limits. April 3. http://chubb.com/corporate/chubb4991.html.

Congressional Research Service. 2005. Federal flood insurance: The repetitive loss problem. RL32972. June 30. http://www.fas.org/sgp/crs/misc/RL32972.pdf.

Dehring, Carolyn A., and Martin Halek. 2008. Do coastal building codes mitigate hurricane damage to residential property? Working paper. Available at http://papers.ssrn.com/sol3/papers.cfm?abstract_id=928009.

Dixon, Lloyd, Noreen Clancy, Bruce Bender, and Patricia K. Ehrler. 2007a. *The lender-placed flood insurance market for residential properties.* Santa Monica, CA: Rand Corporation.

———. 2007b. Private insurers play a limited, but key, role in underwriting residential flood insurance. Santa Monica, CA: Rand Corporation.

Dixon, Lloyd, Noreen Clancy, Seth A. Seabury, and Adrian Overton. 2006. *The national flood insurance program's market penetration rate: Estimates and policy implications.* Santa Monica, CA: Rand Corporation.

Doherty, Neil A. 1997. Financial innovation in the management of catastrophe risk. working paper, Wharton School, University of Pennsylvania.

Drew, Christopher, and Joseph B. Treaster. 2006. Politics stalls plan to bolster flood insurance. *New York Times,* May 15. http://www.nytimes.com/2006/05/15/us/15flood.html?pagewanted=print.

Government Accountability Office. 2008. Flood insurance: FEMA's rate-setting process warrants attention. GAO-09-12. October. http://www.gao.gov/new.items/d0912.pdf.

Hartwig, Robert P., and Claire Wilkinson. 2005. *Public/private mechanisms for handling catastrophic risks in the United States.* New York: Insurance Information Institute.

Jaffee, Dwight M., and Thomas Russell. 1997. Catastrophe insurance, capital markets, and uninsurable risks. *Journal of Risk and Insurance* 64 (2): 205–30.

Kunreuther, Howard. 1978. *Disaster insurance protection: Public policy lessons.* New York: John Wiley.

———. 1984. Causes of underinsurance against natural disasters. *Geneva Papers on Risk and Insurance* 31: 206–20.

———, and Mark Pauly. 2006. Rules rather than discretion: Lessons from Hurricane Katrina. NBER (National Bureau of Economic Research) Working Paper No. 12503, Cambridge, MA.

Lawless, Robert M. 2005. Bankruptcy filing rates after a major hurricane. *Nevada Law Journal* 6: 7.

National Association of Realtors. 2008. Existing home sales. Available at http://www.realtor.org/research/research/ehsdata.

Overby, A. Brooke. 2007. Mortgage foreclosure in post-Katrina New Orleans. *Boston College Law Review* 48 (4): 851–908.

Power, Fred B., and E. Warren Shows. 1979. A status report on the National Flood Insurance Program—Mid 1978. *Journal of Risk and Insurance* 46 (2): 61–76.

Sheehan, Kevin P. 2003. Catastrophe securities and the market sharing of deposit insurance risk. *FDIC Banking Review* 15 (1): 1–16.

Silverman, Rachel Emma. 2005. Flood coverage for costly homes. Wall Street Journal Online, September 2. http://www.realestatejournal.com/buysell/taxesandinsurance/20050902-silverman.html.

Swiss Re. 2006. Securitization—New opportunities for insurers and investors. *Sigma* 7: 1–42.

U.S. Census Bureau. 2008. Census of housing. Available at http://www.census.gov/hhes/www/housing/census/histcensushsg.html.

U.S. Department of Homeland Security. 2008. "Statistics by calendar year." Available at http://www.fema.gov/business/nfip/statistics/statscal.shtm.

U.S. Department of the Treasury. 1999. *Flood disaster protection.* Washington, D.C.: Office of the Comptroller of the Currency.

White, Rodney R, 2001. Catastrophe options: An experiment in the management of catastrophic risk in the United States. *Journal of Environmental Management* 62: 323–26.

6

Private and Public Roles in Providing Agricultural Insurance in the United States

Vincent H. Smith and Barry K. Goodwin

Some form of agricultural insurance has been available to at least some farmers in the United States since 1879, when hail insurance was introduced for tobacco in Connecticut. Until 1938, crop insurance was offered by private companies against the single perils of hail and fire; two efforts by different private companies to offer protection against multiple perils (one in 1919 and another in 1922) failed after one season. In September 1936, hoping the farm vote in the Midwest would help him to win a second term, Franklin Roosevelt announced that he would seek legislation to establish a federal multiple-peril crop insurance program. The initial legislation permitted the introduction of crop insurance programs for wheat and corn in a limited number of counties in the Midwest and Southwest and created the Federal Crop Insurance Corporation (FCIC) to implement the programs. Multiple-peril crop insurance contracts were then developed by the FCIC. These contracts, first offered in 1938, paid indemnities to farmers whose per-acre yields in the insurance year were sufficiently lower than their estimated long-run average yields.

Many changes have been made to the federal crop insurance program since 1938, most of them between 1980 and 2008. In 2008, the U.S. Department of Agriculture (USDA) Risk Management Agency (RMA), the operational arm of the Federal Crop Insurance Corporation, managed and provided federal subsidies for over twenty different types of insurance products covering more than 120 different crops and types of livestock. These products included conventional yield insurance and newer revenue insurance products for individual crops based on individual farms' yield histories and current yields (generally called actual production history or APH products); products that provide indemnities for loss of crop quality at the individual-farm level; area yield and area revenue products that provide indemnities when county-wide average yields or revenues for a crop are sufficiently below their expected levels; pure price insurance products for some livestock (cattle, hogs, and lambs) and dairy products; products that insure expected gross margins (the difference between the price of an animal sold for slaughter and the estimated cost of fattening the animal for slaughter); index-based products tied to weather and vegetation that enable ranchers and farmers to insure against loss of forage; and insurance against declines in whole-farm revenues from their expected levels.

In this study, we begin by providing a history of the evolution and changing role of federal crop insurance programs since 1938 and especially since 1980, when the Carter administration sought to expand the programs and to make ad hoc agricultural disaster programs unnecessary. We then examine the economic issues associated with agricultural insurance, including the reasons why there are private markets for individual-peril crop insurance contracts but not for multiple-peril crop insurance contracts, and alternative rationales for government intervention and support of multiple-peril and other alternative contracts. In the next section we examine more closely the structure of the current program and the various contracts offered by the USDA's Risk Management Agency. We assess the potential of each type of contract (individual farm–based yield and revenue insurance, group-risk or area products, etc.) to encourage adverse selection and moral hazard behavior. Finally, we consider changes to the structure of the current programs that could potentially improve economic efficiency.

A Brief History of U.S. Policy on Agricultural Insurance

Agricultural policy in the United States, widely viewed as having been initiated with the passage of the 1933 Agricultural Adjustment Act, is complex, and agricultural insurance programs are only one component of the myriad of federal policies that support the U.S. agricultural and agribusiness sectors. For example, the 2008 farm bill (the Food, Conservation, and Energy Act of 2008) has fourteen titles, of which only a part of one (Title 12) addresses crop insurance. The other thirteen titles deal with conservation programs, price support and other commodity programs, agricultural trade policy, agricultural credit, nutrition programs, publicly funded agricultural research, agricultural education, and a miscellany of other issues.

The USDA's Commodity Credit Corporation (CCC), the agency largely responsible for disbursing subsidy payments for programs other than agricultural insurance, annually makes payments to U.S. farmers and rural communities through over eighty different policy initiatives (Smith, Goodwin, and Glauber 2006). These disbursements include direct payments (payments largely decoupled from current production but based on historical farm-production records), payments made under price support programs (called loan rate or loan deficiency programs), and countercyclical payments (linked to the same production histories used to determine direct payments). These types of payments are made to producers of "program crops" like corn, wheat, soybeans, cotton, and barley (crops that have received direct support since the 1930s) and, as a result of the 2002 and 2008 farm bills, to producers of minor oilseeds and pulse crops like peas and lentils as well. The CCC also makes payments authorized under ad hoc disaster relief programs and, again largely as a result of the 2008 farm bill, under a new suite of standing disaster programs for crops, livestock, honeybees, and even fish produced by fish farms.[1]

Clearly, in addition to increasing farm incomes, many farm subsidy programs are intended to pay producers when prices are low and/or production losses occur as a result of adverse weather, plant and animal diseases, or insect infestations. Thus several of these programs can implicitly be viewed as providing farmers with some form of insurance (for example, the price support and countercyclical payment programs), while disaster programs can explicitly be viewed as "zero-premium" agricultural insurance programs that do not require farmers to make any up-front payments to obtain the indemnities those programs provide. Moreover, the new ACRE (Average Crop Revenue) program established by the 2008 farm bill will make payments to farmers when state per-acre crop revenues are low relative to their historical average levels, precisely because the farm lobbies sought what they called an "improved farm income safety net" (Smith 2008, 14). None of these programs, however, provides insurance coverage for individual farms through farm-specific insurance contracts.

Insurance coverage is provided by programs authorized by the FCIC and managed on a day-to-day basis by RMA. Multiple-peril crop insurance products, in which indemnities are triggered by low yields on individual farms, have been available to at least some producers since 1938. Since 1980, the scope of the federal crop insurance program has expanded: crop insurance is available for more commodities, the geographic scope of the program is wider, and the range of subsidized insurance products is bigger. Recently, some policymakers have suggested that the federal crop insurance program should be the *only* farm program through which federal subsidies associated with the production of agricultural commodities are paid to farmers.

One potential indicator of the evolution of federal crop insurance programs and their relative importance within the context of U.S. agricultural policy is the share of total farm subsidies attributable to those programs.[2] Figure 6-1 provides information about total federal expenditures on direct government payments to farmers and total federal crop insurance subsidies between 1980 and 2008, the period in which crop insurance programs expanded most rapidly. In 1980, crop insurance subsidies (including both premium subsidies and government payments to insurance companies for administrative and operating expenses) were $28 million and largely consisted of payments to government agencies and government employees to manage and administer the program. In contrast, in the same year, total direct government payments to farmers were $1.3 billion, about fifty times larger than subsidies to the crop insurance program. By 2008, annual federal crop insurance subsidies had increased to $4.7 billion, about 38 percent of the $12.4 billion in total direct government payments received by farmers that year.

Comparisons of expenditures in individual years can be misleading because both direct government payments (which, to a large extent, are inversely related to agricultural commodity-market prices) and crop insurance indemnities (which are linked to sector-wide events such as regional droughts) can vary substantially from one year to the next. Table 6-1 shows

FIGURE 6-1
TOTAL DIRECT GOVERNMENT PAYMENTS TO FARMERS VS. FEDERAL CROP INSURANCE SUBSIDIES, 1980–2008 ($billions)

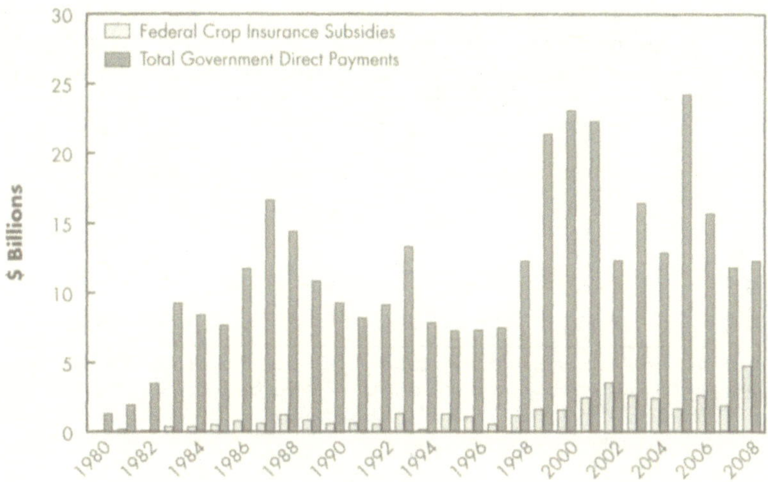

SOURCES: USDA, Risk Management Agency, Summary of Business Reports and Data, various years, available at http://www.rma.usda.gov/data/sob.html; unpublished data from USDA, Risk Management Agency; USDA National Agricultural Statistical Service, annual Agricultural Statistics reports, available at http://www.nass.usda.gov/Publications/Ag_Statistics.

average annual direct government payments to farmers and federal crop insurance subsidies over a series of five-year periods and one four-year period (2005–2008) between 1980 and 2008. Over the period 1980–1984, annual average crop insurance subsidies were $177 million, about 3.6 percent of the $4.9 billion annual average total direct subsidies to farmers. Following the 1985 farm bill up until 1989, however, annual average government payments increased to $12.3 billion, while crop insurance subsidies expanded more rapidly, to an annual average of $748 billion, or 6.1 percent of total direct payments.

The increase in crop insurance subsidies in the 1980s was a direct consequence of the 1980 Federal Crop Insurance Act (FCIA). In 1980, crop insurance was available for only twenty-eight crops in 1,676 of the 3,140 counties in the United States, and prior to 1980, farmers were expected to

TABLE 6-1
DIRECT GOVERNMENT PAYMENTS TO FARMERS VS. FEDERAL CROP INSURANCE SUBSIDIES (annual averages)

Period	Direct government payments to farmers ($billions)	Federal crop insurance subsidies ($billions)	Federal crop insurance subsidies as a percentage of total direct payments
1980–84	4.887	0.177	3.6%
1985–89	12.326	0.748	6.1%
1990–94	9.592	0.602	6.3%
1995–99	11.201	1.111	9.9%
2000–04	17.512	2.514	14.4%
2005–08	16.122	2.715	16.8%

SOURCES: USDA, Risk Management Agency, Summary of Business Reports and Data, various years, available at http://www.rma.usda.gov/data/sob.html; unpublished data from USDA, Risk Management Agency; USDA National Agricultural Statistical Service, annual Agricultural Statistics reports, available at http://www.nass.usda.gov/Publications/Ag_Statistics.

pay all of an actuarially fair premium rate—equal to their expected annual average indemnity payments—for the coverage they purchased (Goodwin and Smith 1995). The 1980 FCIA introduced a 30 percent subsidy for crop insurance premiums paid by farmers, created a mandate for FCIC to expand the number of crops covered by subsidized insurance products, and required that FCIC make subsidized insurance products available on a national basis. By 1989, the number of covered crops had increased to forty-nine, and subsidized insurance coverage for at least some crops was available in 3,026 counties (essentially all U.S. counties with some measurable agricultural activity).

In addition, the 1980 act provided FCIC with some flexibility to introduce area yield insurance products. Individual yield insurance, widely known as multiple-peril crop insurance, had been the only type of federally subsidized contract available to farmers; but in 1993, a new type of yield contract called the Group Risk Plan (GRP) was introduced. The GRP is an area yield insurance plan that pays an indemnity when average yields in a farm's county are sufficiently low relative to their expected levels. The GRP program was first proposed in 1949 by Harold Halcrow, a University of Chicago economist, who argued that it would not result in adverse selection or moral hazard behavior on the part of individual producers because their individual actions would not affect county-wide average yields (Halcrow 1949). However, as Miranda (1991) and Smith, Chouinard, and Baquet (1994) later showed, GRP contracts may be relatively poorly correlated with individual-farm yields in some cases and may therefore have inherent basis risk. Not surprisingly, given the option of multiple-peril crop insurance contracts in which indemnities were perfectly correlated with farm yields (and which made moral hazard behaviors available to producers), the overwhelming majority of farmers ignored GRP contracts in favor of multiple-peril crop insurance contracts until premium subsidies were substantially increased in 2000.

Between 1990 and 1994, both annual average direct government payments ($9.6 billion) and crop insurance subsidies ($602 million) remained relatively stable, at about 20 percent lower than they had been between 1985 and 1989. The decrease in direct government payments was a result of the 1990 farm bill, which reduced some payments to farmers as part of an attempt by the George H. W. Bush administration and Congress to reduce the federal budget deficit. Crop insurance subsidies declined partly because premium rates paid by producers were increased by FCIC, to some extent also in response to congressional and administration concerns about the federal budget costs of the crop insurance program.

In October of 1994, however, Congress passed the Crop Insurance Reform Act (CIRA). The CIRA introduced catastrophic insurance coverage (a modest level of insurance coverage involving no per-acre premiums and available on payment of a $100 administrative fee per crop), which enabled some farmers to increase the proportion of their average yields that could be indemnified (effectively reducing deductibles), required FCIC to develop new insurance products (including revenue products), and also mandated that even more crops be covered under the federal program. As a result, over the period 1995–1999, the annual average cost of federal crop insurance subsidies increased by about 85 percent, to $1.1 billion. In 1996, Congress passed a new farm bill that effectively increased farm subsidies by guaranteeing fixed annual payments (called direct payments) to producers of major crops; and in 1998 and 1999, a period of atypically low corn, wheat, and soybean prices and of federal budget surpluses, Congress provided substantial additional payments to farmers. Thus average annual direct government payments also increased—to $11.2 billion—between 1995 and 1999, but by proportionally less than crop insurance subsidies, and crop insurance subsidies averaged 9.9 percent of direct government payments over that period.

The 2000 Agricultural Risk Protection Act (ARPA) further expanded subsidies for crop insurance premiums to as high as 60 percent of the estimated actuarially fair premium rates for most farmers and also mandated insurance products for livestock and livestock forage (pasture and rangeland). The Risk Management Agency developed a range of livestock-related products, including pure price insurance for hogs, cattle, dairy animals, and sheep; a gross-margin product (mentioned above); and rangeland insurance products indexed to rainfall and vegetation conditions.

Under ARPA, FCIC was also required to develop whole-farm products to protect against shortfalls in revenues from all crops and livestock on a farm. Further, under a provision known as Section 508(h), nongovernment entities were given the right to develop innovative insurance products that, subject to third-party review and approval by the FCIC board, would also be eligible for subsidies and managed on a day-to-day basis by the Risk Management Agency. If a new product was approved by FCIC, the developers could be compensated for the funds they invested in the development process. Subsequently, several new products were developed by nongovernment entities, most of which had close ties to farm organizations whose members would benefit from the development of those products.

The result was further increases in annual average crop insurance subsidies. Over the period 2000–2004, the subsidies averaged $2.5 billion, more than double their level over the previous five years. While annual average direct government payments also increased substantially during this period, to $17.5 billion, the effect of ARPA was to increase crop insurance subsidies to 14.4 percent of annual average direct payments. As the number of crops and livestock enterprises covered by federal crop insurance continued to expand (reaching 135 commodities in 2008), crop insurance subsidies continued to increase, averaging $2.7 billion over the period 2005 to 2008 and, as noted above, reached $4.7 billion in 2008.

Participation rates have been a focus of the federal crop insurance program since its inception. Annual participation rates, as measured by the percentage of acres planted to major crops insured under the federal crop program, are presented in figure 6-2.[3] Although a major objective of the 1980

FIGURE 6-2
PROPORTION OF TOTAL U.S. CROP ACRES INSURED THROUGH SUBSIDIZED FEDERAL CROP INSURANCE PRODUCTS, 1981–2007

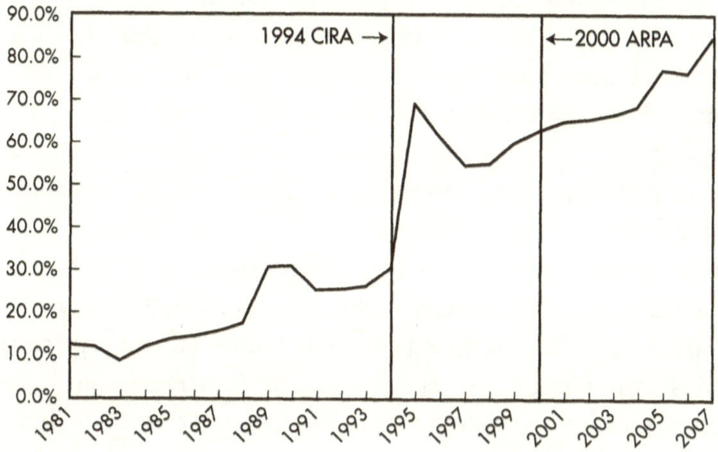

SOURCES: Estimates constructed by the authors using data on insured acres obtained from USDA, Risk Management Agency, Summary of Business Reports and Data, various years, available at http://www.rma.usda.gov/data/sob.html; unpublished data on uninsured acreage from USDA, Risk Management Agency; data on planted crop acres from the USDA National Agricultural Statistical Service, annual Agricultural Statistics reports, available at http://www.nass.usda.gov/Publications/Ag_Statistics.

Federal Crop Insurance Act was to make ad hoc disaster payment programs unnecessary, participation did not increase much in the 1980s, despite the introduction of a 30 percent premium subsidy and the expansion of the program to more crops. Thus in 1980, 12.4 percent of the total area planted to crops was insured, compared to only 17.5 percent in 1988.

Participation rates increased to over 30 percent in 1989 and 1990 because recipients of disaster payments in 1988 (a major drought year) were required to purchase crop insurance to remain eligible for certain program benefits. However, rates subsequently declined to about 25 percent and did not rise until passage of the 1994 Crop Insurance Reform Act, and disaster payments continued to be a regular feature of annual federal outlays on farm programs. The 1994 Crop Insurance Reform Act provided additional impetus for the expansion of crop coverage and the introduction of new products, including revenue products that paid indemnities when per-acre revenues for a crop were relatively low at the farm level. Between 1995 and 1998, several alternative revenue products for major crops like corn, wheat, and soybeans were developed and approved for use by FCIC. These included Revenue Assurance (RA), developed with funding provided by the Iowa Farm Bureau, and Crop Revenue Coverage (CRC), developed by a private insurer but approved for subsidies by FCIC. Both rely on prices at the time of planting for futures contracts with harvest-time settlement dates and a farm's individual yield history to establish expected revenues against which insurance can be purchased.

In response to these innovations, participation by 2000 had increased substantially, to almost 60 percent of total acres planted to crops. Nevertheless, ad hoc agricultural disaster payments continued to be a regular feature of congressional expenditures. The Agricultural Risk Protection Act of 2000 increased premium subsidies for most products to about 60 percent and, as discussed above, encouraged the development of even more types of subsidized insurance products. By 2006, participation had increased to about 77 percent of total crop acres. The House and Senate Agricultural Committees still did not consider this sufficiently large, and so the 2008 farm bill introduced a suite of permanent disaster programs, including the Supplemental Revenue Assurance (SURE) crop disaster program. This program requires farmers to insure all of their economically significant crops (crops expected to contribute more than 5 percent of a farm's revenues from market sales) in order to be eligible for disaster payments. In 2007, participation in crop insurance increased to about 85 percent of the total area planted to crops.

Economic Issues Associated with Agricultural Insurance

Government involvement has characterized agricultural insurance over most of its history, in the United States and elsewhere. Various studies of crop insurance programs around the world—see, for example, Kramer (1983), Goodwin and Smith (1995), and Wright and Hewitt (1994)—have concluded that crop insurance simply would not exist without some form of government intervention. Thus in nearly every country offering crop insurance, the programs are supported and overseen by the government.

In the United States, as we have shown, government intervention in crop insurance is pervasive. The federal program includes large premium subsidies, subsidies to insurance providers who administer and operate the programs, and a number of other measures intended to encourage new crop insurance instruments. In addition, the federal government oversees and manages the operation of the program through an agency of the USDA, the Risk Management Agency. But the fact of government intervention in crop insurance markets does not in itself answer the question of whether such intervention is necessary. In other words, do real market failures exist that preclude the development of a well-functioning private insurance market, or are market failures only perceived to exist?

Several concerns about crop insurance markets are often characterized as market failures, and these are typically used to motivate—and justify—government involvement. These concerns include systemic risk in agricultural production, adverse selection, and moral hazard. Surrounding these concerns and the arguments about them is an overarching question—would farmers be willing to purchase multiple-peril crop insurance if provided at an actuarially viable cost by the private sector (that is, at premium rates which cover both expected indemnities and administrative and operation costs)? Considerable evidence seems to suggest that the demand for accurately priced crop insurance is quite limited in many cases, not least because many alternative risk-management strategies are available to farmers, including, for example, on-farm enterprise diversification (crop and livestock mix), other government programs, spatial diversification, risk-reducing inputs, and off-farm employment for farm household members.[4]

Systemic Risk. Systemic risk plays a prominent role in many current debates regarding economy-wide financial and other macroeconomic conditions and government intervention, and it is frequently cited to justify government involvement in crop insurance. Agricultural risks, which generally involve weather, pests, or natural disasters such as drought and flooding, typically affect large areas and not just an individual farm, and they are therefore described as systemic. A common argument, which has been lucidly described by Miranda and Glauber (1997), focuses only on systemic production risk within the agricultural sector. The proposition is that the systemic nature of risks, together with the very large levels of liability associated with

U.S. agricultural crop production, results in risks that are simply too large for private insurers and reinsurers to handle. In 2008, the U.S. federal crop insurance program covered $89.9 billion in liability for U.S. crops, including liabilities of $37.55 billion for corn, $22.2 billion for soybeans, $8.7 billion for wheat, and $2.3 billion for cotton. Moreover, much of the liability is concentrated in specific growing areas, such as the U.S. Corn Belt, the West Texas cotton region, and the northern Great Plains wheat fields.[5] For example, $20.8 billion of U.S. corn insurance liability (55 percent of the total) is concentrated in four states—Illinois, Indiana, Iowa, and Minnesota. These growing areas often experience similar weather, so that production risks in most years tend to be systemic, at least within individual crops.

Advocates for government provision of agricultural reinsurance therefore maintain that private markets are simply not deep enough to provide coverage for these magnitudes of liability. The systemic argument may appear to be plausible, although Goodwin and Smith (1995), Wright and Hewitt (1994), and others have noted that much larger risks can be spread and diversified across different sectors of the United States and the global economy by international reinsurers. In fact, the systemic risk argument for government intervention might be more credible if couched in terms of the cost of private reinsurance rather than the possibility of obtaining private reinsurance at any price. However, from a market-failure perspective, the case would have to be made that the government can provide such reinsurance at a lower real resource cost than the private market.

In determining the merit of the systemic risk argument, it is useful to compare agricultural crop liability to other forms of liability that have been fluidly traded in international capital markets. Take, for example, the controversial risk-management instruments of credit default swaps (CDSs). Wallison (2008), using Depository Trust and Clearing House Corporation records, estimated that the current outstanding notional amount of liability associated with credit default swaps is about $2.75 trillion. Of course, the systemic nature of risks associated with these instruments and the fact that much of the liability was concentrated in individual firms (for example, Lehman Brothers held $72 billion in CDS liabilities) have played an important role in the current crisis.

The experience with CDSs suggests that international financial markets have substantial capacity to provide coverage of systemic risks, and indeed have insured systemic risks that are orders of magnitude greater than those associated with crop losses in the United States. While annual agricultural insurance liability in the United States was $89.9 billion in 2008, since 1981 indemnities have not exceeded 18 percent of total liability (in 1993, a year in which widespread floods occurred along the Missouri and Mississippi rivers, the loss-cost ratio for the federal crop insurance program was 17.4 percent), which implies that the reinsurance loss exposure risk will be less than $18 billion.

Given that private reinsurance markets are fluid, well developed, and able to assume very large magnitudes of risk, the perception of agricultural reinsurance market failures may reflect concerns about the actual costs associated with the provision of that reinsurance. In private markets, reinsurance costs are embedded in the premium rates that farmers eventually pay for coverage. Significant systemic risks may imply reinsurance premiums that are larger than those associated with cases where risks are diversifiable. Again, the degree to which farmers are risk averse and the overall demand for crop insurance are relevant to the market-failure issue. A simple finding that farmers are not willing to pay for commercial crop insurance does not necessarily imply any failure of the market.

Moral Hazard and Adverse Selection. The twin problems of moral hazard and adverse selection, it is often argued, render private markets unsuitable for crop insurance. The argument is especially prominent with respect to multiple-peril insurance contracts, which may be more difficult to rate and more costly to monitor than single-peril contracts linked to weather indicators (like precipitation and temperature) or to indicators of plant growth within a given area (like vegetation indexes based on satellite data or county-wide average yields reported by a government agency).

Empirical evidence of both adverse selection and moral hazard in U.S. crop insurance markets exists. Evidence of the former is suggested by Goodwin (1993), who reported that high-risk farmers in Iowa who purchased individual multiple-peril contracts had a much less elastic response to premium rate changes than low-risk farmers. Coble et al. (1997) found that farmers were more responsive to subsidy changes than to premium rate changes—a result that may be consistent with differentiated demand responses according to risk. In response to poor actuarial performance, in

1989 the U.S. General Accounting Office recommended across-the-board premium rate increases. As Goodwin (1993) noted, in the presence of adverse selection, such a policy change might actually worsen the actuarial performance of the program through the "death spiral" of adverse selection that reflects such differentiated demand responses.

Evidence of moral hazard in the U.S. crop insurance program was presented by Smith and Goodwin (1996), who found that insured Kansas wheat farms spent an average of $4.23 per acre less on fertilizer and chemicals than did noninsured farms. In a subsequent study based on county-wide data for the entire United States, Goodwin and Smith (2003) reported qualitatively similar findings. Horowitz and Lichtenberg (1993), following an argument presented by Quiggin (1986) that chemical inputs in agriculture tend to be risk enhancing rather than risk reducing, also found evidence of moral hazard, though the hazard was manifest in terms of more inputs rather than less.

Arguments for government intervention to address market failures arising from moral hazard or adverse selection rest upon the assumption that the government is able to measure farm losses and monitor farm behavior more efficiently than private insurance companies, perhaps because of better access to data and complementarities with aspects of other government programs. The government may also have advantages in terms of the coercive power to ensure that no deliberate moral hazard actions are taken. For example, in the U.S. program, farmers found to have committed fraud are likely to lose their eligibility for any government program benefits for several years, in addition to being subject to criminal and civil penalties for abuse. Yet outright fraud and abuse in private insurance are also subject to conventional criminal and civil measures for redress, and it seems unlikely that government bureaucracies possess particular efficiency advantages in managing and monitoring agricultural insurance programs, at least in developed economies such as the United States. In contrast, governments may enjoy such efficiencies in developing countries, where widespread adoption of public crop insurance plans is now taking place. If these governments are inefficient and corrupt, however, crop insurance programs in such settings may be subject to their own particular limitations.

Arguments regarding governmental efficiency advantages in the provision of agricultural insurance, we take this opportunity to note, are also often applied in a broader sense. The arguments assume that the government may simply be more efficient in rate setting, marketing, loss adjustment, and other aspects of agricultural insurance administration and operations. For example, government agencies may be able achieve economies of scale and scope in the use of remote-sensing technology and satellite data that would not be available to private insurance companies. There are also arguments that government administration and operation of agricultural insurance may lower transaction costs or achieve economies of scale in product design and delivery. However, no empirical evidence has been yet provided that demonstrates the government does have such efficiency and cost advantages.

Externality Effects. In a very limited set of circumstances, important externalities may exist that can be best addressed by government intervention in agricultural insurance markets. Specifically, where there are infectious or communicable hazards, government provision of specific-peril insurance plans may improve general welfare. Goodwin and Vado (2007) discuss this issue generally; Goodwin and Piggott (forthcoming) discuss it within the context of citrus canker, an infectious disease which has decimated the Florida citrus industry; and Bekkerman, Goodwin, and Piggott (2008) examine a hypothetical case of soybean rust.

Since some plant and animal diseases have the potential to spread and cause more extensive damage than would occur if immediate mitigation measures were undertaken, producers dealing with diseases are often forced to destroy their commodity and suffer significant and potentially uncompensated losses. Producers thus have strong incentives not to report infections or disease finds. But if the government indemnified farmers against the losses associated with infection, they would have greater incentives to report the disease and adopt protective and loss-mitigating actions, in turn preventing the spread of disease and serving the general welfare. A clear role for the government exists in such cases, though we would argue that such cases are very rare, and even in the case of infectious diseases somewhat limited. Currently, no such specific-peril crop insurance exists in the United States, although ad hoc disaster relief payments are a very common feature associated with such disasters, including disease outbreaks.

We would conclude that private crop insurance market failure is not a common problem. The mere fact that private crop insurance markets are limited is often used as a rationale for government involvement, which is now so pervasive that it is likely to crowd out the development of any purely private markets. That said, private insurers do play a major role in the development, administration, and servicing of the federal crop insurance program. But the claim that systemic risk causes private crop reinsurance markets to fail is suspect. Private markets exist to cover other systemic risks, and they often assume liabilities that are several orders of magnitude greater than those represented by agricultural commodities.

Equity and Social Objectives: The Samaritan Effect. If market failure rationales for government intervention in agricultural insurance seem weak, why are subsidized crop insurance programs such a significant feature of agricultural policy in the United States and elsewhere? The answer is that, while efficiency issues (related to moral hazard, adverse selection, etc.) are important, equity issues and other social objectives also matter. Subsidized agricultural insurance programs are widely viewed as "Good Samaritan" programs that transfer income to farmers experiencing hard financial times through no fault of their own. Crop losses caused by drought, floods, hail, and pest infestations are not viewed by the general public and the body politic as the result of careless management but rather as acts of providence beyond a farmer's control. Helping people when they are in trouble—for example, by providing subsidized crop insurance—is generally viewed as equitable and humane. This Samaritan perspective is politically acceptable not only in the United States but also in many other countries. Hence, for example, the 1994 General Agreement on Tariffs and Trade (GATT) specifically exempted government subsidies for certain forms of crop insurance and disaster relief programs from World Trade Organization disciplines on domestic support for agricultural producers. On equity grounds, then, broad-based congressional support for subsidized crop insurance programs is almost certain to continue for the foreseeable future.

Structure of the Current U.S. Crop Insurance Program

The U.S. federal crop insurance program is impressive in its scope and scale. In 2008, insurance was available for more than 130 crops under twenty-two different insurance plans, and nearly $89.9 billion in total liability was covered by federal crop insurance programs. This included coverage of 272.3 million crop acres on 1.96 million policies. The USDA National Agricultural Statistical Service reported that U.S. farmers planted 320 million crop acres in 2007, implying an insurance participation rate of about 85 percent. The total premium paid into U.S. crop insurance programs in 2008 was $9.9 billion, of which $5.7 billion consisted of premium subsidies provided by the U.S. Treasury. As of March 23, 2009, a total of about $7.5 billion in indemnity payments had been made on 2008 crop insurance policies.[6] Simple arithmetic implies that the typical U.S. farmer received about $1.80 in payments for each $1 of premium (net of subsidies) that he paid into the program. At the same time, it should be noted that the program as a whole reflected actuarial soundness in underlying premium rates, with an implied loss ratio of about 75.7 percent. Significant price volatility led to substantial claims on revenue insurance policies in 2008. However, given the current levels of premium subsidies, an average 80 percent rate of return to participation is not uncommon.

The current federal crop insurance program includes a wide variety of insurance plans. Most offer protection against yields or revenue losses at the individual-farm level. However, index-based insurance has become increasingly popular in the United States, which offers plans that base coverage and indemnities on county-average yields or county-average revenues as well as plans that base coverage on other indexes thought to be correlated with crop risk, such as weather and "greenness" indexes.

Individual-Farm or APH Yield and Revenue Insurance. Multiple-peril crop yield insurance was introduced in 1938 and remained the norm through the mid-1990s. Under conventional crop yield plans, a farmer is guaranteed a preselected percentage of his expected yield for a crop, which is based on the farm's actual yield or production history over the previous four to ten years. Thus conventional yield insurance is often called "actual production history" or APH insurance. Farmers can choose to cover between 50 and 75 percent, or between 50 and 85 percent, of their APH yield.[7] Yield losses are compensated at an insurance price that is announced prior to the season. The insurance price represents a prediction of harvest-time prices and, for major row crops like corn, wheat, and soybeans, is usually based upon futures market projections. It is more difficult to develop appropriate valuations for losses of crops such as fruits and vegetables, for which published prices are less readily available. A farmer who elects an 85 percent level of coverage and has an average yield of one hundred bushels will receive a payment equal to any shortfall in the farm's yields beneath eighty-five bushels multiplied by the insurance price. For example, a corn farmer insured at $4 per bushel who realizes a yield of fifty bushels per acre would be paid an indemnity of $140 per acre for the thirty-five-bushel-per-acre shortfall.

We have already alluded to some of the innovations in U.S. crop insurance offerings in the mid-1990s. These included the development of crop revenue insurance, which offered revenue guarantees that protected against declines in yields or prices (or both); the two basic forms of crop revenue insurance are Crop Revenue Coverage and Revenue Assurance. In 2008, revenue plans, which included CRC, RA, and an index-based plan known as GRIP (Group Risk Income Protection), accounted for 68 percent of the $89.9 billion in total liability in the crop insurance program.[8]

CRC established a revenue guarantee based upon an individual farmer's yield history and forecasts of expected harvesttime prices obtained from futures market contracts. A distinguishing feature of CRC was that it promised to indemnify any yield shortfalls at harvesttime prices, regardless of what actual revenues turned out to be. This feature of CRC was motivated by a desire to ensure that indemnity payments reflected the actual value of lost production at harvesttime.[9] Under standard yield insurance, which bases indemnities on price projections at planting time, farmers forced to replace lost production at harvesttime might have to pay a higher price for replacement than the price at which their yield losses are insured. CRC, which provides a form of basis risk, corrects this situation.

Revenue Assurance establishes a revenue guarantee that is based on the planting-time futures price of a contract that expires at harvesttime, along with the yield guarantee that forms the basis of the underlying yield coverage. RA coverage initially was based only on a revenue guarantee and did not include the provision inherent in CRC that also paid for lost yield at harvesttime prices. An option added latter, called the Harvest Price Option or HPO, provided insurance protection that compensated lost yields at harvesttime prices, just as CRC does. The coexistence of two apparently identical revenue insurance plans with sometimes different premium rates has led to efforts to consolidate RA, CRC, and traditional APH coverage into a single plan called the "Combo" policy, which would make the distinguishing features of each plan an option under the "Combo" umbrella.

Index-Based or Area Insurance. As we have noted, an important limitation of crop insurance plans based on the yield histories and current output levels of individual farms involves their vulnerability to adverse selection and moral hazard. These considerations, along with certain administrative advantages, led to the introduction of a number of index-based insurance plans in the early and mid-1990s. The earliest and most prominent of these plans, the "Group-Risk" or GRP plan, was introduced in 1993. The GRP bases coverage and indemnities on county-average yields for insured crops. These yields are reported by the National Agricultural Statistics Service (NASS) of the USDA. To the extent that any individual farmer is unable to measurably affect those county-average yields, the program is largely immune to moral hazard concerns. Further, county yield data are abundant relative to the data available at the farm level. Thus, it may be possible to develop more accurate premium rates and insurance guarantees for plans based on county-wide yield data. Index programs also have some administrative advantages. Since no individual loss-adjustments are required, no direct farm visit is needed, and the costs of administering and operating the GRP program are significantly lower than those associated with individual-farm insurance plans. In addition, the data demands of a program based on aggregate yield experience are far less than those associated with maintaining ten-year yield histories for each individual farm or insurance unit.

A revenue version of the area-wide GRP program known as GRIP (mentioned briefly above) was introduced in 1999 and has become quite popular with farmers in certain areas. GRP accounted for $2.4 billion and GRIP for $6 billion of the 2008 total crop insurance liability of $89.9 billion.[10] Participation in these plans is largely concentrated in the Corn Belt states.

Index plans have been expanded in recent years to include coverage that is based upon a broader range of indexes, partly in response to concerns by livestock producers that they lacked adequate insurance for forage. Two index-based plans, the Rainfall Index and Vegetation Index programs, were introduced as pilot programs in 2007 to provide coverage for pasture and rangeland. The Vegetation Index plan bases its coverage on a series of

Normalized Difference Vegetation Indexes (NDVIs), measures of greenness derived from satellite images for areas or grids that are roughly five miles square (about the size of a township). The Rainfall Index plan bases coverage on weather data collected and maintained by the National Oceanic and Atmospheric Administration's Climate Prediction Center for areas or grids that are roughly eight miles square.

Crop insurance plans based on weather and other area indexes have become common around the world because they make modest data-collection demands, offer administration advantages, and alleviate concerns about moral hazard. However, the plans do have limitations that influence their use by farmers. In particular, index insurance plans do not provide direct protection against losses by individual farms, so a farmer's actual "on-the-ground" losses are not compensated if the index does not trigger a loss. The design of the insurance, and in particular the degree to which the index happens to be correlated with individual farmers' risk, determines the effectiveness of the insurance as a risk-management mechanism. These plans represent a form of basis risk which has been evaluated in detail for the GRP program by Miranda (1991) and Smith, Chouinard, and Baquet (1994). Plans based upon indexes like the NDVI or rainfall indexes may also suffer from similar limitations. It may be possible to construct and accurately rate an index-based plan, but if it is not highly correlated with the risks that matter to farmers, then—absent substantial premium rate subsidies—demand for the coverage will be low.

Livestock Insurance. The 2000 ARPA established a clear mandate for the development of insurance products that would benefit livestock producers. While forage and hay insurance products had been offered on a limited geographical basis prior to 2000, subsequently RMA supported the development of several new products targeted to cattle, hog, dairy, and sheep operations. These included the rainfall and vegetation index products for forage and hay described above and, in addition, two products providing price-related insurance: Livestock Risk Protection (LRP) and Livestock Gross Margin (LGM), both introduced in 2003.

The LRP product effectively allows farmers to purchase put options contracts for up to 10,000 animals each year, but for no more animals than they market, and to receive a 13 percent subsidy on the premiums charged for the price insurance they obtain. Farmers are prohibited from taking offsetting positions in the private market simply to obtain the subsidy. The LGM product insures the estimated gross margin for animals being fed by a farm or feedlot. At the time the product is purchased, futures market prices for livestock and animal feed (corn) prices are used to establish expected gross margins for the future date when the animals are expected to be sold. Farmers then receive indemnities if estimated gross margins at the date the animals were to be sold are sufficiently lower than the expected gross margin established when the insurance was purchased.

Use of these products has been relatively modest. In 2008, five years after their introduction, only 349 LGM policies and 5,554 LRP policies were purchased; and while total liabilities associated with the products amounted to $245 million, indemnities paid were less than $10 million, and Treasury-paid premium subsidies amounted to $0.6 million.[11] Total annual market receipts from U.S. livestock sales typically exceed $100 billion, indicating that participation rates in these insurance plans are very limited.

Whole-Farm Insurance Plans. As a result of certain ARPA provisions, a number of other forms of crop insurance have been introduced to address the insurance needs of small and specialty-crop producers. One form of whole-farm insurance, the Adjusted Gross Revenue (AGR) plan, was introduced in the late 1990s (before ARPA). AGR bases its coverage on a five-year history of a farm's Schedule F tax return. Loss payments are triggered when the adjusted gross income for the insured year is less than the established AGR guarantee. One issue with this insurance plan is that only losses associated with marketed crops and livestock are covered, so farms that raise substantial amounts of feed and forage for their own use obtain little protection against production losses from the plan (Johnson, Smith, and Hewlett 2009).

Insurable Areas. A number of other structural and operational considerations are relevant to U.S. crop insurance programs. An important distinction involves the crop insurance unit. A policy typically applies to all production of a covered crop within a county. Producers must insure the entire crop within a given county if any insurance is taken. However, farmers can choose the level of aggregation of the insurance guarantee by selecting from among several different available unit structures. The most fundamental unit is the "optional unit," which consists of all acreage owned, cash rented, or crop-share rented within a given section (as defined under the Township/Range/Section legal identification system). For a discounted premium, farmers have the option of combining all optional units within a county into a "basic unit" consisting of all land operated under the same ownership/leasing arrangements. Indemnity payments on basic units will always be lower than (or at least no greater than) on optional units, since production on all the optional units is pooled; thus yield shortfalls on one unit can be offset by production in excess of the insurance coverage level on other units. All land within a county, regardless of ownership structure, can be combined in certain cases to form an "enterprise unit" for even lower premiums. Finally, in a small number of counties in the Corn Belt, a "whole farm" unit can be made up of all corn and soybeans produced on a farm. The 1.96 million crop insurance policies sold in the United States in 2008 were made up of 3.02 million crop insurance units. Some individual farmers have been known to insure their crops through more than 50 different optional units.[12]

Tax-Payer Premium Subsidies. Taxpayer subsidies are also an important structural component of the federal crop insurance program. Table 6-2 presents current premium subsidy rates for different coverage levels that represent the amount of the estimated actuarially fair premium paid by the U.S. Treasury. Catastrophic coverage, which provides 50 percent coverage of yield at 60 percent of the expected price, is provided free of charge except for a fixed administrative fee (currently $300 per crop). Subsidies range from 67 percent of the total premium for 50 percent coverage, to 38 percent of the total premium for 85 percent coverage. On area-wide plans, premium subsidies range from 55 to 64 percent. Gross premiums, net of subsidies, are set to correspond to levels consistent with overall actuarial soundness in the operation of the program.

The Federal Government's Reinsurance Role. Another distinguishing feature of the federal program is incorporated in the Standard Reinsurance Agreement (SRA). The SRA establishes the terms of reinsurance and program operations applicable to the private crop insurance companies that market and service the reinsurance plans. (Companies must also adopt the rates and underwriting procedures established by the USDA's Risk Manage-

TABLE 6-2
U.S. FEDERAL CROP INSURANCE PREMIUM SUBSIDIES FOR APH AND GROUP RISK PRODUCTS IN 2009

Coverage level	APH premium subsidy	Group risk premium subsidies	Administrative fee
Catastrophic	100%	100%	$300
50%	67%	N/A	$30
55%	64%	N/A	$30
60%	64%	N/A	$30
65%	59%	N/A	$30
70%	59%	64%	$30
75%	55%	64%	$30
80%	48%	59%	$30
85%	38%	59%	$30
90%	N/A	55%	$30

SOURCE: USDA Risk Management Agency, http://www.rma.usda.gov/data/premium.html.
NOTE: N/A = Coverage level not available.

ment Agency.) The SRA requires each company to offer coverage to any farmer in a state in which it writes policies, but also provides private companies with advantageous reinsurance considerations that allow them to cede certain risks to the federal government. Companies are allowed to allocate policies among three different insurance funds—the Commercial Fund, the Developmental Fund, and the Assigned Risk Fund. The share of gains and losses that a company must retain differs significantly across funds. The Assigned Risk Fund allows companies to allocate their riskiest policies to the federal government. The maximum possible underwriting loss on Assigned Risk policies is 11 percent of the company-retained premium.[13] As a part of the SRA, private insurance companies also receive an administrative and operating (A&O) subsidy intended to cover the costs of delivering and maintaining the program. In 2006, the A&O subsidy averaged 20.7 percent of gross premium (Collins 2007).

Loss Experience in the Federal Crop Insurance Program. Finally, it is useful to consider the actuarial experience of the modern crop insurance

FIGURE 6-3
LOSS-COST EXPERIENCE: RATIO OF INDEMNITY PAYMENTS TO TOTAL LIABILITY WEIGHTED ACROSS YEARS BY ANNUAL INSURED ACREAGE, 1981–2007

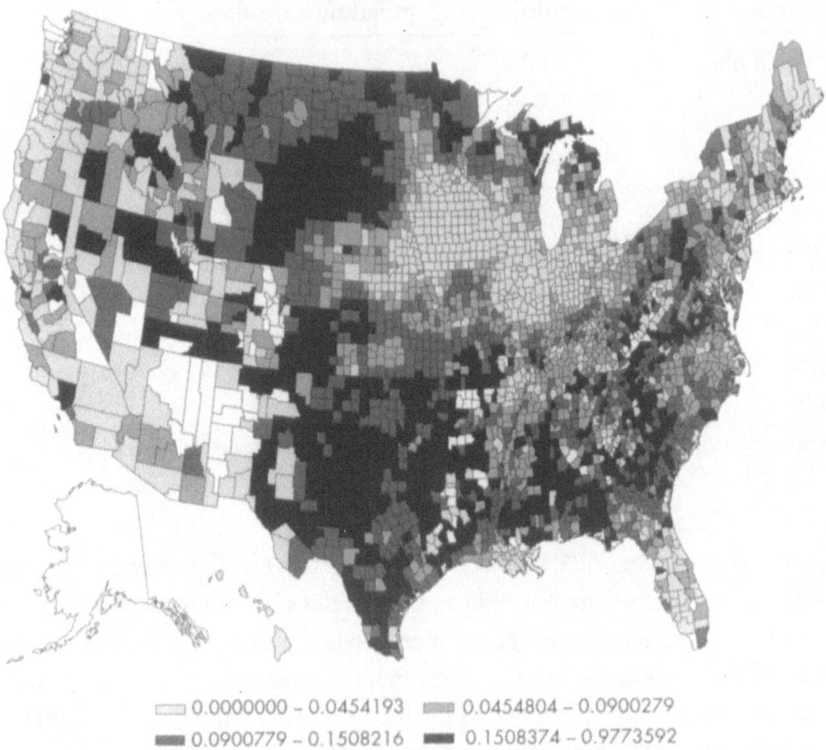

SOURCE: Constructed by the authors from unpublished data obtained from USDA RMA.

program across different years, regions, and crops. Figure 6-3 shows the ratio of total indemnities to total liability by county throughout the United States over the period 1981–2007. The figure illustrates that considerable heterogeneity exists across regions in the risks covered by federal crop insurance, with the lowest levels of agricultural risk occurring in the Corn Belt states. In contrast, the South and Great Plains states tend to have much higher production risks.

Table 6-3 presents loss ratios (the ratio of indemnity payments to total premiums) for major crops. Given the systemic nature of agricultural risks,

TABLE 6-3
LOSS RATIOS BY CROP: RATIO OF INDEMNITY TO GROSS PREMIUMS

Year	Wheat	Cotton	Corn	Soybeans	Other crops
1981	0.97	1.10	0.58	1.81	0.90
1982	0.88	1.89	0.53	2.04	1.46
1983	0.88	1.72	2.74	2.49	2.17
1984	1.60	1.64	0.89	1.90	1.49
1985	2.47	0.55	0.62	1.73	1.78
1986	1.71	2.80	0.83	2.04	1.77
1987	1.03	0.49	0.59	1.32	1.21
1988	3.96	0.88	3.20	1.95	1.91
1989	2.29	2.40	0.91	0.98	1.81
1990	0.91	1.27	0.55	0.85	2.41
1991	1.44	2.00	1.21	1.03	1.15
1992	1.37	3.18	0.81	0.61	0.94
1993	1.66	1.04	3.27	2.50	2.05
1994	1.19	0.64	0.19	0.35	0.91
1995	1.00	1.09	0.93	0.70	1.26
1996	1.47	1.11	0.53	0.39	0.75
1997	0.79	0.68	0.33	0.33	0.65
1998	0.57	1.62	0.67	0.64	1.14
1999	1.50	1.29	0.60	0.76	1.14
2000	1.31	1.57	0.54	0.87	1.30
2001	1.47	1.47	0.65	0.63	1.45
2002	2.04	1.26	1.38	0.99	1.83
2003	0.74	1.19	0.64	1.45	1.14
2004	0.91	0.57	0.58	0.78	1.07
2005	0.60	0.34	0.55	0.30	0.81
2006	1.28	1.19	0.52	0.29	1.14
2007	0.96	0.51	0.35	0.57	0.72
Average	1.37	1.31	0.93	1.12	1.35
Acreage-weighted avg.	1.28	1.18	0.75	0.83	1.20

SOURCES: USDA, Risk Management Agency, Summary of Business Reports and Data, various years, available at http://www.rma.usda.gov/data/sob.html; and unpublished data from USDA, Risk Management Agency.

the sample of twenty-seven years is simply too short to make definite statements about the actuarial soundness of rates. However, the data do suggest that the programs come close to operating on an actuarially sound basis, although differences exist among crops. Wheat and cotton appear to realize larger losses than corn, which operates with an acreage-weighted average loss ratio of about 0.75. When total premiums are adjusted for subsidies, differences are again apparent across crops (table 6-4), with wheat and cotton producers receiving higher indemnities per dollar of premium paid than producers of other crops. Again, this disparity may not result from inaccurate premium rating but may instead reflect the nature of premium subsidies and the weather experiences over the relatively short span of data available.

Policy Issues, Concerns, and Recommendations

In the United States, there appears to be a long-standing political consensus on agricultural insurance: insurance subsidized by taxpayers and/or government borrowing should be available to protect farmers against revenue losses caused by yield shortfalls and/or low prices. The question in the United States is not whether such programs should exist but how they should be structured. The following general principles seem reasonable.

A subsidized crop insurance program should be designed to minimize adverse economic efficiency impacts, specifically moral hazard and fraud. The lost output or unproductively used resources stemming from moral hazard incentives and fraud represent genuine waste and have a clear cost to society.

Deductibles are important in the effort to minimize adverse economic effects. Historically, farmers have not been allowed to insure more than 75 or 85 percent of their expected crop yields. However, the new standing crop disaster program established by the 2008 farm bill—the SURE program—has had an unintended consequence: many producers are able to effectively insure close to 100 percent of their expected yields when they combine SURE payments (which are directly linked to crop insurance decisions) with the indemnities they receive from their crop insurance policies (Smith and Watts 2010). Absent a reasonable deductible, farmers (like other insured individuals) may have substantial incentives to adopt moral hazard behaviors. Farmers are eligible for disaster payments surprisingly often, and so

TABLE 6-4
FARMER-PAID LOSS RATIOS BY CROP: RATIO OF INDEMNITIES TO FARMER-PAID PREMIUMS (premium minus subsidy)

Year	Wheat	Cotton	Corn	Soybeans	Other crops
1981	1.01	1.15	0.61	2.33	1.10
1982	1.15	2.49	0.69	2.62	1.90
1983	1.16	2.28	3.51	3.13	2.79
1984	2.10	2.26	1.15	2.41	1.91
1985	3.27	0.76	0.80	2.23	2.28
1986	2.22	3.89	1.09	2.62	2.28
1987	1.36	0.68	0.78	1.72	1.57
1988	5.26	1.23	4.29	2.57	2.50
1989	3.08	3.40	1.22	1.29	2.40
1990	1.23	1.79	0.74	1.13	3.19
1991	1.95	2.83	1.62	1.38	1.52
1992	1.87	4.50	1.08	0.81	1.25
1993	2.29	1.48	4.40	3.37	2.75
1994	1.64	0.91	0.26	0.47	1.22
1995	2.17	2.95	2.05	1.77	2.86
1996	3.09	2.70	1.14	0.93	1.46
1997	1.52	1.63	0.60	0.66	1.59
1998	1.10	3.96	1.18	1.22	2.52
1999	3.60	3.66	1.30	1.83	3.79
2000	2.74	3.69	0.98	1.76	3.24
2001	3.53	3.61	1.51	1.50	3.29
2002	4.90	3.25	3.16	2.31	3.99
2003	1.73	3.11	1.47	3.38	2.98
2004	2.17	1.52	1.33	1.81	3.03
2005	1.43	0.91	1.27	0.68	3.06
2006	3.08	3.16	1.17	0.67	3.31
2007	2.32	1.38	0.80	1.31	1.94
Average	2.33	2.41	1.49	1.78	2.43
Acreage-weighted avg.	2.42	2.66	1.41	1.61	2.66

SOURCES: USDA, Risk Management Agency, Summary of Business Reports and Data, various years, available at http://www.rma.usda.gov/data/sob.html; and unpublished data from USDA, Risk Management Agency.

this is a real concern. Congress should therefore reconsider the structure of the new disaster program, specifically the interface between it and APH yield and revenue insurance programs. One option, for example, is to remove a provision in the SURE program that establishes a revenue guarantee for each crop at 115 percent of a farmer's insurance liability for that crop. It is this provision of the SURE program that effectively reduces the insurance deductible to zero for farmers located in disaster areas or having individual losses in excess of 50 percent of their normal production (Smith and Watts 2010). Alternatively, the maximum coverage levels allowed under APH yield and revenue insurance contracts could be lowered (although this is likely to be viewed as unacceptable by many farm organizations).

Monitoring and analysis of claims records can also discourage moral hazard practices. Recently, Atwood, Robinson-Cox, and Shaik (2006) as well as others have suggested a suite of statistical techniques for identifying farms where moral hazard and/or fraud appears to be endemic. Such techniques have the potential to substantially mitigate the incidence of those practices and the costs of the program to taxpayers. There is evidence that RMA has been increasingly diligent in addressing these problems since the mid-1990s, partly in response to the mandate in the 1994 CIRA that loss ratios for crop-specific insurance products should not exceed one. However, members of Congress have apparently frequently asked that enforcement (especially in relation to moral hazard concerns) not be vigorously pursued vis-à-vis farmers from their own districts.

Efforts to address adverse selection must recognize that it arises when premium rates do not accurately reflect the expected indemnities which individuals face; that is, when individuals who are heterogeneous with respect to expected losses are placed in the same insurance pool and charged identical premium rates. All of the APH programs appear to be subject to adverse selection problems because rates are generally set on the basis of county-wide loss experiences, with adjustments made to reflect differences in average yields but not farm-specific loss experiences. However, a consideration of actuarial experience (admittedly limited) suggests that the plans tend to operate on a roughly actuarially sound basis. Until premium subsidies were increased to 60 percent as a result of the 2000 ARPA, participation rates were only about 50 percent; prior to 1994, when premium subsidies were 30 percent, participation rates were generally no more than

10 percent of total planted acres and 20 to 30 percent of crop acres eligible for insurance.[14]

One approach to the adverse selection and moral hazard concerns is simply to abandon individual-farm insurance programs and offer only index insurance based on area yields, weather indicators, and plant growth indicators. As discussed above, the index-related data available for actuarial purposes are generally much more extensive and reliable than the information available on individual-farm yields and revenues. As a result, premium rates for index-based agricultural insurance are likely to be more accurate, and adverse selection is therefore less likely to occur. Moral hazard also generally ceases to be an issue because farmers cannot influence the probability or size of their indemnity payments through their own actions.

However, index insurance quite frequently fails to provide indemnities when individual farmers experience on-the-ground losses, and so many farmers, as well as their creditors, prefer to insure individual-farm yields and revenues. From a practical perspective, therefore, an important issue is how premium rates can be tied more closely to individual farmers' likely loss experiences. One approach is to link individual farms' yield histories to the county-wide experiences that are currently used to set APH-based premium rates and to adjust county-wide rates for individual farms accordingly. A second approach is to adjust premium rates for individual farms on the basis of past claims experiences (as is the case for automobile and other forms of insurance) or other characteristics associated with loss probabilities. To some extent, this is already being done. For example, farmers who have very poor yields in certain years are allowed to use "yield plugs" (equal to approximately 60 percent of county-wide historical average yields) in establishing their yield histories but must pay higher premiums for the privilege of using those plugs. In addition, farms with a history of more adverse claims are more likely to have their current-year losses carefully audited. Finally, the RMA recently introduced premium discounts for farmers planting certain genetically engineered corn hybrids that intrinsically have lower yield risk. Currently, however, there is no systematic method by which premium rates are adjusted for individual farms' histories of yield volatility.

Another economic efficiency issue that subsidized insurance programs must take into account is externality effects. Crop insurance programs have been charged with increasing pollution (from on-farm chemical use) and soil erosion. Although research suggests that participation in crop insurance programs appears in fact to reduce agricultural chemical use (see, for example, studies by Babcock and Hennesey [1996], Smith and Goodwin [1996], and Goodwin and Smith [2003]), there is some evidence that farm programs, including crop insurance, have increased soil erosion (Goodwin and Smith 2003), perhaps by encouraging crop production on marginal lands that are more susceptible to soil erosion. Whether crop insurance programs are worse for the environment than other programs that encourage agricultural production is more difficult to assess, although other output-expanding programs uniformly tend to increase agricultural chemical use because they generally encourage more intensive production. On the other hand, crop insurance programs seem to discourage the spread of infectious diseases. As we discussed above, providing farmers with indemnities for losses may increase their willingness to report the incidence of diseases and therefore to mitigate their adverse consequences.

Subsidized crop insurance programs must also address a related concern, the extent to which they encourage higher levels of output and distort the mix of crops and livestock products that are produced. Programs that increase the expected gross returns from agricultural production provide incentives for increased agricultural output. In addition to causing economic inefficiencies, such programs are subject to the disciplines of the 1994 General Agreement on Tariffs and Trade Agricultural Agreement, which restrict any domestic agricultural subsidies that expand agricultural output. Crop insurance subsidies do provide incentives to expand output. However, constraints on the availability of agricultural land may limit impacts on aggregate production. Ideally, in this environment, one goal should be to minimize adverse effects on the mix of crops and livestock enterprises. Currently, most crops and forages can be insured through subsidized insurance programs. Further, as shown in table 6-2, premium subsidy rates, which are closely tied to the value of crops and forages, appear to be similar among APH and index-based insurance. Thus, on the surface, it would appear that proportional subsidies should be quite similar and effects on land allocation decisions and crop mix commensurately modest.

One other feature of federal insurance plans deserves reconsideration. Allowing a farmer to insure optional or basic units instead of the entire crop on his farm allows him to receive indemnities when the farm's overall yields are close to, or even exceed, their expected levels. Moreover, given that actuarially fair premiums are subsidized in proportion to their absolute size for any given coverage level (or proportional deductible), farmers who insure optional units at higher total premium rates (because of higher expected indemnities) on average receive larger subsidies than would otherwise be the case. Certainly, allowing farmers to insure optional or basic units separately may encourage participation in the federal crop insurance program. On either equity or taxpayer-cost grounds, however, it is difficult to see why farms should be allowed to insure different areas planted to the same crop under what amounts to different policies. Subsidized insurance programs should be designed to discourage this practice. Significant increases in subsidies for the highly aggregated "enterprise" units (essentially all acreage of a crop in a county) were introduced for the 2009 crop year to address this concern and are expected to shift participation toward more highly aggregated units.

Two final issues deserve mention here. First, given that the two major APH revenue insurance plans, CRC and RA, are very similar and that both rely on individual-farm yield histories, we think the current proposal to combine the two products with traditional APH yield insurance sensible and equitable.

The second issue concerns systemic risk. Specifically, we do not accept the argument that national and global private reinsurance markets lack the capacity to handle U.S. agricultural systemic risk, which involves a maximum of about $20 billion in total indemnity payments in any given year. Further, we do not believe that reinsurance fees (per dollar of expected indemnity) would necessarily be higher for agricultural contracts than for other forms of contracts involving widespread losses within a sector or geographic region (for example, hurricane insurance in New Orleans or insurance against acts of terrorism in New York). Reinsurance companies are willing to, and do, reinsure liabilities retained by the private agricultural insurance companies that market RMA products. Thus, the absence of purely private multiple-peril agricultural insurance cannot be attributed to a lack of access to reinsurance markets.

Summary

In the United States and elsewhere, private insurance companies have been willing to provide single-peril crop insurance against the consequences of events like fire and hail but not, of their own volition, multiple-peril insurance. They have been willing to offer multiple-peril contracts only when premium rates for those contracts are subsidized by the government and when, in addition, the government itself operates as a reinsurer and accepts a substantial proportion of the financial risks through stop-loss arrangements. There is little evidence that market failure is a major reason why, by itself, the private insurance sector has not offered multiple-peril agricultural insurance. Even systemic risk is not a significant problem for reinsurance markets, as production agriculture accounts for less than 2 percent of gross domestic product (GDP). So conventional economic efficiency arguments for government intervention seem to be relatively weak. The reason the private sector does not usually offer multiple-peril insurance appears to be quite simple; given the likely loading factors (including monitoring, loss adjustment, marketing, and other administrative costs), private multiple-peril insurance is more costly than other forms of risk management available to farmers.

Farmers, however, have actively sought protection from the multiple sources of production and price risks they face, many of which are beyond their control, through a variety of government programs, including ad hoc disaster relief. Policymakers have generally been sympathetic to these concerns, which also resonate with the nonfarm sector. As a result, the federal crop insurance program is widely viewed as a more or less permanent feature of U.S agricultural policy and one likely to grow in importance. Since 1980, Congress and successive administrations have expanded the scope of federal crop insurance programs in three ways: subsidized coverage has been offered for more and more crops, and most recently some livestock; the range of available insurance products has been expanded; and subsidies have steadily been increased, so that for most products, the Treasury now pays about 60 percent of the actuarially fair premium.

The following objectives should be paramount in federal crop insurance program design. First, moral hazard incentives should be kept to a minimum. Insurance contracts that interface with the new SURE disaster program now effectively allow farmers to value crops for loss purposes at close to their expected market value, which is not advisable; deductibles are imposed precisely to minimize moral hazard incentives. Second, crop insurance programs should minimize adverse selection. As Halcrow (1949) noted, area yield programs are more likely to accomplish this objective than programs tied to the yield or revenue performance of individual farms. Third, incentives for distorting agricultural production patterns among crops should be kept to a minimum. Crops should receive insurance subsidies in proportion to their value (to maintain relative prices). Fourth, insurance subsidies should at least be compatible with the World Trade Organization (WTO) rules on agricultural subsidies which the United States agreed to in 1994, when it signed the GATT Agricultural Agreement. Currently, for example, the linkage of the new SURE disaster program to federal crop insurance programs may make the U.S. programs incompatible with current and potential future WTO rules that exclude crop insurance and disaster payments from measures of trade distortion.

Notes

1. Other relatively substantial agricultural subsidies are dispensed through programs that, at least ostensibly, have mainly environmental objectives. These include the Conservation Reserve Program (CRP), under which approximately $2 billion is paid to farmers to place land in conserving uses; the Conservation Stewardship Program (funded at about $500 million a year) which, notionally, pays producers to adopt production practices that conserve environmental amenities; and other programs that conserve wetlands, marshlands, and other environmentally sensitive areas. In addition, many programs that provide considerable economic benefits to farmers involve tariffs and other restrictions on imports (for example, the U.S. sugar program) and/or marketing arrangements that constrain supply (for example, marketing order programs). These programs increase prices paid by consumers and received by farmers (as well as by processors and other agribusinesses in some cases) but do not involve direct government payments, and in the case of tariff-related programs may even generate government revenues.

2. The data presented on federal crop insurance subsidies shown in table 6.1 and figure 6.1 and discussed below were obtained from the USDA RMA home page for the period 1991–2001 (http://www.rma.usda.gov/data/); data for the period 1980–1990 are from unpublished information provided to the authors by RMA. The data on direct government payments were obtained from the USDA National Agricultural Statistical Service home page (http://www.nass.usda.gov/Publications/Ag_Statistics). Percentages were constructed by the authors using these data.

3. The data on participation rates presented in figure 6.2 and discussed in this chapter are estimates constructed by the authors using data on insured acres obtained from USDA, Risk Management Agency, Summary of Business Reports and Data, various years, available at http://www.rma.usda.gov/data/sob.html; from unpublished Risk Management Agency data; unpublished data from USDA, Risk Management Agency and data on planted crop acres obtained from the USDA National Agricultural Statistical Service, annual Agricultural Statistics reports, available at http://www.nass.usda.gov/Publications/Ag_Statistics.

4. For example, Bardsley, Abbot, and Davenport (1984) and Patrick (1988) provide evidence that farmers in drought-prone areas of Australia were not willing to pay loading factors in excess of 4 to 9 percent for otherwise actuarially fair multiple-peril crop insurance. The USDA Risk Management Agency has provided private insurance companies with administration and operations subsidies of no less than 19 percent of the actuarially fair premium.

5. The data on insurance liability, premiums, premium subsidies and subsidy rates, and coverage levels reported in this and subsequent sections of this chapter are from annual RMA Summary of Business Reports, available at http://www.rma.usda.gov/data.

6. Claims are typically settled with some delay, and so this figure likely understates total loss claims for the 2008 crop year. The data discussed in this section are from USDA National Agricultural Statistical Service, annual Agricultural Statistics reports, available at http://www.nass.usda.gov/Publications/Ag_Statistics.

7. Farmers in areas where rainfall is relatively predictable or who raise crops under irrigation are typically able to insure up to 85 percent of their APH yield, while farmers in drought-prone areas are typically able to insure up to 75 percent of their APH yield.

8. See RMA Summary of Business Reports, available at http://www.rma.usda.gov/data.

9. This reflects another aspect of the systemic risk issue discussed above. To the extent that production risks are systemic, aggregate market prices may be inversely related to production, even at a disaggregated level. This correlation suggests that low yields will be accompanied by higher prices, reducing indemnities under revenue insurance plans.

10. Data are from RMA Summary of Business Reports, available at http://www.rma.usda.gov/data.

11. Ibid.

12. Ibid.

13. Fund allocation provisions and the allocation decision are evaluated in detail by Coble, Dismukes, and Glauber (2007).

14. Data are from RMA Summary of Business Reports, available at http://www.rma.usda.gov/data.

References

Atwood, Joseph. A., James F. Robinson-Cox, and Saleem Shaik. 2006. Estimating the prevalence and cost of yield-switching fraud in the federal crop insurance program. *American Journal of Agricultural Economics* 88 (2): 365–81.

Babcock, Bruce A., and David A. Hennesey. 1996. Input demand under yield and revenue insurance. *American Journal of Agricultural Economics* 78 (2): 416–27.

Bardsley, Peter, Arun Abbot, and Scott Davenport. 1984. The economics of insuring crops against drought. *Australian Journal of Agricultural Economics* 28 (1): 1–14.

Bekkerman, Anton, Barry K. Goodwin, and Nicholas E. Piggott. 2008. Spatio-temporal risk and severity analysis of soybean rust in the United States. *Journal of Agricultural and Resource Economics* 33 (3): 311–31.

Coble, Keith H., Robert Dismukes, and Joseph W. Glauber. 2007. Private crop insurers and the reinsurance fund allocation decision. *American Journal of Agricultural Economics* 89 (2007): 582–95.

Coble, Keith H., Thomas O. Knight, Rulon D. Pope, and Jeffrey R. Williams. 1997. An expected indemnity approach to the measurement of moral hazard in crop insurance. *American Journal of Agricultural Economics* 79 (1): 2216–26.

Collins, Keith. 2007. Statement of the chief economist, United States Department Of Agriculture, before the House Agriculture Subcommittee on General Farm Commodities and Risk Management. May 1. agriculture.house.gov/testimony/110/h70501a/DrCollins.doc.

Goodwin, Barry K. 1993. An empirical analysis of the demand for multiple peril crop insurance. *American Journal of Agricultural Economics* 75 (2): 425–34.

———. and N. E. Piggott. Forthcoming. Spatio-temporal modeling of Asian citrus canker risks: Implications for insurance and indemnification fund models. *American Journal of Agricultural Economics.*

Goodwin, Barry K., and Vincent H. Smith. 1995. *The Economics of Crop Insurance and Disaster Relief.* Washington, D.C.: AEI Press.

———. 2003. An ex-post evaluation of the conservation reserve, federal crop insurance, and other government programs: Program participation and soil erosion. *Journal of Agricultural and Resource Economics* 28 (2): 201–16.

Goodwin, Barry K., and Ligia A. Vado. 2007. Public responses to agricultural disasters: Rethinking the role of government. *Canadian Journal of Agricultural Economics* 55 (4): 399–417.

Halcrow, Harold G. 1949. Actuarial structures for crop insurance. *Journal of Farm Economics* 31 (2): 418–43.

Horowitz, John K., and Eric Lichtenberg. 1993. Insurance, moral hazard, and chemical use in agriculture. *American Journal of Agricultural Economics* 75 (4): 926–35.

Johnson, James B., Vincent H. Smith, and John P. Hewlett. 2009. Risk management options for Wyoming ranchers. Agricultural Marketing Policy Paper 27, Montana State University. January. http://www.ampc.montana.edu/policypaper/policy27.pdf.

Kramer, Randall A. 1983. Federal crop insurance: 1938–82. *Agricultural History* 57:181–200.

Miranda, Mario J. 1991. Area-yield crop insurance reconsidered. *American Journal of Agricultural Economics* 73 (2): 233–42.

———, and Joseph W. Glauber. 1997. Systemic risk, reinsurance, and the failure of crop insurance markets. *American Journal of Agricultural Economics* 79 (1): 206–15.

Patrick, George E. 1988. Mallee wheat farmers' demand for crop insurance. *Australian Journal of Agricultural Economics* 32 (1): 37–49.

Quiggin, John. 1986. A note on the variability of rainfall insurance. *Australian Journal of Agricultural Economics* 30 (1): 63–69.

Smith, Vincent H. 2008. Old favorites and new initiatives: Implications of the new farm bill for the Ninth District. *Minneapolis Fedgazette,* 14-18, September.

———, Hayley M. Chouinard, and Alan E. Baquet. 1994. Almost ideal yield crop insurance contracts. *Agricultural and Resource Economics Review* 23 (1): 75–83.

Smith, Vincent H., and Barry K. Goodwin. 1996. Multiple peril crop insurance, moral hazard and agricultural chemical use. *American Journal of Agricultural Economics* 79 (2): 428–43.

———, and Joseph W. Glauber. 2006. Risk management and direct payment programs: Implications for agricultural trade policy. Paper presented to the 2006 International Agricultural Trade Consortium Meetings, May, Capri, Italy.

Smith, V. H., and M. A. Watts. 2010. The new standing disaster program: A SURE invitation to moral hazard behavior. *Applied Economic Perspectives and Policy* 32 (1): 154–69.

Wallison, Peter J. Everything you wanted to know about credit default swaps—but were never told. American Enterprise Institute, *Financial Services Outlook*, Washington D.C., December. http://www.aei.org/outlook/29158.

Wright, Brian D., and Julia A. Hewitt. 1994. All-risk crop insurance: Lessons from theory and practice. In *Economics of agricultural crop insurance: Theory and evidence,* ed. Darell L. Hueth and W. Hartley Furtan, 73–112. Boston: Kluwer Academic Publishers.

Index

About the Authors

Andrew G. Biggs is a resident scholar at the American Enterprise Institute specializing in Social Security and retirement policy. He previously served as the principal deputy commissioner of the Social Security Administration, where he oversaw policy research and led the agency's participation in the Social Security Trustees Working Group. In 2005, he worked on Social Security reform at the White House National Economic Council, and in 2001 he was on the staff of the President's Commission to Strengthen Social Security. Mr. Biggs has written about Social Security reform for numerous publications, including the *Wall Street Journal*, the *Washington Post*, and the *Christian Science Monitor*. He is also the author of AEI's *Retirement Policy Outlook* series.

Jeffrey R. Brown is the William G. Karnes Professor of Finance and director of the Center for Business and Public Policy in the College of Business at the University of Illinois at Urbana-Champaign. He is a research associate at the National Bureau of Economic Research (NBER), where he also serves as the associate director of the NBER Retirement Research Center and as the editor of the *Tax Policy and the Economy* series. Mr. Brown is a trustee for the Teachers Insurance and Annuity Association (TIAA). Previously, he served on the faculty at Harvard University's John F. Kennedy School of Government, on the White House Council of Economic Advisers, and on the staff of the President's Commission to Strengthen Social Security. He was also a member of the Social Security Advisory Board from 2006 until 2008. Mr. Brown has published extensively on topics related to insurance and retirement income security, and was a cofounder and coeditor of the *Journal of Pension Economics and Finance*. In 2008, Mr. Brown received the Early Career Scholarly Achievement Award from the American Risk and Insurance Association, and the TIAA-CREF Paul A. Samuelson Award for outstanding scholarly writing on lifelong financial security.

Mark J. Browne is the Gerald D. Stephens CPCU Chair in Risk Management and Insurance in the Wisconsin School of Business at the University of Wisconsin–Madison. He has served as president of both the American Risk and Insurance Association and the Risk Theory Society. An expert on risk management, insurance, and employee benefits, he teaches courses on these topics and has consulted with businesses on issues related to them. Mr. Browne's research has appeared in many publications, including the *Journal of Risk and Insurance*, of which he is also an associate editor, the *Journal of Insurance Regulation*, and the *CPCU Journal*. Mr. Browne has received numerous awards, including the Beta Gamma Sigma Dean's Award for Teaching Excellence, the Lawrence J. Larson Excellence in Teaching Award at the University of Wisconsin–Madison, and the Shin Award for Research Excellence from the International Insurance Society.

Barry K. Goodwin is the William Neal Reynolds Distinguished Professor in the Departments of Economics and Agricultural and Resource Economics at North Carolina State University. He has published over a hundred journal articles, a large share of which concern public insurance programs. With Vincent Smith, he coauthored *The Economics of Crop Insurance and Disaster Aid* (AEI Press, 1995). He is a fellow at the American Agricultural Economics Association, and his work on crop insurance has received wide recognition and is widely cited. He is a consultant on crop insurance issues for the U.S. Department of Agriculture, private industry, and the World Bank.

Martin Halek has taught in the Actuarial Science, Risk Management, and Insurance Department at the University of Wisconsin since January 2008. He was previously an assistant professor at the University of Georgia and the University of North Carolina–Charlotte. His research and published articles deal with risk behavior, insurance economics, social insurance programs, and ratings effects on financial institutions. In a recent working paper, Mr. Halek examined whether increased coastal building standards imposed by federal and state governments are effective in mitigating hurricane losses. This research topic has generated much interest as high-risk coastal areas continue to experience significant growth. In 2006 he received the Les B. Strickler Innovation in Instruction Award from the American Risk and Insurance Association.

Dwight Jaffee is the Willis Booth Professor of Banking, Finance, and Real Estate at the Haas School of Business at the University of California, Berkeley, where has taught since 1991. Previously, he taught in the Department of Economics at Princeton University. Mr. Jaffee is a member of the Haas School's finance and real estate group and is the cochair of the Fisher Center for Real Estate and Urban Economics. His primary areas of research are insurance—earthquakes, terrorism, and auto—and finance. He has served as an adviser to the World Bank, the Federal Reserve System, the Office of Federal Housing Enterprise Oversight, and the U.S. Department of Housing and Urban Development.

Howard C. Kunreuther is the Cecilia Yen Koo Professor of Decision Sciences and Public Policy at the Wharton School and codirector of the Wharton Risk Management and Decision Processes Center. He has a longstanding interest in ways that society can better manage low-probability/high-consequence events related to technological and natural hazards and has published widely in these areas. Mr. Kunreuther is a fellow of the American Association for the Advancement of Science (AAAS), a member of the National Academy of Sciences Panel on Adaptation Strategies for Climate Change, and a distinguished fellow of the Society for Risk Analysis, receiving the society's Distinguished Achievement Award in 2001. He cochaired the World Economic Forum's Global Agenda Council on "Innovation and Leadership in Reducing Risks from Natural Disasters" and is a member of the OECD's High Level Advisory Board on Financial Management of Large-Scale Catastrophes. His most recent books are *At War with the Weather* (with Erwann Michel-Kerjan, July 2009, MIT Press) and *Learning from Catastrophes: Strategies for Reaction and Response* (with Michael Useem, December 2009, Wharton School Publishing).

Erwann O. Michel-Kerjan's work focuses on managing and financing extreme events, such as natural disasters (such as floods, hurricanes, and earthquakes) and terrorist attacks. He is managing director of the Risk

Management and Decision Processes Center at the Wharton School of the University of Pennsylvania, which for twenty-five years has been at the forefront of research into catastrophes. Mr. Michel-Kerjan also teaches "Value Creation" at Wharton. In 2007, Mr. Michel-Kerjan was named a Young Global Leader (an honor bestowed to recognize and acknowledge the most extraordinary leaders of the world under the age of forty) by the World Economic Forum. In 2008, he was elected chairman of the OECD Secretary-General High Level Advisory Board on Financial Management of Large-Scale Catastrophes, which advises its thirty member countries on these issues. Mr. Michel-Kerjan has authored or coauthored more than fifty publications on financial management and global risk governance, and his views regularly appear in leading media outlets. His books include *Seeds of Disaster, Roots of Response: How Private Action Can Reduce Public Vulnerability* (Cambridge University Press, 2006), *At War with the Weather* (with H. Kunreuther, MIT Press, 2009) and *The Irrational Economist: Making Decisions in a Dangerous World* (with P. Slovis, PublicAffairs, 2010).

George G. Pennacchi is a professor of finance and the codirector of the Office for Banking Research at the University of Illinois at Urbana-Champaign. He is also a research associate at the Federal Reserve Bank of Cleveland and the program coordinator for deposit insurance at the Federal Deposit Insurance Corporation's Center for Financial Research. His research focuses on financial intermediaries and the valuation of fixed-income securities and government guarantees. Currently, Mr. Pennacchi is the managing editor of the *Journal of Financial Intermediation* and an associate editor of the *Journal of Financial and Quantitative Analysis*, the *Journal of Financial Services Research*, and the *Journal of Money, Credit and Banking*. Previously, he was an associate editor for the *Journal of Banking and Finance*, the *Journal of Finance*, the *Review of Financial Studies*, and *Management Science*, and a coeditor of *Advances in Futures and Options Research*. Mr. Pennacchi has consulted for the U.S. Office of Management and Budget, the World Bank, and the International Monetary Fund. He has been a visiting professor at the Università Bocconi in Milan and was a member of the finance faculty at the University of Pennsylvania's Wharton School.

Thomas Russell is an associate professor at Santa Clara University, where he teaches courses in macroeconomics, microeconomics, and decision making.

His numerous scholarly articles have appeared in such publications as the *Journal of Economic Theory*, the *American Economic Review*, *Economic Letters*, the *Journal of International Money and Finance*, and the *Journal of Mathematical Economics*. His current research involves applying differential geometry to the study of rational and nonrational behavior, and analyzing the relationship between capital markets and insurance markets.

Vincent H. Smith is a professor of economics in the Departments of Agricultural Economics and Economics at Montana State University. His research examines agricultural trade and domestic policy issues, with a particular focus on agricultural science policy, domestic and world commodity markets, risk management, and agricultural trade policy. He has authored nine books and monographs and published over one hundred articles. His work has been recognized nationally through numerous awards for outstanding research. In 2008, he became a distinguished scholar of the Western Agricultural Economics Association (the association's highest award for scholarly accomplishment).

The American Enterprise Institute for Public Policy Research

Founded in 1943, AEI is a nonpartisan, nonprofit research and educational organization based in Washington, D.C. The Institute sponsors research, conducts seminars and conferences, and publishes books and periodicals.

AEI's research is carried out under three major programs: Economic Policy Studies, Foreign Policy and Defense Studies, and Social and Political Studies. The resident scholars and fellows listed in these pages are part of a network that also includes ninety adjunct scholars at leading universities throughout the United States and in several foreign countries.

The views expressed in AEI publications are those of the authors and do not necessarily reflect the views of the staff, advisory panels, officers, or trustees.

www.ingramcontent.com/pod-product-compliance
Lightning Source LLC
LaVergne TN
LVHW090322210926
848480LV00001B/329